Ethereum Cookbook

Over 100 recipes covering Ethereum-based tokens, games, wallets, smart contracts, protocols, and Dapps

Manoj P R

BIRMINGHAM - MUMBAI

Ethereum Cookbook

Commissioning Editor: Pravin Dhandre
Acquisition Editor: Namrata Patil
Content Development Editor: Eisha Dsouza
Technical Editor: Ishita Vora
Copy Editor: Safis Editing
Project Coordinator: Namrata Swetta
Proofreader: Safis Editing
Indexer: Aishwarya Gangawane
Graphics: Jisha Chirayil
Production Coordinator: Nilesh Mohite

First published: August 2018

Production reference: 1310818

Published by Packt Publishing Ltd.
Livery Place
35 Livery Street
Birmingham
B3 2PB, UK.

ISBN 978-1-78913-399-8

www.packtpub.com

To my father.

– Manoj

`mapt.io`

Mapt is an online digital library that gives you full access to over 5,000 books and videos, as well as industry leading tools to help you plan your personal development and advance your career. For more information, please visit our website.

Why subscribe?

- Spend less time learning and more time coding with practical eBooks and Videos from over 4,000 industry professionals

- Improve your learning with Skill Plans built especially for you

- Get a free eBook or video every month

- Mapt is fully searchable

- Copy and paste, print, and bookmark content

Packt.com

Did you know that Packt offers eBook versions of every book published, with PDF and ePub files available? You can upgrade to the eBook version at `www.packt.com` and as a print book customer, you are entitled to a discount on the eBook copy. Get in touch with us at `customercare@packtpub.com` for more details.

At `www.packt.com`, you can also read a collection of free technical articles, sign up for a range of free newsletters, and receive exclusive discounts and offers on Packt books and eBooks.

Contributors

About the author

Manoj P R is a tech-savvy person who has been working with distributed ledger technology for more than three years. His passion for the latest technology trends in the market has made him an avid learner and contributor in this space. He specializes in Ethereum, JavaScript, and Go. A self-taught programmer, Manoj started his programming career as a freelancer during his early academic life. He has developed many scalable enterprise blockchain solutions for various clients across the globe. He is currently associated with Conduent Labs as a Blockchain SME. He loves solving real-life problems using technology and is a lively contributor towards open source projects. Apart from work, Manoj likes traveling and writing.

About the reviewer

Mayukh Mukhopadhyay is an assistant consultant at Tata Consultancy Services who works on the big data and revenue assurance projects of the world's oldest telecommunication company, where he tames messy data to generate tangible insights. He has authored the book *Ethereum Smart Contract Development* and engages in occasional pro-bono consultation on blockchain implementation. He has a master's in Software Engineering from Jadavpur University and is an executive MBA candidate at IIT Kharagpur.

> *I want to thank my daughter, Abriti, who, even at the tender age of 11 months, supports her papa and his foolish endeavours. To my wife, Mrittika, all I want to say is, "Despite our superficial differences, we share the same soul."*

Packt is searching for authors like you

If you're interested in becoming an author for Packt, please visit `authors.packtpub.com` and apply today. We have worked with thousands of developers and tech professionals, just like you, to help them share their insight with the global tech community. You can make a general application, apply for a specific hot topic that we are recruiting an author for, or submit your own idea.

Table of Contents

Preface

With this practical guide, you will learn how to set up Ethereum and connect to a network, write and deploy quality smart contracts, use Truffle and Ganache to manage your development, create your own Tokens and ICOs, build decentralized games and organization, create your own wallet that supports multiple tokens, and much more.

You'll also learn about the security vulnerabilities that can arise and various other protocols of Ethereum. Moving on, you'll learn the various design decisions and tips to make your application scalable and secure. With this book and the advanced topics it covers, you can get well versed with the Ethereum principles and ecosystem.

Who this book is for

If you want to set up an Ethereum blockchain network, write and deploy smart contracts, build decentralized applications (DApps) or facilitate peer-to-peer transaction, then this book is for you. It is recommended that the readers should be familiar with basic blockchain concepts and knowledge of JavaScript and NodeJS.

What this book covers

Chapter 1, *Getting Started*, covers the very basics of Ethereum and its tools. You will find the steps required to set up and run a network and interact with it.

Chapter 2, *Smart Contract Development*, contains a set of recipes that will help you write smart contracts. It also covers the steps to compile, deploy, and test the contracts that you have written.

Chapter 3, *Interacting with the Contract*, covers the topics that are essential for building a decentralized application (DApp) that can interact with blockchain and the contracts.

Chapter 4, *The Truffle Suite*, explains a popular tool in the Ethereum ecosystem. This chapter also explains the use cases that will help you to have a better development workflow and build better DApps.

Chapter 5, *Tokens and ICOs*, covers the topics necessary for you to build your own Ethereum-based token and distribute it through ICO.

Chapter 6, *Games and DAOs,* takes you through a series of interesting recipes that will help you create your own decentralized game or organization.

Chapter 7, *Advanced Solidity,* contains more advanced recipes about the smart contract language that will help you to achieve more complex tasks efficiently in the Blockchain.

Chapter 8, *Smart Contract Security,* is designed to help you understand more about the common vulnerabilities and ways to avoid them. It also takes you through the set of tools you can use to analyze the code.

Chapter 9, *Design Decisions,* contains the recipes to help you decide between the common design questions you may come across while developing a fully functional DApp.

Chapter 10, *Other Protocols and Applications,* walks you through some of the other Ethereum protocols and applications that might come in handy while building your DApp.

Chapter 11, *Miscellaneous,* includes a few additional recipes that can help you build better DApps.

To get the most out of this book

It is recommended to have a basic idea about blockchain and its concepts to get the most out of this book. This book does not cover the basics of how blockchain works but focuses more on working with Ethereum.

Basic knowledge of JavaScript and NodeJS would be good to have since interaction with Ethereum happens mostly through JavaScript. Support for other languages is also explained.

Download the example code files

You can download the example code files for this book from your account at www.packtpub.com. If you purchased this book elsewhere, you can visit www.packtpub.com/support and register to have the files emailed directly to you.

You can download the code files by following these steps:

1. Log in or register at www.packtpub.com.
2. Select the **SUPPORT** tab.
3. Click on **Code Downloads & Errata**.
4. Enter the name of the book in the **Search** box and follow the onscreen instructions.

Once the file is downloaded, please make sure that you unzip or extract the folder using the latest version of:

- WinRAR/7-Zip for Windows
- Zipeg/iZip/UnRarX for Mac
- 7-Zip/PeaZip for Linux

The code bundle for the book is also hosted on GitHub at `https://github.com/PacktPublishing/Ethereum-Cookbook`. In case there's an update to the code, it will be updated on the existing GitHub repository.

We also have other code bundles from our rich catalog of books and videos available at `https://github.com/PacktPublishing/`. Check them out!

Download the color images

We also provide a PDF file that has color images of the screenshots/diagrams used in this book. You can download it here: `http://www.packtpub.com/sites/default/files/downloads/EthereumCookbook_ColorImages.pdf`.

Conventions used

There are a number of text conventions used throughout this book.

`CodeInText`: Indicates code words in text, database table names, folder names, filenames, file extensions, pathnames, dummy URLs, user input, and Twitter handles. Here is an example: "Mount the downloaded `WebStorm-10*.dmg` disk image file as another disk in your system."

A block of code is set as follows:

```
pragma solidity ^0.4.21;
contract HelloWorld {
    function printSomething() returns (string) {
        return "hello world";
    }
}
```

When we wish to draw your attention to a particular part of a code block, the relevant lines or items are set in bold:

```
pragma solidity ^0.4.21;
contract HelloWorld {
    string textToPrint = "hello world";
    function changeText(string _text) public {
        textToPrint = _text;
    }
    function printSomething() public view returns (string) {
        return textToPrint;
    }
}
```

Any command-line input or output is written as follows:

```
$ npm install -g remixd
```

Bold: Indicates a new term, an important word, or words that you see onscreen. For example, words in menus or dialog boxes appear in the text like this. Here is an example: "Select **System info** from the **Administration** panel."

 Warnings or important notes appear like this.

 Tips and tricks appear like this.

Get in touch

Feedback from our readers is always welcome.

General feedback: Email `feedback@packtpub.com` and mention the book title in the subject of your message. If you have questions about any aspect of this book, please email us at `questions@packtpub.com`.

Errata: Although we have taken every care to ensure the accuracy of our content, mistakes do happen. If you have found a mistake in this book, we would be grateful if you would report this to us. Please visit `www.packtpub.com/submit-errata`, selecting your book, clicking on the Errata Submission Form link, and entering the details.

Piracy: If you come across any illegal copies of our works in any form on the Internet, we would be grateful if you would provide us with the location address or website name. Please contact us at `copyright@packtpub.com` with a link to the material.

If you are interested in becoming an author: If there is a topic that you have expertise in and you are interested in either writing or contributing to a book, please visit `authors.packtpub.com`.

Reviews

Please leave a review. Once you have read and used this book, why not leave a review on the site that you purchased it from? Potential readers can then see and use your unbiased opinion to make purchase decisions, we at Packt can understand what you think about our products, and our authors can see your feedback on their book. Thank you!

For more information about Packt, please visit `packtpub.com`.

Getting Started 1

In this chapter, we will cover the following recipes:

- Choosing a client for Ethereum
- Setting up a node and participating in a network
- Working with the JavaScript console
- Saving time and money with INFURA
- Creating your own private Ethereum network
- Creating a blockchain network for development
- Using Azure Ethereum as a service
- Using MetaMask and other wallets
- Using block explorer
- Understanding everything about accounts
- Installing a solidity compiler

Introduction

It is really important to understand how to configure and work with various implementations of the Ethereum protocol before developing applications in it. There are several flavors, which can be used interchangeably for development, testing, and deployment. Keywords in Ethereum might be very new to a person who is just getting started, so it is important to understand and use the tools and services in the Ethereum ecosystem.

Ethereum is a distributed public ledger, like Bitcoin. Bitcoin acts more like a peer-to-peer electronic cash system, whereas Ethereum is a decentralized platform for building applications. Ethereum has a built-in Turing complete programming language (solidity), which can be used to write smart contracts. This means that Ethereum has a broader application than other traditional blockchains. Ethereum also has a cryptocurrency (Ether), which can be traded for value or to pay the transaction fee for applications and services in Ethereum.

POW (Proof of Work), **POS (Proof of Stake)**, **IBFT (Istanbul Byzantine Fault Tolerance)**, Raft, and so on are different commonly used consensus algorithms. These algorithms are used to achieve agreement on a data value among distributed systems. Each algorithm has their own advantages and disadvantages, and various blockchain platforms use them based on their requirements.

A smart contract is a computer program that outlines the rules in a relationship. Smart contracts work exactly as intended and cannot be changed at a later point in time. Once deployed, these smart contracts cannot be changed. This gives users trust and transparency. With the help of Ethereum smart contracts, you can create your own tradable tokens, raise funds for your startup, build a decentralized organization, or even make a fun game.

The recipes in this chapter will primarily focus on Ethereum configuration and platform tools, which will help the reader understand more about the Ethereum ecosystem before starting to develop applications.

While the recipes in this chapter will give you an overview of Ethereum and working with various clients, we encourage you to adopt this proposal according to your needs. Since the software used is still in development and gaining in popularity, some organization's policies and antivirus software will prevent you from using this. In such cases, it is typically a good idea to discuss this with your IT security department—if your company happens to have one—well in advance, to prevent lengthy discussions later on.

Choosing a client for Ethereum

In this recipe, we will focus on installing various clients that implement the Ethereum protocol. This will help you learn what each client has to offer, and will enable you to choose and work with an efficient implementation based on your requirements.

Getting ready

If you are using macOS, you will need `homebrew` to install the packages.

How to do it...

There are several clients that implement the Ethereum protocol and we will mainly focus on `geth` and `parity`. You can get more information about the remaining protocols from the official Ethereum documentation (`http://www.ethdocs.org/`).

Geth

Geth is the official `Go` implementation of Ethereum:

1. To install `geth` on macOS, the easiest way to follow is using `homebrew`. Run the following commands in your Terminal to download and install `geth`:

```
brew tap ethereum/ethereum
brew install ethereum
```

This command will install the latest stable version of `geth` on your Mac. If you want to install the development version of `geth`, then add the `--devel` flag to the `install` command:

```
brew install ethereum --devel
```

2. To install `geth` on Ubuntu, run the following commands:

```
sudo apt-get install software-properties-common
sudo add-apt-repository -y ppa:ethereum/ethereum
sudo apt-get update
sudo apt-get install ethereum
```

3. If you are using Windows, it is suggested to download the binary from `https://geth.ethereum.org/downloads/` and install it by double-clicking the `geth.exe` file.

4. Verify the installation by running the `geth` command:

```
geth version
```

It will show the current client details, as displayed here:

```
$ geth version
Geth
Version: 1.8.2-stable
Architecture: amd64
Protocol Versions: [63 62]
Network Id: 1
Go Version: go1.10
Operating System: darwin
GOPATH=
GOROOT=/usr/local/opt/go/libexec
```

 Since `geth` is a development version and still gaining in popularity, some antivirus software may consider it a virus. Also, make sure that you are not violating your organization's policies by using this software.

Parity

Parity is an Ethereum client that is built by Parity Technologies. It is a rust-based implementation and offers some additional functionalities over Go Ethereum:

1. The easiest way to install `parity` on Mac or Ubuntu is to use the one-line binary installer. This will handle all the hassle of downloading and installing the package:

```
bash <(curl https://get.parity.io -kL)
```

2. If you are using Windows, then download the binary releases from `https://github.com/paritytech/parity/releases` and install them. You can also see supported binaries for other operating systems as well.

There's more...

You can build and run the client directly from its source code. To build `geth` from the source in Ubuntu, follow the steps given later. Make sure you have `Go` and the `C` compilers installed:

```
git clone https://github.com/ethereum/go-ethereum
cd go-ethereum
make geth
```

Setting up a node and participating in a network

Here, you will learn how to set up a node using the `geth` command-line tool. You will also see how to connect to a public network and perform operations such as ledger syncing and mining.

Getting ready

You will need a working installation of the `geth` command-line interface. You can also start a node with `parity` or any other Ethereum protocol implementation, but the steps may differ for each client.

Commands starting with $ have to be run on the command prompt/terminal and those starting with > will work only on the `web3` JavaScript console.

How to do it...

1. Verify your installation by running the following version command:

   ```
   $ geth version
   ```

2. Start your node with the following command:

   ```
   $ geth
   ```

   This will start an Ethereum node and will connect with the main network. As soon as it finds any peer nodes, it will start downloading the blocks from them.

   You can configure the parameters before starting a node. This will help you do things like connect to a different network, expose APIs, and much more. Let's look at a sample initialization and the parameters used in it:

   ```
   $ geth --networkid 3 --datadir "./ropsten-db" --keystore
   "./ropsten-keys" --syncmode "fast" --rpc --rpcport "8546" --rpcapi
   "web3,eth,miner,admin" --rpccorsdomain "*" --port 30301 console
   ```

Let's look into each parameter in detail:

- `--networkid <id>`: A parameter to identify each network. You can either connect to the main/test network (1=Frontier(default), 2=Morden (disused), 3=Ropsten(PoW), 4=Rinkeby(PoA)) or any private network that you have set up.
- `--datadir <path>`: Directory path for storing the blockchain database and keystore. You can change the default `keystore` directory with the `--keystore` parameter.
- `--syncmode <mode>`: A parameter to specify the type of `sync` method. You can choose fast, full, or light, based on your needs.
- `--rpc`: Enables an RPC server through HTTP. You can also change parameters such as `--rpcaddr`, `--rpcport`, and `--rpcapi`.
- `--rpccorsdomain <list>`: Domains from which cross-domain requests are accepted. Use * as a wildcard or specify domains as a comma-separated list.
- `--port <port>`: Changes the default network listening port (`30303`).
- `--console`: Starts the `web3` JavaScript console.

If you get stuck anywhere, you can always make use of the inbuilt help interface. Just enter `geth help` and it will return a comprehensive list of all commands with their respective description that you can run using `geth`.

3. It might take a few minutes to identify the peers that are already on the network. Run the following command to return the list of peers that are currently connected to your node. Your node will start syncing once it finds at least one peer:

```
> admin.peers
```

4. Check the current syncing status by running the following command. It will return false if not syncing:

```
> eth.syncing
```

5. Run the `geth attach` command if you would like to connect to this node from a different console. You can also explicitly specify the host and the port. In our case, it is `localhost` and `8546`:

```
$ geth attach http://localhost:8546
```

Your firewall may restrict the node from communicating with an external peer. This can cause issues with the synchronization process. Also, ensure that you are not exposing your RPC APIs to the internet, which can result in attacks.

Working with the JavaScript console

The `geth` command-line utility has an inbuilt **JavaScript Runtime Environment** (**JSRE**). This JavaScript console exposes all `web3js` objects and methods. You can use this JSRE as a **REPL** (**Read**, **Execute**, **Print**, **Loop**) console.

In this recipe, we will learn how to connect and use the JSRE in interactive (console) and non-interactive (script) modes.

Getting ready

You should have the `geth` command-line tool installed on your system to test this recipe. You can either start a node along with the console or connect to an already existing node.

How to do it...

1. Start the Ethereum console with the `console` or `attach` subcommand. The console command starts the `geth` node and opens the JavaScript console along with it. The `attach` command is used to connect to an existing node. Here, we will connect to an already running node that you started earlier:

```
$ geth attach http://localhost:8545
```

2. If you are starting a new node and would like to see the log information, start the node with this:

```
$ geth --verbosity 5 console 2>> /tmp/eth-node.log
```

Too many logs can pollute your console. To avoid this, start the node with a specific verbosity value:

```
$ geth --verbosity 0 console
```

3. Take a look at the `web3` object, which is available for you to interact with:

    > **web3**

4. For managing the node, you can make use of the `admin` API. For the list of supported admin operations, run the following command:

    > **admin**

    You can check the current node information with this:

    > **admin.nodeInfo**

    This will return an object with properties such as `enode`, `protocols`, `ports`, `name`, and other details related to the current node, as displayed here:

```
> admin.nodeInfo
{
  enode: "enode://315d8f023dfa1ae1b59dc11462f3e13697fc8fe4886034e01530ebe36b2f8cc154a8dd9c21f5b42564668f22ae71
73943b9dd9a0fbfc1430cca8c471968729140[::]:30303",
  id: "315d8f023dfa1ae1b59dc11462f3e13697fc8fe4886034e01530ebe36b2f8cc154a8dd9c21f5b42564668f22ae7173943b9dd9a
0fbfc1430cca8c47196872914",
  ip: "::",
  listenAddr: "[::]:30303",
  name: "Geth/v1.8.2-stable/darwin-amd64/go1.10",
  ports: {
    discovery: 30303,
    listener: 30303
  },
  protocols: {
    eth: {
      config: {
        byzantiumBlock: 0,
        chainId: 1100,
        eip150Hash: "0x0000000000000000000000000000000000000000000000000000000000000000",
        eip155Block: 0,
        eip158Block: 0,
        homesteadBlock: 0
      },
      difficulty: 400,
      genesis: "0x21894755552cd3e11dc93ccaaefa1f3778157dff2a555a7d20a85e1327436734",
      head: "0x21894755552cd3e11dc93ccaaefa1f3778157dff2a555a7d20a85e1327436734",
      network: 1100
    }
  }
}
```

To see the list of peers connected to the current node, use the `peers` object:

> **admin.peers**

You also have access to methods that can help you enable or disable RPC/WS.

5. For handling Ethereum blockchain-related tasks, use the `eth` object. Run the following command to see the methods supported by it:

```
> eth
```

You can check the latest block number (block height) with this:

```
> eth.blockNumber
```

You have an option to read the contents of a block. You can pass any block number as a parameter:

```
> eth.getBlock(301)
```

In the following screenshot, you can see the block number, difficulty, gas details, miner, hash, transactions, and much more:

```
> eth.getBlock(301)
{
  difficulty: 131072,
  extraData: "0xd783010800846765746887676f312e392e32856c696e7578",
  gasLimit: 1600353550,
  gasUsed: 21000,
  hash: "0x667629a5a4f92723ef9601d3d7baa61e5235b81b56b4a55ac4b1c37ea393052c",
  logsBloom: "0x000000000000000000000000000000000000000000000000000000000000000000000000000000000000000000000000000000000000000000000000000000000000000000000000000000000000000000000000000000000000000000000000000000000000000000000000000000000000000000000000000000000000000000000000000000000000000000000000000000000000000000000000000000000000000000000000000000000000000000000000000000000000000000000000000000000000008",
  miner: "0xb8a7483ace529de28d1d9f8860a298d94e451892",
  mixHash: "0x85e8a46e15a8b3421143c63b520c415c9bb05da662b4d7fe52b0d28a23f21e21",
  nonce: "0x7d73192b6dcd55e9",
  number: 301,
  parentHash: "0x9494c5c74d306f23a769353374c6e61429419531aa62668c9e2d6969ebd0a76b",
  receiptsRoot: "0xc8a8d86c683e17c3832fb19e2b0e700915bc51c09ccfa8aad2abad75beaa3d3c",
  sha3Uncles: "0x1dcc4de8dec75d7aab85b567b6ccd41ad312451b948a7413f0a142fd40d49347",
  size: 657,
  stateRoot: "0x6b7b76bf6546e186c39f66b73023cd88643805ecad7253aa97c9f74a4aa45658",
  timestamp: 1521928050,
  totalDifficulty: 39460096,
  transactions: ["0x653d0bcbc5f155c541635c21fd9f5e898f920932df15147a268ad07d89f55359"],
  transactionsRoot: "0x3010a61f727038215f217307840a73c0508e45e79eb60c6a57dc622cfdf1a6ac",
  uncles: []
}
```

`eth` also has methods related to accounts, transactions, and contracts. We will talk more about those later in this book.

6. To manage Ethereum accounts, you can make use of the `personal` method. It has options for creating an account, unlocking the account, sending/signing a transaction, and so on:

```
> personal
```

7. You can play around with mining and its methods through the console:

```
> miner
```

8. This console also has an option to monitor the transaction pool through the `txpool` object:

```
> txpool
```

9. `web3` also offers some generic methods to help you with the interaction. Some of the examples include conversion of values, encoding, and hashing. One such example to convert `ether` to `Wei` is given here:

```
> web3.toWei(1, "ether")
```

Since it is a JavaScript console, you have complete ECMA5 functionality (Go Ethereum uses Otto JS VM, which is a JS interpreter written in Go). You can declare variables, use control structures, define new methods, and even use any of `setInterval`, `clearInterval`, `setTimeout`, and `clearTimeout`.

There's more...

You can also execute JavaScript commands in a non-interactive way. There are two different approaches to doing this:

1. Use the `--exec` argument, which takes JavaScript as input. This will work with both the `console` and `attach` commands:

```
$ geth --exec "eth.accounts" attach http://localhost:8545
```

This will print the list of accounts stored in the current node.

2. You can execute more complex scripts with the `loadScript` method. The path to your scripts folder can be specified with the `--jspath` attribute:

```
$ geth --jspath "/home" --exec 'loadScript("sendTransaction.js")'
attach http://localhost:8545
```

Saving time and money with INFURA

If you don't want to set up a full node for you decentralized application, then this is the recipe for you. INFURA provides an infrastructure for Ethereum and you can make use of it for free.

How to do it...

1. Go to the INFURA signup page (`https://infura.io/signup`) and enter your name and email.
2. Once you acknowledge the terms and conditions and have signed up, you will receive an email from INFURA with the providers for each network.
3. For each network, you will receive an endpoint and an API key:
   - **Main Ethereum network**: `https://mainnet.infura.io/<api-key>`
   - **Test Ethereum network (Ropsten)**: `https://ropsten.infura.io/<api-key>`
   - **Test Ethereum network (Rinkeby)**: `https://rinkeby.infura.io/<api-key>`
   - **Test Ethereum network (INFURAnet)**: `https://infuranet.infura.io/<api-key>`

   You can interact with the providers just like you do with your local node. You can use JSON RPC, Web3JS, or even the REST API provided by INFURA to interact with the nodes.

4. Get the current block number with JSON RPC using cURL:

```
curl -X POST -H "Content-Type: application/json" --data
'{"jsonrpc": "2.0", "id": 1, "method": "eth_blockNumber", "params":
[]}' "https://mainnet.infura.io/<your-api-key>"
```

   This will return the current block number, as follows:

```
{"jsonrpc":"2.0","id":1,"result":"0x512bab"}
```

5. INFURA also provides an easy-to-use REST API interface for JSON RPC commands. You can use the JSON RPC methods as the path to get the result:

```
https://api.infura.io/v1/jsonrpc/mainnet/eth_blockNumber?token=<your-api-key>
```

6. To use INFURA with your `web3js` application, you can set the endpoints as HTTP providers:

```
web3 = new Web3(new Web3.providers.HttpProvider
("https://mainnet.infura.io/<your_api_key>"));
```

There's more...

INFURA also provides support for IPFS and you can use their server as a gateway:

- **IPFS Gateway**: `https://ipfs.infura.io`
- **IPFS RPC**: `https://ipfs.infura.io:5001`

Creating your own private Ethereum network

This recipe helps you create your own private POW-based Ethereum blockchain. Here, we will be creating an entirely new custom blockchain that cannot interact with the Ethereum main-net. You will have the flexibility to control parameters such as mining and peers. This will come in handy when you want to have a consortium of your own or even for testing purposes.

Getting ready

To step through this recipe, you will need a working installation of the `geth` command-line interface. No other prerequisites are required.

How to do it...

1. Create a directory to save your blockchain data:

   ```
   $ mkdir datadir
   ```

2. Create an account and save it to the directory:

   ```
   $ geth account new --datadir datadir
   ```

You will be asked to enter a password for the account. An address will be displayed once the account is created. The key file for this account will be stored in the `/datadir/keystore/` location.

3. Create a `genesis.json` file with the following contents:

```
{
    "config": {
        "chainId": 1100,
        "homesteadBlock": 0,
        "eip155Block": 0,
        "eip158Block": 0,
        "byzantiumBlock": 0
    },
    "difficulty": "400",
    "gasLimit": "2000000",
    "alloc": {
        "87db8fceb028cd4ded9d03f49b89124a1589cab0": {
            "balance": "1000000000000000000000000000"
        }
    }
}
```

Various parameters in the genesis files are explained here. You can make changes as per your requirements:

- `config`: The config object defines the settings for our custom blockchain. `chainId` is used to identify our network. Set it to a unique value for our private network. Other parameters are related to forking and versioning. Let's not worry about them, since we are starting a network from scratch.
- `difficulty`: This value is used to control the block generation time of a blockchain. The higher the difficulty, the longer it will take to mine each block. In a test network, try to keep it low to avoid long waiting times.
- `gasLimit`: This value denotes the total amount of gas that can be used in each block. We will keep it high enough to avoid any bottlenecks during testing.
- `alloc`: This object allows us to pre-fill accounts with Ether. This won't create accounts for you. Since we already have an account created in step 2, use it here to allocate some `wei` (1 Ether = 10^{18} wei).

4. Initialize your genesis file using the following command:

```
$ geth --datadir ./datadir init ./genesis.json
```

5. Start your network:

```
$ geth --datadir ./datadir --networkid 1100 console 2>> network.log
```

Running this command will display a console like this in your terminal/command prompt:

```
Welcome to the Geth JavaScript console!

instance: Geth/v1.8.2-stable/darwin-amd64/go1.10
coinbase: 0x87db8fceb028cd4ded9d03f49b89124a1589cab0
at block: 0 (Thu, 01 Jan 1970 05:30:00 IST)
 datadir: /Users/manoj/Desktop/blockchain/datadir
 modules: admin:1.0 debug:1.0 eth:1.0 miner:1.0 net:1.0 personal:1.0 rpc:1.0 txpool:1.0 web3:1.0

>
```

You can use this console to interact with your private blockchain. To give you a brief idea, execute the following command to see the list of accounts:

```
> eth.accounts
```

6. If you would like to add another peer to the network, open a second terminal/command prompt to create a second peer with a different data directory and port:

```
$ geth --datadir ./datadir2 init ./genesis.json
$ geth --datadir ./datadir2 --networkid 1100 --port 30302 console
2>> network.log
```

7. Find out the enode address of the first node using the first JavaScript console:

```
> admin.nodeInfo.enode
```

This will return the enode address of the current node:

```
enode://315d8f023dfa1ae1b59dc11462f3e13697fc8fe4886034e01530ebe36b2
f8cc154a8dd9c21f5b42564668f22ae7173943b9dd9a0fbfc1430cca8c471968729
14@[::]:30303
```

8. Use the second node's JavaScript console to connect with the first node:

```
> admin.addPeer(
"enode://315d8f023dfa1ae1b59dc11462f3e13697fc8fe4886034e01530ebe36b
2f8cc154a8dd9c21f5b42564668f22ae7173943b9dd9a0fbfc1430cca8c47196872
914@127.0.0.1:30303")
```

We replaced [::] with the IP address and port of the first node.

9. Verify the connection from both nodes by listing the connected peers:

```
> admin.peers
```

How it works...

In steps 1 through 5, we created a private Ethereum network. This should be enough for you to run a single-node network. With the minimum difficulty and maximum gas limit, this network is ideal for development and testing. At this point, your application can connect to the network with the default Ethereum port, `8545`.

In steps 6 to 9, we are creating another peer and connecting it to the first node. This allows you to have a multi-node Ethereum network. All the blocks will be synced between these two nodes and will be accessible from both nodes. You can create and connect as many nodes as you want with the procedure explained here. Make sure to set appropriate firewall rules to ensure proper communication.

There's more...

`puppeth` is a command-line tool that comes with `geth`. It can help you create a new Ethereum network, down to the genesis block, bootnodes, miners, and ethstats servers, in a user-friendly way. Start `puppeth` using the following command:

```
$ puppeth
```

You will be asked to enter a network name. You can either enter a new network name or use the one that you already created using `puppeth`. Once you enter it, you can see the list of things that `puppeth` can do.

Create a new genesis file using `puppeth` and use Proof of Authority (clique) as the consensus algorithm. Try creating a private network with the generated genesis file.

See also

This recipe explains how you can create a private network using `geth`. There are other options for various use cases, such as development and production. You can check out the following recipes to learn more:

- Creating a blockchain network for development

- Using Azure Ethereum as a service

Creating a blockchain network for development

You don't always have to create a fully functioning node to support your development. There are development networks that can simulate an Ethereum network. In this recipe, you will learn about `ganache-cli` (previously TestRPC), which is part of the Truffle suit of Ethereum development tools and is a command-line tool that you can use to create your personal blockchain network for Ethereum development.

Getting ready

Since the tool is written in JavaScript and distributed via `npm`, you will need `Node.js` (>= v6.11.5) installed on your machine to try this recipe.

How to do it...

Follow these steps to install and create a test Ethereum network using `npm`:

1. Install `ganache-cli` using `npm`:

```
npm install -g ganache-cli
```

2. Starting a basic blockchain network is as simple as running this command:

```
ganache-cli
```

You will know that your blockchain is ready when you see this screen:

```
Ganache CLI v6.1.0 (ganache-core: 2.1.0)

Available Accounts
==================
(0) 0x678f048d923dcc6241cbbcecf66f2031cc5148ae
(1) 0xf76b850677593cc986c5457f3df38f4da91780d9
(2) 0xe8cb4c908dc844e7e414fb21a62a269a12482205
(3) 0xcda7446095a17b0bbb0a89beb05f7efa3ffe6ff2
(4) 0x627b8654fb66a0dd71e373412465dcf6ec6d5e01
(5) 0xb452289857495a2cc38d49b2306181b76ca62412
(6) 0xa1ead7940996e93ee7ef886377e41a9d419f5f04
(7) 0x6e81429c2c6b77db69d44e8cfeb24d41d21812dc
(8) 0xde34067ebd4f0b5b03e6b80864015889c977ce25
(9) 0x74aa772ec451c8fcf516108de1d0e881e2425435

Private Keys
==================
(0) 0578e786a0f850e9a8ec21be8f8781616ea863417d59581a04683df58d0ed7af
(1) d6d015e21181ec7fe4fa10bc5b49c89c126b214130eacd59a2b02624688f2b09
(2) 8a9d169b5e3a3dd2e7e4daad97814fb2c8286cd0b7294c3cb426d60d7029c174
(3) ebddb3e53d470b37fcd48ccc0665a0fc0e931f833d6401298c469f55d4870f7f
(4) 0112072b63db2c1ccc5ca0cb5a2fcfcfee7b1fb8713152f07bb7745d098bb058
(5) e72f0c814a96cc7c23b6e69be7412826750fa4eef8af67785f22637bfd705f3e
(6) 32341bc68af5b57f65386aa45dbf75178cbd5150e0b93241bbaaee2ae665ead1
(7) 4f375355ba49e754ee1cfc00538f6f19bea58458f6824f904ac376c54a8a78e9
(8) bf0803802831fab52f49e3e40cfc18232e2e5daf7bd5a28a1351f3d14f38c7fb
(9) 533d3acb39defca3933fc507de44b3725590a64c7bf4f6ea60aefb309537f5b0

HD Wallet
==================
Mnemonic:      kick relax space measure door number process slot tragic rude taxi voyage
Base HD Path:  m/44'/60'/0'/0/{account_index}

Listening on localhost:8545
```

Ganache creates a virtual Ethereum blockchain, and it generates some sample accounts for you to use during development. Each account is filled in 100 Ether so that you only have to focus on development. You can access the network from `http://localhost:8545`.

3. You can use a few parameters to customize the blockchain. Here's one such example:

   ganache-cli -a 5 -e 2000 -p 8080 -l 999999

   - -a: Number of accounts to generate while starting the network. The default is *10*.
   - -e: Amount of Ether to allocate for each account. The default is *100* Ether.
   - -p: Port number for listening to RPC requests. The default is *8,545*.
   - -l: Gas limit for each block. The default is *90,000*.

You can find the complete list of parameters to configure here:

`https://github.com/trufflesuite/ganache-cli`.

 By default, accounts are unlocked and you can do the transaction from any account without a password. You can change this by using the `--secure` or `-n` flag. This will lock all accounts by default and you need to unlock each one to send a transaction.

There's more...

There is a GUI for ganache that offers an easy-to-use interface for creating Ethereum networks. It even offers an intuitive **User Interface (UI)** for browsing blocks and transactions.

You can download and install the ganache GUI from `http://truffleframework.com/ganache/`.

Using Azure Ethereum as a service

Azure offers cloud solutions to deploy and configure Ethereum consortiums with a simple single-click deployment through the Azure portal. In this recipe, you will learn how to deploy a flexible Ethereum network, consisting of a set of load-balanced transaction nodes, with which an application or user can interact to submit transactions, and a set of mining nodes to record transactions.

Getting ready

You will need an Azure subscription to create an Ethereum consortium. Other dependencies will be configured by the provider itself.

How to do it...

Follow these steps to create an Ethereum POW blockchain in Azure:

1. Log in to the Azure portal and click on **Create a resource** from the left navigation bar.

2. Select **Create Ethereum Proof-of-Work Consortium** under **Blockchain**.

   Once you click Create, you can see a five-step wizard that will guide you through the setup process. The first step will ask you to choose a username, password, subscription, location, and so on. Provide the appropriate values and click **OK**:

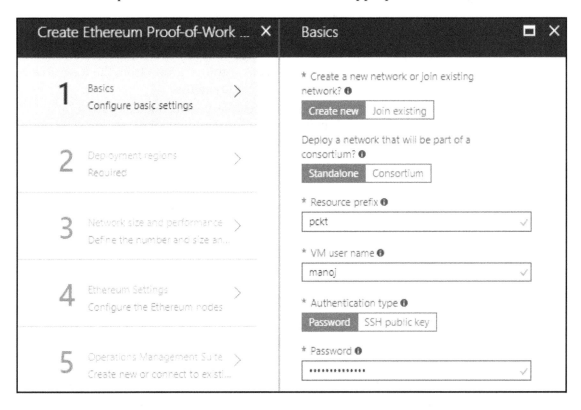

3. Step 2 will ask you to configure the regions in which the nodes should be deployed. For a simple network, one region should be enough.
4. Step 3 is all about configuring the number of nodes that should be dedicated to mining and transactions. Mining nodes do all the heavy lifting of creating blocks, and transaction nodes take care of broadcasting the transaction from your application. Choose the number of nodes for each category and their respective configuration to meet your needs.
5. Step 4 focuses more on the parameters of blockchain that you are about to create. You can compare it with the genesis file you will create during private network configuration.

6. Once you are finished on the Ethereum settings tab, you can choose the **Operations Management Suite** for your Azure resource. Create a new one if you are new to Azure and creating resources for the first time.

7. If everything goes well, then the verification process in the **Summary** tab will be successful and you can proceed to purchase the service.

8. Read through the **Terms and Conditions** and click **Create**. This will start deploying your resources and can take a few minutes to finish.

9. Once the deployment is finished, you can see your resources in the resource group that you created/selected. Select your resource group from the **Resource groups** tab in the left navigation bar and **Deployments**.

10. This will display the set of deployments that has been created as part of Ethereum consortium's deployment. Select the deployment name that starts with **microsoft-azure-blockchain-ethereum**:

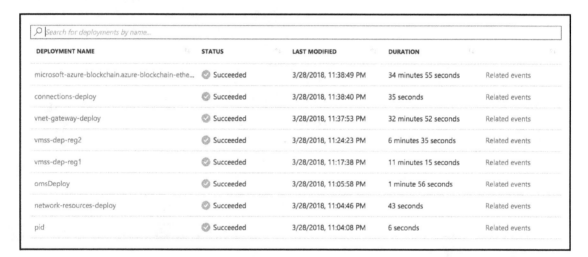

DEPLOYMENT NAME	STATUS	LAST MODIFIED	DURATION	
microsoft-azure-blockchain.azure-blockchain-ethe...	Succeeded	3/28/2018, 11:38:49 PM	34 minutes 55 seconds	Related events
connections-deploy	Succeeded	3/28/2018, 11:38:40 PM	35 seconds	Related events
vnet-gateway-deploy	Succeeded	3/28/2018, 11:37:53 PM	32 minutes 52 seconds	Related events
vmss-dep-reg2	Succeeded	3/28/2018, 11:24:23 PM	6 minutes 35 seconds	Related events
vmss-dep-reg1	Succeeded	3/28/2018, 11:17:38 PM	11 minutes 15 seconds	Related events
omsDeploy	Succeeded	3/28/2018, 11:05:58 PM	1 minute 56 seconds	Related events
network-resources-deploy	Succeeded	3/28/2018, 11:04:46 PM	43 seconds	Related events
pid	Succeeded	3/28/2018, 11:04:08 PM	6 seconds	Related events

11. Select **output** from the window, and now you can see the access credentials for the resources that you created:

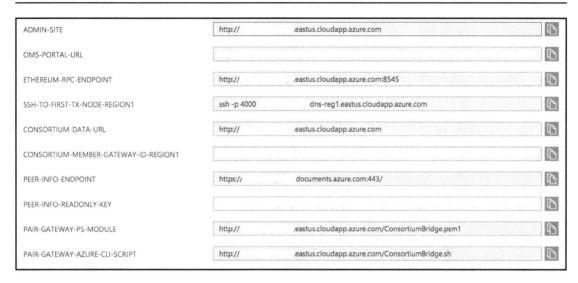

ADMIN-SITE	http://	.eastus.cloudapp.azure.com	
OMS-PORTAL-URL			
ETHEREUM-RPC-ENDPOINT	http://	.eastus.cloudapp.azure.com:8545	
SSH-TO-FIRST-TX-NODE-REGION1	ssh -p 4000	dns-reg1.eastus.cloudapp.azure.com	
CONSORTIUM-DATA-URL	http://	.eastus.cloudapp.azure.com	
CONSORTIUM-MEMBER-GATEWAY-ID-REGION1			
PEER-INFO-ENDPOINT	https://	documents.azure.com:443/	
PEER-INFO-READONLY-KEY			
PAIR-GATEWAY-PS-MODULE	http://	.eastus.cloudapp.azure.com/ConsortiumBridge.psm1	
PAIR-GATEWAY-AZURE-CLI-SCRIPT	http://	.eastus.cloudapp.azure.com/ConsortiumBridge.sh	

These are some of the credentials you can use in the Azure blockchain service:

- **ADMIN-SITE**: Admin portal that you can use to view the current node status and send Ether to newly created accounts
- **OMS-PORTAL-URL**: Azure Operations Management Portal for your resources
- **ETHEREUM-RPC-ENDPOINT**: Ethereum RPC port for you to interact with the blockchain you created
- **SSH-TO-FIRST-TX-NODE-REGION1**: Credentials for connecting to a transaction node that is in the first region

How it works...

Steps 1 to 9 guide you through the process of creating a private Ethereum consortium using services offered by Azure. This will create and deploy multiple peers across various regions behind a load balancer for you to interact with. Steps 10 to 12 describe the process of using these services. This helps you understand various services and where to use them.

Using MetaMask and other wallets

You will need a wallet to send and receive the cryptocurrency used in Ethereum. In this recipe, you will learn to install and use MetaMask or another wallet, which can be used for managing accounts and transactions.

Getting ready

MetaMask is a browser-based wallet and it currently works with both Chrome and Firefox. Other wallets are either browser-based or need additional downloads.

How to do it...

MetaMask, Mist, and MyCrypto are some of the popular wallets in the Ethereum ecosystem. Let's look into these options in detail.

MetaMask

1. Install MetaMask for Chrome or Firefox from the respective app store.
2. Select MetaMask from the extensions tab and **Accept** both **Privacy** and **Terms and Conditions** after carefully reading them. Then, you will be asked to create a password to encrypt your wallet storage:

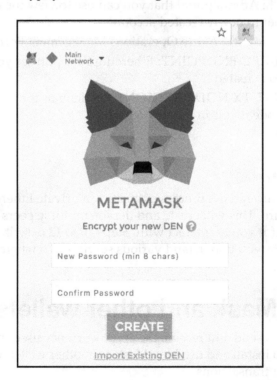

3. MetaMask will generate a random 12-word mnemonic that you can use to restore your account at a later point in time. Save it somewhere safe and secret as this is the only way to regain access to your account:

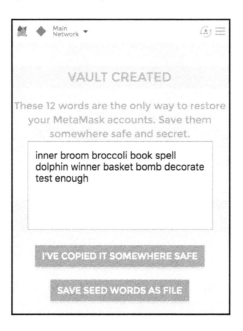

4. Your account has now been successfully created. You can now use MetaMask with all supported websites for signing transactions:

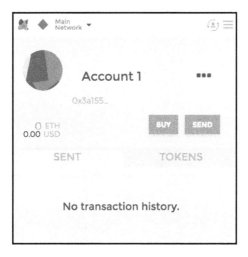

5. You can connect to various Ethereum networks using MetaMask. This includes connecting to the main-net, test nets, or any other RPC ports you have access to. This can be configured from the network selector drop-down in the top-left corner.

6. You also have the option to add additional accounts or to export the private key of the current account. These options let you configure MetaMask as per your requirements.

MyCrypto

1. Using **MyCrypto** is as simple as navigating to `https://mycrypto.com/`. It offers an intuitive UI to interact with Ethereum:

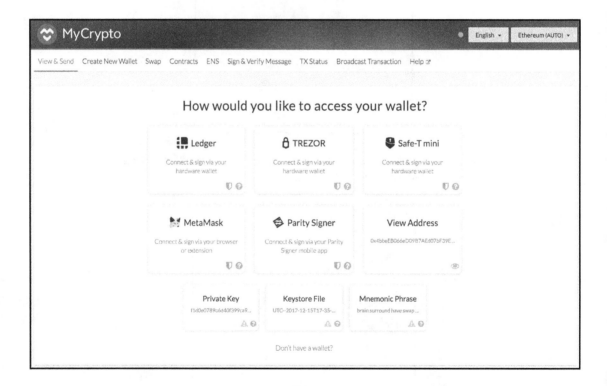

2. Either use an existing wallet or create a new one. The web interface of MyCrypto has limited support for creating/using wallets through PrivateKey, Mnemonic, or keyfile. This restriction is enabled to use a strong password while creating your wallet. Once your wallet is created, you can export your private key and KeyFile. Save it in a secure place and do not lose it. It cannot be recovered!

3. To use MyCrypto, you can import the private Key/KeyFile you created in step 2 or use external wallets such as MetaMask/Mist/Hardware.

4. MyCrypto also has options to deploy and interact with contracts, use Ethereum name service, or even swap your Ether for other cryptos.

Ethereum wallet–Mist

1. Download and install the Mist or Ethereum wallet from `https://github.com/ethereum/mist/releases`. Mist is a browser for decentralized web apps. The Ethereum wallet is a Mist implementation that can only access a single **Decentralized Application** (**DApp**), which is the wallet DApp.

2. You can select the network from **Network** under the **Develop** menu of Mist. You can choose between the main network, test networks, or your own private network.

> Using the Ethereum wallet DApp, you can send/receive transactions and deploy/interact with smart contracts.

Never send your account credentials to anyone or use them with unknown websites. Make sure that you are using a trusted wallet or exchange while using cryptocurrencies. Typos in addresses can make you lose your funds. Double-check the address before making any transactions.

Using block explorer

There are many ways to read data from a transaction or a block in Ethereum. Etherscan is one block explorer and analytics platform for Ethereum. In this recipe, you will learn about the platform and how you can make use of it.

How to do it...

1. Go to `https://etherscan.io/` to access the block explorer. You will see a dashboard that displays the network state:

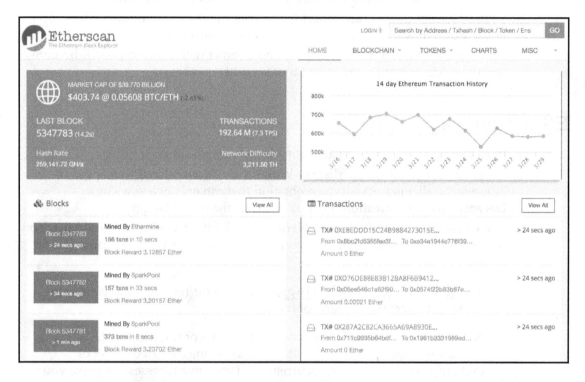

2. On the top left, you can see a card that displays the current Ethereum market share along with the exchange rate. You can also see a transaction history chart for the last 14 days.

3. Search for a block number or select it from the recent blocks list to view the contents of the block. You can see details such as time, miner, hash, transactions, size, gas, and so on:

Height:	**< Prev** **5347843** **Next >**
TimeStamp:	1 day 5 hrs ago (Mar-30-2018 08:13:29 AM +UTC)
Transactions:	181 transactions and 16 contract internal transactions in this block
Hash:	0xc575e73f67f34985cf689e150d95cd0a070613e3c7d7c8de68fc731ca3bd03ee
Parent Hash:	0x67eea7814feda29fef4ffb0aa83dd12c7107dc04ae00262fbe6e2141b67e0ab9
Sha3Uncles:	0x1dcc4de8dec75d7aab85b567b6ccd41ad312451b948a7413f0a142fd40d49347
Mined By:	0x52bc44d5378309ee2abf1539bf71de1b7d7be3b5 (**Nanopool**) in 12 secs
Difficulty:	3,179,980,184,825,897
Total Difficulty:	3,346,245,058,223,482,114,549
Size:	23778 bytes
Gas Used:	7,960,499 (99.51%)
Gas Limit:	8,000,029
Nonce:	0x61fff3f00de99a12
Block Reward:	3.065574029116866653 Ether (3 + 0.065574029116866653)
Uncles Reward:	0
Extra Data:	nanopool.org (Hex:0x6e616e6f706f6f6c2e6f7267)

4. By searching a transaction, you can view transaction details such as from address, to address, the value transferred, gas, and other details.

5. Etherscan also offers a details page for both **Externally Owned Addresses** (**EOA**) and contract addresses. To see the balance, list of transactions, and even tokens owned by that address, navigate to the EOA details page.

6. The contract page also shows the balance, transactions, and even a contract code if it is a verified contract. To interact with verified contracts through Etherscan, use this page.

7. The platform also offers charts for analytics. Use the charts to get an idea about the currency, network, mining, blocks, transactions, and other general information.

8. Click the **MISC** tab to use tools such as the mining calculator, bytecode converter, and transaction broadcaster.

9. Etherscan also has a free to use API for reading data from Ethereum. Sign up to Etherscan to use the API and use the free API key that can be generated from the portal itself. Make sure that you are not making more than five requests per second. You will be blocked if this is exceeded.

10. Signing up with Etherscan will allow you to watch specific addresses and create email alerts. You can even add a private note for each transaction.

There's more...

Eth-netstats is a visual interface for tracking an Ethereum network status. To access the public status page, go to `https://ethstats.net/`. Note that the portal does not represent the entire state of the Ethereum main net. This is because of the voluntary listing of nodes in the portal.

You can use netstats to visualize your private Ethereum network:

1. Download the source code from the repository. Make sure to verify the license:

```
git clone https://github.com/cubedro/eth-netstats
```

2. Install the dependencies:

```
sudo npm install -g grunt-cli
cd eth-netstats
npm install
```

3. Build the project using grunt and use `npm` to run it:

```
grunt
npm start
```

Understanding everything about accounts

Ethereum accounts are made up of 20-byte addresses, and you can exchange data and values between two accounts with state transitions. In general, there are two types of account in Ethereum: EOA and contract accounts. Depending on the type of account, there are four fields associated with each account: balance, contract code, storage, and nonce.

EOAs are controlled by a private key, and contract accounts are controlled by the contract code. A normal user can create an EOA by using a wallet such as MetaMask or MyCrypto. As a developer, you need to know more about these accounts and other ways to create them. In this recipe, you will learn how to create and maintain EOAs in Ethereum.

Getting ready

You will need a working installation of `geth` in your system to run `web3` commands. Other prerequisites, if any, are listed along with each command.

How to do it...

1. Create an account using the account command in the `geth` command-line tool. This will create an Ethereum account for you and will return the EOA address:

   ```
   $ geth account new
   ```

   If you are using the JavaScript console or Web3JS, use the following command to create an account:

   ```
   > web3.personal.newAccount("<password>")
   ```

2. Before you do any transaction from this account, unlock it using the password. Use the third parameter to control the duration of unlocking. To lock the account after the transaction, use the `lockAccount` function:

   ```
   > personal.unlockAccount("<address>", "<password>")
   > personal.lockAccount("<your_address>")
   ```

3. Creating an account using this method also creates an encrypted KeyFile. The file is located in your key store with the format `UTC--{year}-{month}--{account}`. The contents of the file also includes an encrypted version of your private key:

   ```
   {
     "address":"4f9e3e25a8e6ddaf976dcbf0b92285b1bb139ce2",
     "crypto":{
        "cipher":"aes-128-ctr",
   "ciphertext":"0b0ae5548acc4d08134f4fe...53cb8c08eb9563a76aeb082c",
           "cipherparams":{
              "iv":"6079a38e159b95f88e0f03fbdae0f526"
           },
           "kdf":"scrypt",
           "kdfparams {
              "dklen":32,
              "n":262144,
              "p":1,
              "r":8,
   ```

```
                    "salt":"7ed09d37d80048c21490fc9...dc10b3cef10e544017"
                },
            "mac":"0d8ac3314c4e9c9aaac515995c...43bf46f17d2d78bb84a6"
        },
        "id":"7b6630ea-8fc8-4c35-a54f-272283c8f579",
        "version":3
    }
```

4. You can also create a private key externally and import it into other wallets. Ethereum follows the elliptical curve for private keys. You can either create one with OpenSSL or with wallets such as MyCrypto. Once a private key is created, you can import it using the following command. Make sure to give it a strong password to encrypt it:

   ```
   $ geth account import <path to PrivateKey file>
   ```

   You can also import the private key using the JavaScript console:

   ```
   > web3.personal.importRawKey("<private key>", "<password>")
   ```

 Please do not share your private keys with any website, business, or individual. You may need to provide your private keys to MetaMask and other similar wallets, which exist to manage accounts, in order to use them. Do this with caution and ensure that you can trust them.

5. If you want to find the address from the private key, a series of steps have to be followed. Convert the private key to a 64-byte-long public key. Then, take the Keccak-256 hash of the public key, and the last 20 bytes will be the Ethereum address for that private key.

6. You can also create an account securely by using the mnemonic phrase. This mnemonic is a 12-word phrase that can be used as a seed to create EOAs. This is easy to store and wallets such as MetaMask follow this pattern.

There's more...

If you need a safe and secure way to store your private key or account, then the recommended way is to use a hardware wallet. The only way someone can use the account is by physically interacting with the wallet. This reduces the potential security threat if someone gets into your system maliciously.

Installing a solidity compiler

You have multiple options when it comes to compiling smart contracts written in solidity. In this recipe, you will learn about installing a solidity compiler and using it to compile your smart contract.

Getting ready

If you are using macOS, you will need `homebrew` to install the binary compiler. There are other options, such as using `npm` or `docker`, which require `Node.js` and `Docker`, respectively, installed on your machine.

How to do it...

1. If you are in Ubuntu, use `ppa` to install the compiler by running the following command:

```
sudo add-apt-repository ppa:ethereum/ethereum
sudo apt-get update
sudo apt-get install solc
```

2. If you are using macOS, install the compiler using `brew`:

```
brew update
brew tap ethereum/ethereum
brew install solidity
```

3. Verify the installation with the following command:

```
solc --version
```

4. Use this command to compile a contract and print the binary:

```
solc --bin SampleContract.sol
```

5. You want to get some of the more advanced output from `solc`:

```
solc -o outDirectory --bin --ast --asm --abi --opcodes
SampleContract.sol
```

We can configure it using these provided flags:

- `--ast`: Abstracts the syntax trees of source files
- `--asm`: EVM assembly of the contracts
- `--abi`: ABI specification of the contracts
- `--opcodes`: Opcodes of the contracts

You can get the complete list of operations supported by the `solc` compiler by running `solc --help`.

There's more...

There is also a JavaScript-based solidity compiler available for you to use. You can install `SolcJS` using `npm`. The `solc-js` project is derived from the C++ `solc` project and can be used in JavaScript projects directly:

```
npm install -g solc
```

To see all the supported features, run the following command:

```
solcjs --help
```

Smart Contract Development 2

In this chapter, we will cover the following recipes:

- Choosing an IDE wisely
- Writing your first smart contract
- Testing your contract with Remix
- Static and dynamic types in solidity
- Constructor and fallback functions
- Working with struct and enum
- Control structures in solidity
- Writing functions in solidity
- Deciding between arrays and mappings
- Where to use function modifiers
- Using visibility modifiers efficiently
- Essential events: EVM logger
- Efficiently using memory and storage
- Compiling your contract with the solc compiler
- Deploying the contract using geth

Introduction

Smart contracts enable you to solve common problems in a way that maximizes trust. The purpose of contracts is to reduce ambiguity and inclination so that a predictable set of outcomes is produced, and these outcomes can be depended upon. In Ethereum, you can write smart contracts with the built-in Turing complete programming language (solidity). The language can create its own arbitrary rules for ownership, transaction formats, and state transition functions. Smart contracts in Ethereum are written in solidity and targeted to run on the Ethereum Virtual Machine (EVM). To actually execute smart contract code, someone has to send enough Ether as a transaction fee. The fee is calculated based on the computing resources required. This pays the miner nodes for participating and providing their computing power.

This chapter covers all the essentials of writing a smart contract from scratch, compiling the contract, and deploying it to an Ethereum network. You will also learn various design choices to write an efficient smart contract.

Smart contracts given in this chapter are targeted towards the solidity compiler 0.4.23, which is the latest version as of writing this book. New versions are being released quickly and we recommend you check the changelog for Ethereum and solidity in their respective GitHub repositories. Smart contracts in this book are for illustration purposes only. It is strongly advised to test and audit your code for bugs before deploying it to the main network.

Choosing an IDE wisely

Developing a distributed application often requires the developer to interact with multiple tools and languages. There are efficient Integrated Development Environments (IDE) that can help you accomplish most of the work related to developing an application. IDEs usually combine code editors, compilers, debuggers, and other useful tools. Some may find it comfortable using a simple text editor and related command-line tools for development.

In this recipe, you will learn about a few tools that can support Ethereum development.

How to do it...

One of the most popular and widely used IDEs for solidity is Remix. Let's see how you can use it for your development:

1. Access Remix by navigating to `https://remix.ethereum.org`. Remix is a web-based IDE that you can use to write, test, debug, and deploy your smart contracts.

2. Use the file view from the left panel to create and delete files. Use the right-hand panel for tools that will help your development. Write code in the editor window and use the console window to see the result. The console window can also help in executing web3 commands in real time:

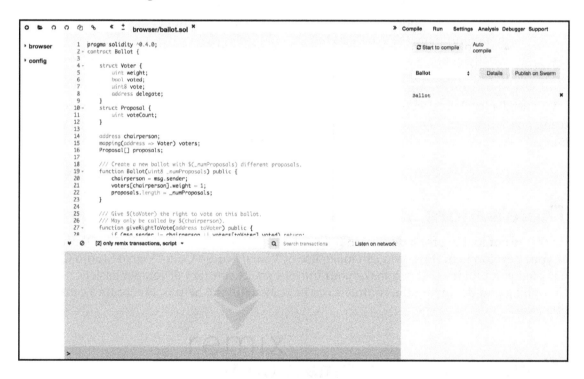

3. Remix has a JavaScript-based solidity compiler working in the background; use this feature to find errors and suggestions in real time.

4. The files are on the left panel. Use the option to import your existing project as well.

5. Use the console window to see logs for events triggered by the IDE, and you can execute Web3JS commands in **REPL** (**Read-Evaluate-Print-Loop**) mode, which takes single expressions, evaluates them, and returns the result.

6. Use the **Compile** tab in the right panel to perform tasks related to compiling your contract. You can see a list of errors during compilation and the complete output once it finishes.

7. Deploy and test your smart contract from the **Run** tab. Choose your own network using the **Environment** option and use the **Create** button to deploy your contract. Point your contract to an existing deployment using the **At Address** option. You can use this to test and debug your existing contract.

8. Use the **Setting** tab to change IDE-related settings, such as changing the theme, choosing a different compiler, or other general settings.

9. Analyze your code, which will help you identify potential bugs and best practice violations using the **Analysis** tab.

10. Finally, there is a **Debugger** tab, which will help you debug your code. We will discuss the debugging process in `Chapter 11`, *Miscellaneous*.

If you need a local version of Remix, it is available as an `npm` module, and you can get it using `npm install remix-ide -g`. Also, you can download and build it from its source (`https://github.com/ethereum/remix`) if you need more flexibility and control over the code.

There's more...

If you are not looking for a dedicated IDE and need a text editor to use along with the rest of your development flow, you can make use of Visual Studio Code. Visual Studio Code has plenty of plugins that can make your life as a smart contract developer easier. Compiling and deploying the contracts can be done with the help of Ethereum's command-line tools.

Writing your first smart contract

Solidity is the language of choice for writing smart contracts in Ethereum. A solidity smart contract is a collection of code (functions) and data (state) that resides at a specific address in the Ethereum blockchain.

Solidity is a statically typed, high-level language which is influenced by JavaScript, Python, and C++. Solidity supports inheritance, libraries, and user-defined types, and is designed for EVM.

Getting ready

It is recommended to use Remix (`https://remix.ethereum.org`) for writing smart contracts in solidity. Remix is a browser-based IDE that supports writing, compiling, testing, and deploying solidity smart contracts. Remix provides all of these features in an easy-to-use interface and can be accessed quickly without any installation.

You can also use any text editor along with Ethereum command-line tools to write and deploy contracts.

How to do it...

Follow these steps to write your "hello world" contract:

1. Specify the target compiler version using version pragma. It is recommended to specify the target compiler version for each contract. This will avoid the contract getting compiled on future or older versions, which might have incompatible changes:

```
pragma solidity ^0.4.21;
```

    This source code will not compile with a compiler with a version lower than 0.4.21 or greater than 0.5.0.

2. Create a contract with the `contract` keyword followed by the contract name:

```
contract HelloWorld {
    // Here goes your smart contract code
}
```

3. Write a method that we can use for printing "hello world." The method declaration starts with the `function` keyword:

```
function printSomething() {
    // things to do
}
```

4. Return "hello world" from the method with the `return` keyword:

```
return "hello world";
```

5. Specify the return type for each method using `returns`:

```
function printSomething() returns (string) { }
```

6. This is how your contract will look now:

```
pragma solidity ^0.4.21;

contract HelloWorld {
    function printSomething() returns (string) {
        return "hello world";
    }
}
```

Remix provides real-time errors and warnings as you write your contract. This option can be toggled using the **Auto compile** checkbox under the **compile** tab. A contract can be manually compiled with the **Start to compile** button.

7. Let's try to do a little more with your first contract. Add a method that modifies the text to print based on user input. For storing the string value, add a state variable of type string:

```
string textToPrint = "hello world";
```

8. Add a method that accepts user input and changes the default value of the text:

```
function changeText(string _text) {
    textToPrint = _text;
}
```

9. Finally, change the `printSomething` method to return the string state variable than print static text:

```
function printSomething() returns (string) {
    return textToPrint;
}
```

10. Make sure that you also tag this method as a read-only method using view. view restricts the method from modifying the state of the contract. These methods don't consume any gas and are free to use:

```
function printSomething() view returns (string) { }
```

12. Methods have different levels of visibility and default to public. It is a good idea to specify this explicitly. We will discuss the other keywords used later in this chapter.

13. This is how your contract should look after adding these parameters:

```
pragma solidity ^0.4.21;

contract HelloWorld {

    string textToPrint = "hello world";

    function changeText(string _text) public {
        textToPrint = _text;
    }

    function printSomething() public view returns (string) {
        return textToPrint;
    }
}
```

How it works...

EVM is the runtime environment for Ethereum smart contracts. Contracts running inside EVM have no access to the network, filesystem, or other processes. This is because of the isolated and sandboxed nature of EVM.

The first line in this smart contract tells us that the source code is written for compiler version 0.4.21 or anything newer (such as <0.5.0) that does not break any functionality. The pragma keyword is used because pragmas are instructions for the compiler about how to treat the source code.

The line string textToPrint = "hello world"; declares a state variable called textToPrint and assigns a value to it. You can think of it as a slot in a database that can be queried and altered by calling the functions in the code that manage the database. To access the variable inside the contract, you don't need to use this as in other languages.

This is a simple contract that allows anyone to store a string that is accessible by anyone in the world, without a way to prevent you from publishing this value. Anyone could just use a different value and overwrite your string, but the old string will still be stored in the history of the blockchain. You will learn to restrict write access to a contract in a different recipe.

There's more...

If you want to change something in the blockchain, you have to create a transaction, which has to be accepted by all participants. As an example, imagine a bank table that lists the balances of all accounts. The transactional nature of the database ensures that if an amount is subtracted from one account, it is always added to the other account. It also ensures that only the person holding the keys to the account can transfer money from it. This is ensured with the process of signing a transaction cryptographically by the owner.

A transaction can include both binary data and Ether. If the target account contains code, that code is executed and the payload (binary data) is provided as input data. If the target account is non-existent, the transaction creates a new contract. The payload of such a contract creation transaction is executed. The output of this execution is permanently stored as the code of the contract.

Each transaction is charged with a certain amount of gas, which limits the amount of code to execute and what to pay the miner for its execution. The gas price is a value set by the transaction sender. The sender has to pay an initial price, which is calculated by *gasPrice * gas*. During the execution, if the gas provided is not enough, then it triggers an exception and will revert any state changes made during the call. If any gas is left after the execution, it will be refunded to the sender's account. All the values are represented in Wei, which is the smallest denomination of Ether (*10^{18} Wei = 1 Ether*).

Testing your contract with Remix

In this recipe, you will learn how to test your smart contract using the Remix IDE. Remix is a browser-based IDE that enables users to write Ethereum contracts in the solidity language and debug transactions. Remix has an inbuilt JavaScript-based solidity compiler and EVM to compile and run smart contracts.

How to do it...

1. Open Remix (`https://remix.ethereum.org`) in your desktop browser.
2. Copy your smart contract to Remix and it will automatically compile your code. Warnings and errors, if any, will be displayed in the right panel.
3. Remix has an inbuilt JavaScript VM for testing smart contracts. Ensure that you have selected JavaScript VM as the default environment under **Run**:

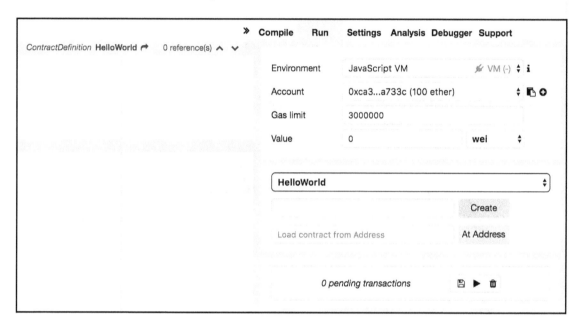

4. Select an account from which the contract will be deployed. You can select an account from the list of default accounts provided by Remix. Each account is loaded with enough Ether for testing.
5. The gas limit specifies the maximum amount of gas (unit for calculating the execution cost) that has to be used for deployment. For our HelloWorld contract, the default value should be enough.
6. To send some Ether to the contract while deploying, use the **Value** field to specify the amount of Ether to send.
7. Deploy your contract using the **Create** button. Ensure that the drop-down menu above the **Create** button has your contract name selected.

8. Once you have successfully deployed your contract, you can see the transaction and other logs in the console window. Click on the **Details** button to view more information:

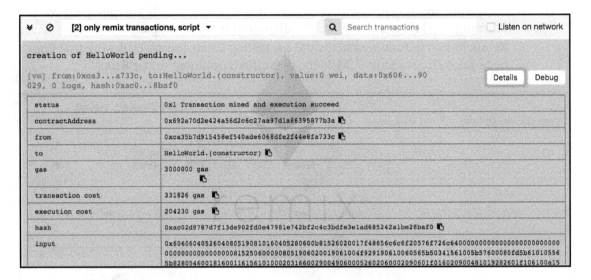

9. Once the contract is deployed, Remix will also generate an interactive contract instance UI for you to interact with:

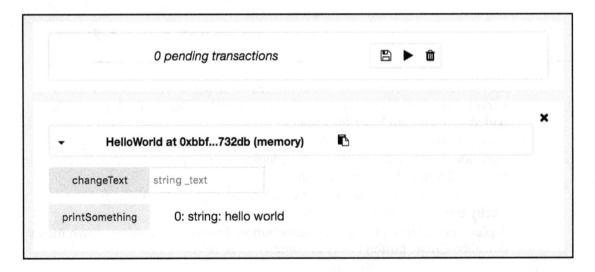

10. The contract instance UI generated by Remix will display the contract address, along with the relevant controls for all public and external methods. Blue controls are read-only methods, which are free to use, and red controls are used to modify the state of the contract.
11. Test the `printSomething` method by clicking its button and it will display the default value, which is "hello world".
12. Try changing the default value with the help of the `changeText` method. Input values are provided in the input box, which is next to each button. Ensure that you are entering the string value in double quotes ("new text").
13. The **Account**, **Gas Limit**, and **Value** fields at the top also apply while interacting with your contract.

Remix will work over both HTTP and HTTPS protocols. This can come in handy if you are connecting to a local node that may not always have an HTTPS connection.

There's more...

You can create multiple contract files in Remix and even open files from your local storage. Remix can also interact with your filesystem with read/write permission. This will help you to work on files stored in your filesystem without copying them to remix.

`Remixd` is the `npm` module that gives the remix IDE access to a folder from your local computer. To install `remixd` globally in your system, use the following command. Unix/Mac users might want to use `sudo` for permission:

```
npm install -g remixd
```

To start sharing your files for Remix, use the following command. This will share the files using a `WebSocket` connection:

```
remixd -s <Path-to-the-folder>
```

Once file sharing has started, click on the **connect to localhost** button under the left panel to connect to the shared filesystem.

Static and dynamic types in solidity

Statically typed programming languages do the type checking at compile time. Since solidity is a statically typed language, the type of each variable has to be specified at compile time. Solidity also provides an option to create complex user-defined types and type conversion.

In this recipe, you will learn about the basic elementary types of solidity, such as int, bool, array, byte, and address.

Getting ready

Remix is the best way to quickly write a test smart contract. Remix is a browser-based IDE that supports writing, compiling, testing, and deploying solidity smart contracts. Remix provides all these features in an easy-to-use interface and can be accessed quickly without any installation.

You can also use any text editor along with the solidity compiler to write and compile your contract.

How to do it...

1. Create a state variable to store Boolean values in the contract. Use the bool keyword and initialize it using either true or false. The Boolean type supports basic operators such as - !, &&, !!, ==, and !=:

   ```
   bool isAvailable = false;
   ```

2. To create a variable to store integer values using either int or uint keyword, use int to store unsigned integers and uint to store signed integers of various memory sizes. You can store integers ranging from uint8/int8 to uint256/int256 in steps of 8:

   ```
   // uint/int are aliases for uint256/int256
   uint256 a = 9607111;
   int32 b = 102;
   ```

Use the following supported operators to perform comparisons or arithmetic operations:

- **Comparisons**: <=, <, ==, !=, >=, >
- **Bit operators**: &, |, ^ (bitwise exclusive or), ~ (bitwise negation)
- **Arithmetic operators**: +, -, unary -, unary +, *, /, % (remainder), **
  (exponentiation), << (left shift), >> (right shift)

Integers in solidity are susceptible to overflow/underflow. It is strongly recommended to include such conditions in your contract. You can also use well-tested third-party libraries such as openzeppelin's `SafeMath` (`https://github.com/OpenZeppelin/zeppelin-solidity`) for performing arithmetic operations safely.

3. Now, we can create a fixed-point variable using fixed/ufixed. Since they are not completely supported by Solidity, you can only declare them, but cannot be assigned to or from.
4. Create an address variable with the address keyword. The address type is unique to solidity and holds an Ethereum address of 20 bytes. The address type also supports the <=, <, ==, !=, >=, and > operators:

```
address owner = 0x05ee546c1a62f90d7acbffd6d846c9c54c7cf94c;
```

The following members are part of each address:

- `<address>.balance`: Can be used to query the balance of the address. Returns value in Wei.
- `<address>.transfer(<amount>)`: Sends Ether (in Wei) to an address. If the execution fails, the contract will stop with an exception:

```
owner.transfer(1 ether); // Throws an exception if failed
```

- `<address>.send(<amount>)`: Similar to transfer, but returns false on failure and will not stop the execution:

```
owner.send(1 ether); // Returns true or false
```

- `<address>.call()`: Issues a low-level call. It is generally used to interact with a contract that does not specify an ABI. Call accepts an arbitrary number of arguments of any type and returns false on failure:

```
address productStore = 0x4db26171199535b2e4bae6615c9b8ffe33c41d74;
productStore.call("getProduct", "product_id_001");
```

Adjust the supplied gas and value for call():

```
productStore.call.gas(2000000).value(1 ether).("buyProduct",
"product_id_001");
```

The ABI, or Application Binary Interface, is the standard for encoding or decoding data to or from machine code. Data in Ethereum is encoded according to its type, and this encoding is not self-describing. It requires a schema in order to decode, which is obtained from the ABI.

- `<address>.delegatecall()`: delegatecall uses the code of the target address, taking all other aspects (storage, balance, and so on) from the calling contract. The purpose of delegatecall is to use library code that is stored in another contract. For delegatecall, the user has to ensure that the layout of storage in both contracts is suitable to be used. You can adjust the supplied gas and value like so:

```
contract A {
    uint value;
    address public sender;
    // address of contract B
    address a = 0xef55bfac4228981e850936aaf042951f7b146e41;

    function makeDelegateCall(uint _value) public {
        // Value of A is modified
        a.delegatecall(bytes4(keccak256("setValue(uint)")),
_value);
    }
}

contract B {
    uint value;
    address public sender;

    function setValue(uint _value) public {
        value = _value;
        // msg.sender is preserved in delegatecall.
        // It was not available in callcode.
        sender = msg.sender;
    }
}
```

msg.sender is a global variable in solidity that has the address of the message/transaction sender. You can also make use of msg.value, msg.data, msg.gas, and msg.sig.

- <address>.callcode(): Prior to homestead, only a limited variant called callcode was available, which did not provide access to the original msg.sender and msg.value values. It is not recommended to use callcode.

5. Create an array with a static or dynamic length. Solidity also supports two-dimensional arrays and, unlike other programming languages, the notation is reversed. For example, an array of three dynamic arrays of int is int[][3]. To read the third int in the second dynamic array, you can use a[1][2]:

```
uint[] dynamicSizeArray;
uint[7] fixedSizeArray;
```

Solidity will generate a getter method for arrays if you mark them as public. The index will become the input parameter for that method. If you want to return the whole array at once, create an explicit getter method that returns the required array.

6. Create a fixed byte array in solidity using the bytes keyword. It ranges from bytes1 to bytes32 in steps of 1. These arrays are compatible with Comparisons (<=, <, ==, !=, >=, >) and Bit operators (&, |, ^ (bitwise exclusive or), ~ (bitwise negation), << (left shift), >> (right shift)).
7. Now, we can create an arbitrary length raw byte data type using bytes and for arbitrary length UTF-8 data, use string. These are used as dynamic byte arrays in solidity. String literals are written with either single or double quotes. They are implicitly convertible to bytes if they fit.
8. If we try creating array literals that are written as expressions and are not assigned to a variable right away, the type of an array literal is memory of a fixed size. For example, the type of [2, 4, 8, 5] is uint8[4] memory.

There's more...

Solidity also supports conversions between elementary types. Both implicit and explicit conversions work with data types in solidity.

If different types of values are used with assignment or arithmetic operations, the compiler tries to implicitly convert one value to the type of the other. An implicit conversion is possible if it matches semantically and no information is lost during the conversion. For example, `uint128` can be converted to `uint256` and `int16` to `int32`, but `int` is not convertible to `uint` because `uint` cannot store *-1*. Furthermore, any unsigned `integers` can be converted to `bytes`, but not vice versa:

```
int8 a = 1;
uint b = a + 1200;
```

You can also perform explicit type conversion to supported variables. Only do it if you know what you are doing, and perform enough tests to validate this:

```
int u = -1;
uint v = uint(v);
```

Constructor and fallback functions

In this recipe, you will learn about two important methods in a contract: `constructor` and `fallback` functions.

How to do it...

The declaration and workings of these methods are very similar to other object-oriented languages. Let's look into each one individually.

Constructor

The constructor is a function that is executed when a contract is created. It cannot be called explicitly and is invoked only once during its lifetime. Every contract can have exactly one constructor and if no constructor is declared, the contract will use the default constructor.

1. Create a constructor in solidity using the `constructor` keyword:

```
contract A {
    constructor() {
        // Constructor
    }
}
```

2. Then, write some logic that should get executed during contract creation inside the constructor:

```
contract A {
    address owner;

    constructor() {
        owner = msg.sender;
    }
}
```

3. Now, decorate the constructor as either public (default) or internal. A constructor set as internal causes the contract to be marked as abstract:

```
contract C {
    uint n;

    constructor(uint _n) internal {
        n = _n;
    }
}
```

4. If there is no constructor specified, the contract will execute the default constructor:

```
contract X {
    // Default constructor
    constructor() public { }
}
```

5. Now, we can specify the base contract `constructor` parameters, if any, while inheriting. This can be done in two ways, during inheritance or as part of the `constructor` function:

```
contract A {
    uint someValue;
    constructor(uint _value) public {
        someValue = _value;
    }
}

contract B is A(10) {
    // Base contract argument during inheritance
}

contract C is A {
    constructor(uint _anotherValue) First(_anotherValue) public {
```

```
                        // Base contract argument in constructor
        }
    }
```

Creating a constructor with the same name as the contract is now deprecated. Starting from solidity version 0.4.22, the `constructor` keyword is available for creating a constructor.

Fallback function

Each contract can have one unnamed function called the `fallback` function. It is executed if no other function matches the given signature or plain Ether is sent to the contract:

1. Create a `fallback` function by declaring an unnamed function:

   ```
   function() {
       // fallback function
   }
   ```

2. In order to receive Ether, mark the `fallback` function as a payable function. An exception will be thrown by the contract if it does not have a `fallback` function declared as payable:

   ```
   function() payable {
       // fallback function which can receive Ether
   }
   ```

   A contract without a payable `fallback` function can still receive Ether as a result of self-destruct or mining. Such Ether transfers cannot be rejected by a contract and it is not recommended to use the contract balance as a requirement for execution.

3. By default, the `fallback` function only has 2,300 gas available for execution, which cannot be used for tasks other than basic event logging. This restriction helps in avoiding execution of any unknown malicious code present in the target contract. Refer to Chapter 8, *Smart Contract Security*, for more information on the vulnerabilities that can occur:

   ```
   function() payable {
       // takes only 2300 gas.
       emit EtherReceived(msg.sender);
   }
   ```

4. Now, to perform gas consuming tasks such as writing to storage and creating another contract using the `fallback` function, ensure that there is enough gas sent along with the transaction:

```
contract Receiver {
    uint count;
    event EtherReceived(address indexed from);

    function() payable {
        count++;
        emit EtherReceived(msg.sender);
    }
}
```

`Fallback` methods cannot accept arguments or return anything. One can still use `msg.data` to retrieve the payload sent with the call as parameters. Event logs can be used as a workaround to return values from the function.

Working with struct and enum

There are several elementary types in solidity that can be used together to form various complex user-defined types. In this recipe, you will learn about two user-defined types in Solidity: `struct` and `enum`.

How to do it...

Let's create and work with various user-defined types using `struct` and `enum`.

Structs

Structs provide a way to define new types of solidity:

1. Use the `struct` keyword for creating user-defined types in solidity:

```
struct Person { }
```

2. Create a `struct` with a name and the associated properties inside it:

```
struct Person {
    uint16 id;
    bytes32 fName;
    bytes32 lName;
}
```

3. Structs can also include `arrays`, `mapping`, or other user-defined types:

```
struct Person {
    uint16 id;
    bytes32 fName;
    bytes32 lName;
    Contact phone;
}

struct Contact {
    uint countryCode;
    uint number;
}
```

4. You cannot create a `struct` member with its own type. This helps in limiting the size of the struct to a finite value.

5. Create a variable of the `struct` type as follows:

```
Person owner;
Person[] contributors;
```

6. Directly access or modify the values of a `struct` as follows:

```
contributors[2].fName = "John";
contributors[2].lName = "Doe";
```

7. Create a local variable of `struct` type and use the data location of storage. This only stores a reference and does not copy the `struct` so that assignments to members of the local variable actually write to the state:

```
Person storage contributor = contributors[2];
contributor.fName = "John";
contributor.lName = "Doe";
```

8. To initialize a `struct` variable, use any of the following methods:

```
Contact memory myContact = Contact(91, 23232323);
// OR
Contact memory myContact = Contact({
    countryCode: 91,
    number: 23232323
});
```

9. Use the following contract as a reference to understand more about the use of structs:

```
pragma solidity ^0.4.21;

// This contract is for illustration purpose only.
contract CrowdFunding {

    // Defines a new type with two fields.
    struct Funder {
        address addr;
        uint amount;
        bool isApproved;
    }

    // Array of user defined type
    Funder[] contributors;

    function contribute() public payable {
        // Creates a new temporary memory struct
        // Initializes with the given values
        // You can also use Funder(msg.sender, msg.value).
        Funder memory contributor = Funder({
            addr: msg.sender,
            amount: msg.value,
            isApproved: false
        });

        contributors.push(contributor);
    }

    // Function that changes a specific value of struct
    function approve(uint id) public {
        Funder storage contributor = contributors[id];
        contributor.isApproved = true;
    }

    // Function which returns struct value
```

```
function getContributor(uint id) public view
    returns (address, uint, bool) {
    Funder memory contributor = contributors[id];
    return (contributor.addr,
            contributor.amount,
            contributor.isApproved);
}
}
```

Ordering storage variables and struct members can optimize gas usage if tightly packed. For example, declare your storage variables in the order of `uint128`, `uint128`, `uint256` instead of `uint128`, `uint256`, `uint128`, as the former will only take up two slots of storage whereas the latter will take up three.

Enums

Enums are generally used for creating custom types with a limited set of values:

1. Create an enum in solidity with the `enum` keyword:

```
enum Direction {
    // Options
}
```

2. Enums should contain at least one member:

```
enum Direction {
    North,
    East,
    South,
    West
}
```

3. You can initialize enums directly:

```
Direction path = Direction.North;
```

4. Enums support explicit conversion to and from all integer types:

```
function getCurrentChoice() view public
    returns (uint) {
    return uint(path);
}
```

5. Use the following contract as an example of enums:

```
pragma solidity ^0.4.23;

contract Navigation {

    // enum declaration
    enum Direction {
        North,
        East,
        South,
        West
    }

    // Default direction
    Direction path = Direction.North;

    // Function which accepts enum as input
    function changeDirection(Direction dir) public {
        path = dir;
    }

    // Function which returns enum. Since enum is not part of ABI,
return type will be changed to uint
    function getCurrentDirection() view public
        returns (Direction) {
        return path;
    }
}
```

Control structures in Solidity

Most of the control structures from other languages are also supported in solidity. In this recipe, you will learn about supported control structures in solidity, along with examples. The semantics are very similar to C or JavaScript.

How to do it...

1. If-else condition statements are used to perform different actions based on different conditions. Create a function, isValid, which returns true for input values greater than 10 and returns false otherwise:

```
pragma solidity ^0.4.23;
```

```
contract test {
    function isValid(uint input) public pure
        returns (bool) {
        if (input > 10) {
            return true;
        } else {
            return false;
        }
    }
}
```

Solidity doesn't support type conversion from Boolean to non-Boolean types as in other languages like JavaScript. So, if(1) { } is not a valid condition in solidity.

2. A `while loop` allows code to be executed repeatedly based on a Boolean condition. Create a while loop to send Ether to all addresses present in the array:

```
pragma solidity ^0.4.23;

contract test {
 function refund(address[] users) public {
        uint i = 0;
        while (i < users.length) {
            users[i].transfer(1 ether);
            i++;
        }
    }
}
```

3. A `for` loop is the control structure generally used when you want to create a loop. Modify the previous example to use a `for` loop:

```
pragma solidity ^0.4.23;

contract test {
    function refund(address[] users) public {
        for(uint i = 0; i < users.length; i++) {
            users[i].transfer(1 ether);
        }
    }
}
```

Using uint8 in for loops is not a good idea since uint8 can easily under/overflow due to its limited size. Also, it is strongly recommended to check the gas usage in loops to avoid the contract getting stuck in the middle.

4. do while works just like in JavaScript and C. The code is executed first and then the expression is evaluated. Use the do while control to transfer Ether:

```
pragma solidity ^0.4.22;

contract test {
    function refund(address[] users) public {
        uint input = 0;
        do {
            users[input].transfer(1 ether);
            input++;
        } while (input < 10);
    }
}
```

5. Use the continue and break statements as follows:

```
pragma solidity ^0.4.22;

contract test {
    function refund(address[] users) public {
        for (uint i = 0; i < 20; i++) {
            if (i % 2 == 0)
                continue;
            users[i].transfer(1 ether);
        }
    }
}
```

6. Use the conditional operator as follows. It takes three arguments. The first argument is a comparison argument, the second is the result of a true comparison, and the third is the result of a false comparison:

```
pragma solidity ^0.4.22;

contract test {
    function isValid(uint value) public pure
        returns (bool) {
        bool result = (value > 10) ? true : false;
        return result;
    }
}
```

Solidity supports most of the control structures implemented in JavaScript, except switch and goto. These are currently under consideration, and future versions may include support for them.

Writing functions in solidity

A function is a unit of code designed to do a particular task within a larger contract. In this recipe, you will learn about creating and interacting with functions in solidity.

How to do it...

1. Create a function in solidity with the `function` keyword to perform a specific task. The following example demonstrates how we can create a simple function:

```
contract Test {
    function functionName() {
        // Do something
    }
}
```

2. Create another function to accept input parameters. These parameters can be declared just like variables. The following example accepts two parameters of type `uint`:

```
contract Test {
    function add(uint _a, uint _b) public {
        // Do something
    }
}
```

3. Define output parameters with the same syntax. The `returns` keyword is used to specify the return. The following function returns a variable of type `uint`:

```
contract Test {
    function add(uint _a, uint _b) public pure
        returns (uint sum)
    {
        sum = _a + _b;
    }
}
```

4. Declare `return` types without a name. They will use the same name as the variable returned:

```
contract Test {
    function add(uint _a, uint _b) public pure
        returns (uint)
    {
```

```
            uint sum = _a + _b;
            return sum;
        }
    }
```

5. Create a function with multiple output parameters. You can see a function returning two `uint` values in the following example:

```
contract Test {
    function arithmetics(uint _a, uint _b) public pure
        returns (uint, uint)
    {
        return (_a + _b, _a - _b);
    }
}
```

6. Try calling the functions of the current contract internally by its name. The example described here shows a function, `addTwo`, calling another function, `addOne`, which is declared within the same contract:

```
contract Test {
    function addOne(uint _a) public pure
        returns (uint)
    {
        return _a + 1;
    }

    function addTwo(uint _b) public pure
        returns (uint)
    {
        return addOne(_b) + 1;
    }
}
```

7. Try calling functions declared within other contracts externally with this `.f()` or `<contractInstance>.f()`. In this example, the `addOne` and `addTwo` functions are declared within different contracts but called externally using the contract instance:

```
contract Basic {
    function addOne(uint _a) public pure
        returns (uint)
    {
        return _a + 1;
    }
}
```

```
contract Advanced {
    Basic basic;
    function addTwo(uint _b) public view
        returns (uint)
    {
        return basic.addOne(_b) + 1;
    }
}
```

Calls to external contracts can cause several unexpected security issues. Untrusted contract calls may execute malicious code in that contract or any other contract that it depends upon. It is recommended to strictly validate such calls.

8. Create a function that accepts Ether and has to be marked with payable. Non-payable functions will throw if someone tries to send Ether to it:

```
contract test {
    mapping(address => uint) donors;
    function donate() public payable {
        donors[msg.sender] = msg.value;
    }
}
```

9. In a function call, argument names can be specified by name. This allows the user to follow a different order for passing parameters:

```
contract Test {
    function add(uint _a, uint _b) public {
        // Do something
    }

    function calc() public {
        add({_b: 5, _a:10});
    }
}
```

10. Unused parameter names can be omitted from the function:

```
contract test {
    function calc(uint _a, uint) public returns (uint) {
        // Do something
    }
}
```

11. Functions can be declared as view (an alias for constant, which is deprecated) if they do not modify the state. State modification includes tasks such as writing to a state variable, emitting events, and sending Ether:

```
contract test {
    uint multiplier = 10;
    function fun(uint _a, uint _b) public view
        returns (uint) {
        return (_a + _b) * multiplier;
    }
}
```

12. Functions can be declared as pure if they do not read or modify the state. The following example does not read from or write to the contract state:

```
contract test {
    function fun(uint _a, uint _b) public pure
        returns (uint) {
        return _a + _b;
    }
}
```

There's more...

Functions can be overloaded with function overloading. Functions can have the same name but different arguments. Consider the following example of overloading the `fun` function:

```
contract Test {
    function fun(uint _a) public {
        // Do something
    }

    function fun(uint _b, uint _c) public {
        // Do something
    }
}
```

Deciding between arrays and mappings

Arrays and mappings in solidity are the most commonly used data types to store complex data. There are trade-offs in using one over the other, and each has its own advantages. In this recipe, you will learn about common use cases for `arrays` and `mappings`.

How to do it...

`Arrays` and `mappings` are used for a series of objects, all of which are the same size and type. Arrays store data sequentially with an incrementing index, whereas mappings store data as key-value pairs (which can also be seen as hash tables).

Arrays

Follow these steps to create arrays in solidity and to perform read/write operations:

1. Arrays can be created with a fixed or dynamic length. Arrays can also hold user-defined types:

```
uint[10] numbers;

struct Person {
    uint id;
    string name;
}
Person[] candidates;
```

2. The creation of multidimensional arrays is supported by solidity:

```
// array of 3 dynamic arrays of bool
bool[][3] table;
```

Note that the index value is reversed when compared with other languages. For example, to access the first element in the third array, you use *a[2][0]*:

3. Arrays have a length parameter to store the number of elements in the array. Changing the length parameter of dynamic storage arrays can resize the arrays:

```
contract test {
    address[] contributors;

    function donate() public payable {
        contributors.push(msg.sender);
    }
    function getContributorsCount() view public
        returns (uint) {
        return contributors.length;
    }
}
```

Dynamic arrays have a member called push, which can be used to append an element to the array. The function returns the new length of the array.

4. One of the main advantages of using an array is the iteration. Array iteration has to be done carefully so that it does not throw an out-of-gas error during execution. An attacker can even fill up the array to create a denial-of-service attack.

Each block has a gas limit, and exceeding this limit during a transaction will throw an out-of-gas exception. Such an exception will revert the whole transaction, and the value transferred is sent back to the sender's address.

Mapping

Follow these steps to create mappings in solidity:

1. Mappings are created with key-value pairs. A mapping can be compared with a hash table or dictionary. The following example creates a mapping of an address and a user-defined type, and another mapping with an address and an unsigned integer. These are used for storing employee data:

```
contract test {

    struct Person {
        uint id;
        string name;
    }
    mapping(address => Person) employees;
    mapping(address => uint) balances;
    function insert(address _employee, uint _id,
        string _name, uint _balance) public {
        employees[_employee] = Person({
            id: _id,
            name: _name
        });
        balances[_employee] = _balance;
    }
}
```

2. Mappings can be nested to create a more complex data structure:

```
contract test {
    mapping(address => mapping(uint => bytes32)) dataStore;
    function insert(uint _id, bytes32 _value) public {
        dataStore[msg.sender][_id] = _value;
    }
}
```

3. In a mapping, the key can be anything except a mapping, a dynamically sized array, a contract, an `enum`, or a `struct`. The value can be of any type.

4. The key data is not actually stored in the mapping, as only its `keccak256` hash is used to look up the value. Because of this, mappings do not have a length associated with them.

5. Mappings are not iterable, but we can design a data structure to allow such operations.

Declaring an array or mapping as a public variable generates a `getter` method for it. In a mapping, the key will become a parameter for the `getter` and it will return the value. For an array, the index will become the parameter.

Where to use function modifiers

Function modifiers are simple snippets that can change the behavior of a contract. In this recipe, you will learn how to create and use function modifiers in solidity.

How to do it...

1. Modifiers are declared with the `modifier` keyword as follows:

```
modifier modifierName {
    // modifier definition
}
```

2. The function body is inserted where the _ symbol appears in the definition of a modifier:

```
modifier onlyOwner {
    require(msg.sender == owner);
    _;
}
```

3. Modifiers can accept parameters like functions do. The following example creates a generic modifier to verify the caller address:

```
contract Test {
    address owner;
    constructor() public {
```

```
        owner = msg.sender;
    }
    modifier onlyBy(address user) {
        require(msg.sender == user);
        _;
    }
    function donate() onlyBy(owner) public {
        // do something
    }
}
```

4. Multiple modifiers can be specified in a function. They will be evaluated in the order given:

```
contract modifierContract {
    address owner;
    constructor() {
        owner == msg.sender;
    }

    modifier onlyOwner {
        require(msg.sender == owner);
        _;
    }

    modifier valueGreaterThan(uint value) {
        require(msg.value > value);
        _;
    }

    function sendEther() onlyOwner valueGreaterThan(1 ether) public
    {
        // Function body
    }
}
```

5. Modifiers can be inherited from other contracts and can also be overridden:

```
contract Ownership {

    address owner;
    function Ownership() public {
        owner = msg.sender;
    }

    modifier onlyOwner {
        require(msg.sender == owner);
        _;
```

```
        }
    }

    contract Donate is Ownership {

        bool locked;
        modifier noReentrancy() {
            require(!locked);
            locked = true;
            _;
            locked = false;
        }

        function claim() onlyOwner public {
            require(msg.sender.call());
        }

        function donate(address _user) noReentrancy public {
            require(_user.call());
        }

    }
```

It is recommended to use modifiers often to validate function execution, as they express what actions are occurring in a readable and declarative manner.

Using visibility modifiers efficiently

Functions and state variables can have visibility modifiers. There are four visibility modifiers in solidity. Functions can be specified as `public`, `private`, `internal`, or `external`. State variables support all visibility levels except external. In this recipe, you will learn about visibility modifiers and how to use them.

How to do it...

1. If you want the function to be accessible both externally and internally, it has to be marked as `public`. Public state variables will generate a `getter` function automatically:

```
pragma solidity ^0.4.21;
contract Visibility {
    // Public state variables generate an automatic getter
```

```
uint public limit = 110021;

// Accessible externally and internally
function changeLimit(uint _newLimit) public {
    limit = _newLimit;
}
}
```

You can see the `getter` methods generated from the ABI output of this contract:

```
[{
    "constant":false,
    "inputs":[{
        "name":"_newLimit",
        "type":"uint256"
    }],
    "name":"changeLimit", // public function
    "outputs":[],
    "payable":false,
    "stateMutability":"nonpayable",
    "type":"function"
},{
    "constant":true,
    "inputs":[],
    "name":"limit", // public state variable
    "outputs":[{
        "name":"",
        "type":"uint256"
    }],
    "payable":false,
    "stateMutability":"view",
    "type":"function"
}]
```

2. If you want your function to be only accessible from other contracts and via transactions, use external. This only works with functions:

```
pragma solidity ^0.4.21;
contract Visibility {
    // External function
    function f() external {
        // Do something
    }
}
```

An external function `f()` cannot be directly used internally. You need to use this.f() while calling from the same contract. External functions can also help save some gas for large inputs. It is recommended to use external whenever possible.

3. Internal functions can only be accessed from within the contract or the contracts inheriting from it. State variables are internal by default:

```
pragma solidity ^0.4.21;

contract Base {
    // Internal state varible
    uint internal limit = 110021;
    function update(uint _newLimit) internal {
        limit = _newLimit;
    }
}

contract Visibility is Base {
    function increment() public {
        uint newLimit = limit + 1;
        update(newLimit);
    }
}
```

4. If you want the function or state variable to be used only within the contract and not for external or inherited contracts, mark them as `private`:

```
pragma solidity ^0.4.21;

contract Visibility {
    // Private state varible
    uint private limit = 110021;
    function update(uint _newLimit) public {
        limit = _newLimit;
    }
}
```

Defining a state variable as private only prevents others from modifying it. Everyone in the network can read what data is stored in a `private` variable. This is often overlooked and can cause security flaws in the contract. More details are explained in Chapter 8, *Smart Contract Security*.

Essential events – EVM logger

EVM provides logging facilities through events. When events are called, the arguments that are passed along with them will be stored in the transaction log. This also helps listeners in the distributed application to trigger an action based on a transaction. These logs are associated with the address of the respective contract. The contract itself cannot access any log information stored in the transaction.

In this recipe, you will learn about logging and events, and listening to them from the JavaScript console of geth.

Getting ready

You will need a working installation of geth to test the event listener scripts given in this tutorial. Commands starting with > are executed from the geth JavaScript console.

How to do it...

Follow these steps to create and emit events from the contract:

1. Events are declared with the event keyword. The following example creates an event with three parameters:

```
event Transfer(
    address _from,
    address _to,
    uint _value
);
```

2. Events are emitted/logged with the emit keyword:

```
function transfer(address _to, uint _value) public {
    // Function body
    emit Transfer(msg.sender, _to, _value);
}
```

3. Up to three parameters can be indexed in an event. We can use indexed parameters to filter events based on requirements. If `arrays`, `strings`, or `bytes` are used as indexed arguments, the `Keccak-256` hash of it is stored as a topic:

```
event Transfer(
    address indexed _from,
    address indexed _to,
    uint _value
);
```

4. By default, all events will have a topic, which is the function signature. Use anonymous to log events without a topic. Anonymous events will also be part of ABI:

```
event Deposit(
    address _from;
    uint _value;
) anonymous;
```

5. You can use the `geth` JavaScript console (or other RPC methods) for listening to events. Let's consider the following contract as an example:

```
pragma solidity ^0.4.21;

contract Token {
    address owner;

    event Transfer(address indexed _from, address indexed _to, uint
_value);
    modifier onlyOwner {
        require(msg.sender == owner);
        _;
    }
    function Token() public {
        owner = msg.sender;
    }
    mapping(address => uint) public balances;
    function mint(address _to, uint _value) public onlyOwner {
        balances[_to] += _value;
        emit Transfer(address(0), _to, _value);
    }
    function transfer(address _to, uint _value) public {
        require(balances[msg.sender] >= _value);
        balances[msg.sender] -= _value;
        balances[_to] += _value;
```

```
            emit Transfer(msg.sender, _to, _value);
        }
    }
```

6. Create an instance of this contract using ABI and the deployed address:

```
> var tokenContract = web3.eth.contract(<ABI>);
> var tokenInstance = tokenContract.at(<Address>);
```

7. Create an instance of the event:

```
> var transferEvent = tokenInstance.Transfer({}, {
    fromBlock: 0,
    toBlock: 'latest'
});
```

Filters for indexed parameters can be added to the event listener. Consider the following example, which listens to events with a specific from address:

```
> var transferEvent = tokenInstance.Transfer({
    _from: web3.eth.accounts[0]
}, {
    fromBlock: 0,
    toBlock: 'latest'
});
```

8. Start watching the event and pass a `callback` that will be executed once an event is logged:

```
> transferEvent.watch(function(error, result) {
    console.log(result);
});
```

9. Make a call to any state changing method to see the event listener in action:

```
> tokenInstance.mint(web3.eth.accounts[1], 100, {
    from: web3.eth.accounts[0]
});
```

10. The events that have been logged will have the following structure:

```
{
    "address":"0x94b993cb18bd880e3ea4a278d50b4fb0cb4cb143",
    "args":{
        "_from":"0x0000000000000000000000000000000000000000",
        "_to":"0x87db8fceb028cd4ded9d03f49b89124a1589cab0",
        "_value":"100"
```

```
    },
    "blockHash":"0x817ab7205fe54c78b1d3e45358a350669714188bab4af78aaecd
    f200fa334f67",
    "blockNumber":1605,
    "event":"Transfer",
    "logIndex":0,
    "removed":false,
    "transactionHash":"0x5b487f78045ef2e96d460b65a5d0c1a28a4ed12a3d38f0
    e16ccd529bff1fb42d",
    "transactionIndex":0
}
```

11. To get all past event logs, use this:

```
> var transferLogs = transferEvent.get(function(error, logs){
    console.log(logs);
});
```

12. You can stop watching an event with this:

```
> transferEvent.stopWatching();
```

Events are widely used in distributed applications to communicate between smart contracts and their user interfaces. Events emitted from smart contracts are processed from the frontend to read the return values or to trigger an asynchronous operation.

Using storage and memory efficiently

There are two types of memory area associated with contracts: storage and memory. Storage is a value store where all contract state variables are stored and are only changed by a transaction. Memory is a temporary storage location that is cleared for each message call. In this recipe, you will learn how to use these types efficiently, based on your requirements.

How to do it...

1. State variables are always stored in storage, and function arguments are always in memory.

2. The memory location of a variable can be explicitly specified with the storage or memory keywords:

```
uint storage sum;

uint memory calc;
```

3. Local variables created for `struct`, `array`, or mapping types always reference storage by default. Modifying this local variable changes the actual storage data:

```
pragma solidity ^0.4.22;

contract Storage {

    struct Name {
        string fName;
        string lName;
    }

    mapping(address => Name) public names;

    function setName(string _fName, string _lName) public {
        // Declared as a storage pointer
        Name n = names[msg.sender];
        // Modifies state variable
        n.fName = _fName;
        n.lName = _lName;
    }
}
```

4. Variables can be declared as memory by specifying them explicitly. Memory can only be used in methods, not at the contract level:

```
pragma solidity ^0.4.22;

contract Memory {

    struct Name {
        string fName;
        string lName;
    }

    mapping(address => Name) public names;

    function setName(string _fName, string _lName) public {
        Name memory n = Name({
            fName: _fName,
```

```
                lName: _lName
        });
        names[msg.sender] = n;
    }
}
```

There's more...

EVM is a stack machine and the operations are performed on the stack memory. The stack data store is limited to *1,024* and stack elements can be moved to memory or storage. It is not possible to access arbitrary elements from the stack without removing the top of the stack.

The stack is generally used to hold small local variables and it is almost free to use. Local variables of value types except for `arrays`, `structs`, and mappings are stored in the stack.

Compiling your contract with the solc compiler

Solidity is a high-level language and has to be compiled before being deployed to Ethereum. In this recipe, you will learn how to use the `solc` command-line compiler to compile your smart contract to its binary and ABI.

Getting ready

You need to have a working installation of the `solc` compiler to step through this recipe. You can also make use of the JavaScript-based `solcjs` to compile solidity. These commands may not work in `solcjs` and you have to follow its documentation.

How to do it...

1. Consider the following smart contract, `HelloWorld.sol`, as an example:

```
pragma solidity ^0.4.22;

contract HelloWorld {
    string public greeting = "Hello World";
```

```
    event greetingChanged(address by, string greeting);
    function changeGreeting(string _newGreeting) public {
        greeting = _newGreeting;
        emit greetingChanged(msg.sender, _newGreeting);
    }
}
```

2. Verify your `solc` installation with the following command. It will show you all the parameters supported by the compiler:

    ```
    $ solc --help
    ```

3. For deploying and interaction, we need the ABI and binary of a smart contract. Use the `--abi` and `--bin` flags to generate them using the `solc` compiler:

    ```
    $ solc --bin --abi HelloWorld.sol
    ```

4. Compiling the contract with `--bin` and `--abi` will produce an output like this:

```
MANOJs-MacBook-Pro:Desktop manoj$ solc --bin --abi HelloWorld.sol

======= HelloWorld.sol:HelloWorld =======
Binary:
60606040526040805190810160405280600b81526020017f48656c6c6f20576f726c6400000000000000000000000000000000000081525060000908059
190602001906100049f2919061006065655b50341561005b57600080fd5b610105565b828054600181600116156101000203166002900490600052602060000020909
601f016020900481019282601f106100a157805160ff1916838001178556100cf565b828001600101855582156100cf579182015b828111156100ce5782518
25591602001919600010190600100b3565b5b5090506561060c919061000e0565b509005655b61010291905b808211156100fe576000816000905550600010161061000e656
5b5090565b90565b610958061011460000396000f3006060604052600436106101004c576000357c0100000000000000000000000000000000000000000000
000000000900463ffffffff1168063d28c25d414610051578063ef690cc0146100ae575b600080fd5b341561005c57600080fd5b6100ac6004808035906020001
9082018035906020019080806601f016020806910402602001604051908101604052809392919081815260200183838082843782019150505050505091950506506
1013c565b005b34156100b00957600080fd5b6100c1610226565b60405180800602001828103825283818151815260200191508051906020019080838360005b83
81101561010157808201518184015260208101905060100e6565b50505050509050908109190601f16801561012e578082038005160018360200361010000a031916
15260200191505b509250505060040518091039107f35b80600090805190602001906101052929190610102c4565b507f410cfa20c248f7be0b5ec30c2399200f17c1
ea8520d5d36e50bb61015dac9e14338260405180837ffffffffffffffffffffffffffffffffffffffffffffffffff1673ffffffffffffffffffffffffffffffffffffffff
f168152602001806020018281038252838181515181526020019150805190602001908080838360005b83811015610101e857808201518184015260208101905061011
cd565b5050505050905090810190601f16801561021557808203805160018360200036101000a031916815260200191505b50935050505060405180910390a1505
65b6000805460018160011615610100020316600290004806011f0160208091040260200160405190810160405280929190811526020018280546001018160011
156101000203166002900480156102bc5780600f10610291576101008083540280353529160200019161102bc565b820191906000526020600020905b815481529
0600010196020018083116102f578290003601f16820191505050505050081565b828054600181600116156101000203166002900490600052602060000020906
1f01602090004810192820601f10610305557805160ff1916838001178556561018360200361000a031916815b826019820015b828111115610332578251825
59160200191906001019060310317565b5b5090506561034091906103a565b5090565b5090600a0165627a7a7230582021eee6c2cb728aa0025e2915e130f21c528955a9b65bb274cd948c3e5e6322c00029
Contract JSON ABI
[{"constant":false,"inputs":[{"name":"_newGreeting","type":"string"}],"name":"changeGreeting","outputs":[],"payable":false,"sta
teMutability":"nonpayable","type":"function"},{"constant":true,"inputs":[],"name":"greeting","outputs":[{"name":"","type":"stri
ng"}],"payable":false,"stateMutability":"view","type":"function"},{"anonymous":false,"inputs":[{"indexed":false,"name":"by","ty
pe":"address"},{"indexed":false,"name":"greeting","type":"string"}],"name":"greetingChanged","type":"event"}]
```

5. **ABI (Application Binary Interface)** defines how your `call` functions are called and in which format the parameters should be passed from one component to the next. `Binary` or `bytecode` is the compiled output, which is deployed to Ethereum.

6. Use -0 along with the path to save the output to separate files:

```
$ solc -o <path_to_output_directory> --bin --abi HelloWorld.sol
```

7. The compiler will automatically read imported files in the contract. It is also possible to provide custom path redirects using the `prefix=path` command:

```
$ solc github.com/OpenZeppelin/zeppelin-
solidity=/usr/local/zeppelin =/usr/local/others contract.sol
```

This asks the compiler to search for files in `/usr/local/zeppelin` when it finds imports with the prefix `github.com/OpenZeppelin/zeppelin-solidity`. If there are no files there, then it looks in `/usr/local/others`. The non-specified prefix will only work if you specify `=/` as a remapping.

8. If libraries are used in the contracts, `bytecode` will have substrings of the form `__LibraryName____`.

9. `solc` can also be called with the `--link` flag, which interprets all input files to be unlinked binaries in the `__LibraryName____` format and is linked in place (if the input is read from `stdin`, it is written to `stdout`). All options except `--libraries` are ignored in this case.

10. Use `--optimize` during compilation if you are planning to use the binary for deployment:

```
$ solc --optimize --bin HelloWorld.sol
```

11. `solc` also supports more advanced outputs, and a few of them are listed here:

```
--ast       AST of all source files.
--asm       EVM assembly of the contracts.
--opcodes   Opcodes of the contracts.
--hashes    Function signature hashes of the contracts.
--userdoc   Natspec user documentation of all contracts.
--formal    Translated source suitable for formal analysis.
```

There's more...

You can also use Remix, or Truffle, which uses `solcjs`, to compile solidity smart contract. It can also provide similar outputs for contracts. Compiler output in Remix can be viewed by clicking the **Details** button under the **Compile** tab.

Deploying contracts using geth

After writing your smart contract, it is time to deploy it in Ethereum. In this recipe, you will learn about deploying your smart contract and testing it to ensure that it works as intended.

Getting ready

You will need a working installation of the `solc` compiler to compile your contract and `geth` to deploy it. We will be using the `geth` JavaScript console to run the deployment and transaction scripts.

How to do it...

1. Here is our simple smart contract example:

```
pragma solidity ^0.4.21;

contract HelloWorld {
    string public greeting = "Hello World";
    function changeGreeting(string _newGreeting) public {
        greeting = _newGreeting;
    }
}
```

2. Use `solc` or other alternatives to compile the contract into ABI and bytecode:

```
$ solc --optimize --bin --abi HelloWorld.sol
```

3. Start the `geth` node with the web3 console:

```
$ geth console 2>> ./geth.log
```

4. Make sure that you have enough Ether for deployment. If you are using a private network, make sure to start mining before performing any transactions.
5. Unlock the account from which you want to deploy the contract:

```
> web3.personal.unlockAccount(web3.eth.accounts[0], "<password>");
```

6. Create an object of the contract with ABI:

```
> var helloWorldContract = web3.eth.cointract(<ABI>);
```

7. Deploy the contract bytecode from an unlocked account:

```
> var helloworld = helloworldContract.new({
    from: web3.eth.accounts[0],
    data: <Bytecode>,
    gas: '4700000'
  }, function (e, contract){
    if (typeof contract.address !== 'undefined') {
        console.log('Address: ' + contract.address);
    }
});
```

8. If the constructor accepts arguments, then those have to be specified during deployment:

```
> var helloworld = helloworldContract.new("<paramerer1>",
    "<parameter2>", {
    from: web3.eth.accounts[0],
    data: <Bytecode>,
    gas: '4700000'
  }, function (e, contract){
    if (typeof contract.address !== 'undefined') {
        console.log('Address: ' + contract.address);
    }
});
```

The gas amount can vary for each transaction, based on the tasks it has to perform in the contract. `web3.eth.estimateGas()` can be used to estimate the gas required for each call.

9. One the contract is mined, you can see its address in the console. Use the address to create a new instance of the contract:

```
> var greet = web3.eth.cointract(<ABI>).at(<Address>);
```

10. To read data from the contract, use this:

```
> greet.greeting();
// Hello World
```

11. To call a state changing method in the contract, use this:

```
> greet.changeGreeting("Meow!", {
    from: web3.eth.accounts[0],
  });
```

There's more...

You can use Remix to generate the web3 deployment script. After compiling the contract in Remix, click on the **Details** button under the **Compile** tab. Scroll down to see the web3deploy section, which has the script to deploy your contract.

You can also deploy the smart contract directly from Remix or with frameworks such as Truffle. You can get more information about this in other related recipes.

Interacting with the Contract 3

In this chapter, we will cover the following recipes:

- Installing and configuring web3.js
- Using MetaMask as an injected provider
- Managing accounts and sending transactions
- Compiling and deploying your smart contract
- Reading data from smart contracts
- Writing data into a smart contract
- Watching events from your DApp
- Sending a raw transaction
- Batch requests using web3.js
- Interacting with Ethereum using JSON-RPC
- Other ways to interact with your contract

Introduction

We don't expect an end user to be interacting with the `geth` console to access the smart contract or other Ethereum properties. It generally happens through a user interface. So, there needs to be a way by which applications can interact with the Ethereum blockchain. Ethereum allows connections via RPC and IPC, using which an application or user can interact with the distributed ledger.

This chapter mainly focuses on several ways to interact with your smart contract, which is deployed on the Ethereum main network. You will learn about `web3.js` and other libraries that will help you to build a decentralized application.

Installing and configuring web3.js

Web3.js is a JavaScript library that implements the JSON RPC specification of Ethereum. This library allows you to interact with a local or remote Ethereum node, using an HTTP or IPC connection. The following recipe will guide you through installing and configuring web3.js, as well as provide examples to use in your **Decentralized Application (DApp)**.

Getting ready

Since the library is written in JavaScript and distributed via npm, you will need Node.js installed on your machine to use the library. Bower and Meteor versions are also available and you need to have the respective tools to download them.

There are two web3.js releases in use: 0.2x.x, which is the current stable version, and 1.x.x, which is an upcoming release that is currently in beta. We will learn to install and configure both of these versions.

How to do it...

Here are the steps to install web3.js and then configure it:

1. Install web3 using the npm install command:

    ```
    npm install web3
    ```

    This will download the latest package available in the npm directory. Specify the version along with the install command to download a different release. Try installing the 0.2x.x release by specifying its version:

    ```
    npm install web3@0.20.6
    ```

    Run the following command to view the list of packages and select the one that suits your needs:

    ```
    npm view web3 versions
    ```

2. Use the library as a browser module by downloading the JavaScript version directly from the web3.js repository at github.com/ethereum/web3.js. Navigate to the dist folder to find the web3.js files. Once you have downloaded them, import them into the HTML with a regular script tag:

    ```
    <script src="./dist/web3.min.js"></script>
    ```

3. Import `web3` into your application using the `require` function. If you are using it as a browser module, it will be available as a global object:

```
var Web3 = require("web3");
```

4. If you are using web3.js 1.x.x, reference individual packages under `web3` using their module names. For example, you can directly import `we3.eth` using `web3-eth`:

```
var Eth = require("web3-eth");
var Bzz = require("web3-bzz");
var Shh = require("web3-shh");
```

5. Set a provider for the `web3` instance so that it can access the Ethereum node:

```
// For v0.2x.x
var web3 = new Web3(
    new Web3.providers.HttpProvider("http://localhost:8545")
);

// For v1.x.x
var web3 = new Web3("ws://localhost:8546");
```

6. If you are using version `1.x.x`, setting the provider for the `web3` module will also set the provider for submodules such as `web3.eth` and `web3.shh`, except `web3.bzz`, which needs to be specified explicitly:

```
var eth = new Eth("ws://localhost:8546");
var bzz = new Bzz("http://localhost:8500");
var shh = new Shh("ws://localhost:8546");
```

7. Once the provider is set up, use the `web3` object to interact with the Ethereum network.

8. Try reading some data using the `web3` object to ensure that it is working as expected:

```
// For v0.2x.x
console.log(web3.eth.coinbase);
console.log(web3.eth.getBalance("<address>"));

// For v1.x.x
web3.eth.getCoinbase().then(console.log);
web3.eth.getBalance("<address>").then(console.log);
```

Using MetaMask as an injected provider

MetaMask and the Mist browser can be used as a provider for the web3 object. These services expose the web3 API and allow your application to connect to an Ethereum node. In this recipe, you will learn to use Mist or MetaMask as an injected provider for your application, along with other options.

Getting ready

You need to have the MetaMask extension installed in your browser to try this recipe. MetaMask supports Chrome, Firefox, Opera, and Brave browsers. Make sure that you are connected to your network of choice in MetaMask.

These scripts will also work with the Mist browser.

How to do it...

Now, we will start with the steps that are needed to use MetaMask as an injected provider:

1. Initialize web3 using the provider object injected by the browser providers:

```
// For v0.2x.x
var web3 = new Web3(web3.currentProvider);

// For v1.x.x
var web3 = new Web3(Web3.givenProvider);
```

2. Check for existing providers to ensure that you are not overwriting the existing Mist or MetaMask provider:

```
// For v0.2x.x
if (typeof web3 !== 'undefined') {
  web3 = new Web3(web3.currentProvider);
} else {
  web3 = new Web3(
      new Web3.providers.HttpProvider("http://localhost:8545")
  );
}

// For v1.x.x
var web3 = new Web3(Web3.givenProvider || "ws://localhost:8546");
```

MetaMask cannot communicate to applications running directly from a filesystem through `file://`. This is because of the security restrictions in the browser. Run a local server during development to avoid this issue.

3. Use asynchronous callbacks to read data from Ethereum via providers. This is because the browser does not have the full blockchain in local and MetaMask has to get the data from a remote server:

```
// For v0.2x.x
web3.eth.getBalance(<address>, function (error, result) {
    if (!error) {
        console.log(result);
    }
});

// For v1.x.x
web3.eth.getBalance("<address>").then(console.log);
```

There are some exceptions to asynchronous commands in MetaMask. The following methods can return value synchronously: `web3.eth.accounts`, `web3.eth.coinbase`, `web3.eth.uninstallFil ter`, `web3.eth.reset`, and `web3.version.network`.

4. MetaMask also handles user accounts and private keys. Any time you make a transaction (Ether transfer or contract call), MetaMask will automatically prompt the user for permission. Based on the user input, it will forward the call to the Ethereum node. This avoids the need to sign and send the transaction from the application.

How it works...

The MetaMask extension or Mist browser writes a script tag into the **Document Object Model (DOM)** of every web page you visit. This script tag exposes the web3 API, which allows your decentralized application to read and write data to and from Ethereum.

MetaMask is a widely used tool for connecting to Ethereum nodes. It makes life easier by exposing providers for the main-net, test-nets, and other custom nodes you have set up. You can also use MetaMask as a wallet and transaction signer.

Managing accounts and sending transactions

Web3JS exposes several APIs used to create and interact with accounts in Ethereum. In this recipe, you will learn how to work with Ethereum accounts using the `web3` object.

Getting ready

You need to have web3.js in your application to use these scripts. Make sure that you have a valid provider set up for the library to work. You can get more details about this from the first two recipes of this chapter.

Some methods used in the recipe may need access to the `personal` API. You have to expose it via `rpc`. This can be done in two ways. The first method is to use the `--rpcapi` flag to expose the personal API while starting the node:

```
$ geth --rpc --rpcapi="db,eth,net,web3,personal"
```

Or, you can use `web3.admin` to start the API from the geth JavaScript console:

```
> admin.startRPC("<ip_address>", <rpc_port>, "*",
"db,eth,net,web3,personal")
```

It is not recommended to exposes personal APIs over the internet. This allows anyone to read/create accounts or try to brute-force your passwords and steal your Ether. Either expose it in a closed network, after considering all the security consequences, or use IPC to make requests. Moreover, you can make use of MetaMask or Mist as a wallet, which allows the user to manage their own accounts.

How to do it...

We are now going to learn how to manage accounts and send transactions:

1. To view the list of accounts available in the connected node, use the following command:

```
// v0.2x.x
web3.eth.accounts;

// v1.x.x
```

```
web3.eth.getAccounts().then(console.log);
```

2. To create an account using the `web3` object, run the following command. Starting from 1.x.x, web3.js includes added support for account management:

```
// For v1.x.x
web3.eth.accounts.create();
web3.eth.accounts.create("<random entropy>");
```

The `create` function accepts an entropy as input for randomness. If not specified, it will generate a random hex of 32 bytes by using `web3.utils.randomHex(32)` and will use it as the entropy input. This method will return the new address, private key, and methods associated with it:

```
{
    address: '0x824e470cCac64CC5fa4Abe953e64FA360EA11366',
    privateKey: '0x782174a3e404424af...499baffd30e6105f',
    signTransaction: [Function: signTransaction],
    sign: [Function: sign],
    encrypt: [Function: encrypt]
}
```

3. If you already have a private key, import it using the `privateKeyToAccount` function:

```
// For v1.x.x
web3.eth.accounts.privateKeyToAccount("<privateKey>");
```

4. Unlock your account with the passphrase before sending a transaction. Authentication works differently for a raw transaction, which we will focus on in the *Sending a raw transaction* recipe later in this chapter. You can try unlocking your account with the following scripts:

```
// For v0.2x.x
web3.personal.unlockAccount("<address>", "<password>", <duration>);
```

```
// For v1.x.x
web3.eth.personal.unlockAccount("<address>", "<password>",
<duration>)
    .then(console.log);
```

It is recommended to reduce the unlock duration or to lock the account immediately after a transaction with `lockAccount`. If you are in a development environment and don't want to lock and unlock an account frequently, then specify the duration as 0 to avoid automatic locking after a certain period.

5. To send a transaction, use the `sendTransaction` method with the required parameters:

```
web3.eth.sendTransaction(transaction_object [, callback])
```

You can use the following parameters to create the transaction object:

- `from`: Address of the sending account. The default is `web3.eth.defaultAccount`.
- `to` (optional): Address of the destination account. Leave it blank if you are creating a contract.
- `value` (optional): The value transferred through the transaction in Wei.
- `gas` (optional): The maximum amount of gas to use for the transaction.
- `gasPrice` (optional): The price of gas for this transaction in Wei. The default is `web3.eth.gasPrice`.
- `data` (optional): Either the data of the function call or the contract initialization code.
- `nonce` (optional): Nonce value for the transaction. You can use this to overwrite a transaction by providing the same nonce value as the older transaction.

Here is an example that uses these parameters:

```
web3.eth.sendTransaction({
    from: "0xce5C2D181f6DD99091351f6E6056c333A969AEC9",
    to: "",
    gas:21000,
    gasPrice: 20000000000, // 20 Gwei
    value: 200000
}, function(error, transactionHash) {
    if(!error)
        console.log(transactionHash);
})
```

6. Starting from web3.js 1.0.0, the `sendTransaction` method returns a promise combined with an event emitter. This can help perform different tasks based on various stages of a transaction. Consider the following example:

```
web3.eth.sendTransaction({
    from: "0xce5C2D181f6DD99091351f6E6056c333A969AEC9",
    to: 0x71495cd51c5356B1f0769dB5027DC0588010dC14,
    value: '10000000000000000'
})
.on('transactionHash', function(hash){
    console.log(hash);
```

```
})
.on('receipt', function(receipt){
    console.log(receipt);
})
.on('confirmation', function(confirmationNumber, receipt){
    console.log(confirmationNumber);
})
.on('error', console.error);
```

Let's look into each event in detail:

- transactionHash: It is fired immediately after a transaction hash is available.
- receipt: It is fired when the transaction receipt is generated.
- confirmation: It is fired for every confirmation up to the 12th confirmation, starting from 0th confirmation.
- error: It is fired if an error occurs during the transaction. For out of gas errors, the second parameter is the transaction receipt.

Compiling and deploying your smart contract

You can compile your solidity smart contract with the help of the solc compiler and deploy it using the geth JavaScript console. In this recipe, we will focus on compiling and deploying the contract from your decentralized application using solc.js and web3.js.

Getting ready

Make sure that you have web3.js available in your application to run these scripts. You will also need to install solc.js in order to compile your contract. You can install solc.js using npm:

```
npm install solc --save
```

Every transaction has to mine before you can see the result of the execution. In the Ethereum main or test networks, there are other miners to take care of this. If you are using a private network, you can start and stop the mining process from the web3 JavaScript console using the following commands:

```
miner.start() // starts mining
miner.stop() // Stops mining
```

How to do it...

These steps are used to compile and deploy smart contracts:

1. Consider the following contract as an example:

```solidity
pragma solidity ^0.4.21;

contract HelloWorld {

    string textToPrint = "hello world";

    function changeText(string _text) public {
        textToPrint = _text;
    }

    function printSomething() public view returns (string) {
        return textToPrint;
    }
}
```

2. Import the contract into your source by either reading it from a file or directly assigning it to a variable as a string:

```
var contract = "pragma solidity ^0.4.21; contract HelloWorld {
string textToPrint = "hello world"; function changeText(string
_text) public { textToPrint = _text; } function printSomething()
public view returns (string) { return textToPrint; } }";
```

3. Compile the contract using `solc.compile()`. Specify 1 as the second parameter to include optimization while compiling:

```
var solc = require("solc");
var output = solc.compile(contract, 1);
```

4. It supports multiple files with automatic import resolution:

```
var solc = require("solc");

var contracts = {
  "library.sol": "library Lib { function f() pure returns (uint) {
return 1; } }",
  "contract.sol': "import 'library.sol'; contract Test { function
g() pure { Lib.f(); } }"
};

var output = solc.compile({ sources: contracts }, 1);
```

5. The compiler returns an object with the contract name as the key and the compiled output as the value. Iterate through each value to print the result:

```
for (var contractName in output.contracts) {
    console.log(contractName);
    // Bytecode
    console.log(output.contracts[contractName].bytecode);
    // ABI
    console.log(output.contracts[contractName].interface);
}
```

6. If there are no errors in your contract, it should compile fine and you will get the standard compiler outputs. You can deploy this contract using the bytecode generated.

7. To deploy the contract to the Ethereum network, send a transaction without the to address, but with the compiled contract code in the data field:

```
var bytecode = output.contracts["HelloWorld"].bytecode;

web3.eth.sendTransaction({
    from: "0xce5C2D181f6DD99091351f6E6056c333A969AEC9",
    data: bytecode,
    gas: "4700000"
}, function(err, transactionHash) {
  if (!err)
    console.log(transactionHash);
});
```

8. Get the deployed contract address from the receipt once the transaction is mined. If you are using v1.x.x, you can use the event emitter to get the contract address:

```
var bytecode = output.contracts["HelloWorld"].bytecode;

web3.eth.sendTransaction({
    from: "0xce5C2D181f6DD99091351f6E6056c333A969AEC9",
    data: bytecode,
    gas: "4700000"
})
.on('receipt', function(receipt){
    console.log(receipt);
});
```

9. Now, use the address and ABI to read from and write to the deployed contract.

There's more...

You can also deploy the contract using the contract instance. Consider the following example of deploying a contract in both v0.2x.x and v1.x.x to understand more:

```
var bytecode = output.contracts["HelloWorld"].bytecode;
var abi = output.contracts["HelloWorld"].interface;

// For v0.2x.x
var helloworldContract = web3.eth.contract(abi);
var helloworld = helloworldContract.new({
        from: "0xce5C2D181f6DD99091351f6E6056c333A969AEC9",
        data: byteCode,
        gas: 4700000
}, function (e, contract){
    if (typeof contract.address !== "undefined") {
        console.log("address: " + contract.address);
    }
});

// For v1.x.x
var helloWorld = new web3.eth.Contract(abi);
helloWorld.deploy({
    data: byteCode,
    arguments: [] // Constructor arguments
})
.send({
    from: "0x12345678901234567890123456789012345678901234567891",
    gas: 4700000
})
.on("error", function(error){
    console.error(error);
})
.on("receipt", function(receipt) {
    console.log(receipt.contractAddress);
});
```

For larger contracts, you may have to increase the gas amount for execution. This can be estimated with the contract instance:

```
// For v0.2x.x
var gas = web3.eth.estimateGas({
    data: byteCode
});
console.log(gas);

// For v1.x.x
helloWorld.deploy({
```

```
    data: byteCode,
    arguments: []
})
.estimateGas(function(err, gas){
    console.log(gas);
});
```

Reading data from smart contracts

The best way to interact with your contract from your application is by using web3.js. This library offers plenty of feature sets that you will need while building a DApp. In this recipe, you will learn to read data from the deployed smart contract.

Getting ready

You need to have web3.js installed on your application to use these methods. Ensure that your Ethereum node is running. You can also use Ganache to create a development node.

How to do it...

In order to read data from smart contracts, we will have to perform these steps:

1. Create a contract instance with the ABI and the deployed address. If you are using web3.js v0.2x.x, use the following methods to create an instance:

```
// Create a contract object
var MyContract = web3.eth.contract(<ABI>);

// Create an instance with address
var contractInstance = MyContract.at("<Address>");
```

For those who are using the upcoming version of web3js (v1.x.x), use the following method to create an instance:

```
var contractInstance = new web3.eth.Contract(
    "<ABI>",
    "<Address>"
);
```

2. Read data from the smart contract using the `call` method. This executes the code in the **Ethereum Virtual Machine (EVM)** and returns the value. This method does not modify the state of the contract.

3. Consider the following contract method, which accepts a parameter and returns a value:

```
// Solidity contract
contract Test {
    function sample (uint _a) pure public returns (uint) {
        return _a * 2;
    }
}
```

4. Call the `sample` function from the preceding contract using the contract instance, as illustrated here:

```
// For v0.2x.x
var result = contractInstance.sample(10);
console.log(result) // 20

// For v1.x.x
MyContract.methods.sample(10).call()
        .then(console.log); // 20
```

5. Let's examine another example, which returns multiple values:

```
// Solidity contract
contract Test {
    function sample () pure public
            returns (string testString, uint testNumber) {
        return ("hello", 100);
    }
}
```

6. The following web3.js script can be used to call the `sample()` method in the preceding `Test` contract:

```
// For v0.2x.x
var result = contractInstance.sample();
console.log(result);
// Output
> {
  '0': 'hello',
  '1': '100'
}
```

```
// For v1.x.x
MyContract.methods.sample().call()
    .then(console.log);
// Output
> Result {
    '0': 'hello',
    '1': '100',
    testString: 'hello',
    testNumber: '100'
}
```

Writing data into a smart contract

Reading data from a smart contract does not modify the state, while writing data into the contract modifies it. State changing methods can be called only by a transaction and with enough gas for execution. The state will be changed if the transaction satisfies all the conditions placed in the contract method.

In this recipe, you will learn how to interact with the contract using state changing methods.

Getting ready

Ensure that your Ethereum node is running. You can also use Ganache to create a development node.

How to do it...

For writing data to smart contracts, we have to follow this procedure:

1. Consider the following example contract:

```
pragma solidity ^0.4.21;

contract HelloWorld {
    // State variable
    string textToPrint = "hello world";

    // State changing function
    function changeText(string _text) public {
        textToPrint = _text;
    }
```

```
        // Read-only function
        function printSomething() public view returns (string) {
            return textToPrint;
        }
    }
```

2. Create the contract instance with the ABI and the deployed address. The method to create an instance is slightly different between web3.js v0.2x.x and v1.x.x:

```
// For v0.2x.x
var helloWorld = web3.eth.contract(<ABI>);
var helloWorldInstance = helloWorld.at("<Address>");

// For v1.x.x
var helloWorldInstance = new web3.eth.Contract(
    "<ABI>",
    "<Address>"
);
```

3. If you are using web3.js v0.2x.x, call the contract method with input parameters and a transaction object. Make sure to unlock the account before calling the contract:

```
// Method syntax - v0.2x.x
contractInstance.stateChangingMethod.sendTransaction(
    param1 [, param2, ...] [, transactionObject] [, callback]
);

// Example - v0.2x.x
helloWorldInstance.changeText.sendTransaction("Greetings!", {
    from: "0xce5C2D181f6DD99091351f6E6056c333A969AEC9",
    gas: 470000
}, function(error, result) {
    ...
});
```

4. For `web3.js` v1.x.x, state changing methods can be called, as shown here:

```
// Method syntax - v1.x.x
myContractInstance.methods
    .stateChangingMethod([param1[, param2[, ...]]])
    .send(options [, callback]);

// Example - v1.x.x
helloWorldInstance.methods
    .changeText("Greetings!")
    .send({
        from: "0xce5C2D181f6DD99091351f6E6056c333A969AEC9"
```

```
    }, function(error, transactionHash){
        ...
    });
```

5. Use the event emitters to perform various tasks based on actions logged in the
   blockchain:

```
helloWorldInstance.methods.changeText("Greetings!").send({
    from: "0xce5C2D181f6DD99091351f6E6056c333A969AEC9"
})
.on('transactionHash', function(hash){
    ...
})
.on('confirmation', function(confirmationNumber, receipt){
    ...
})
.on('receipt', function(receipt){
    console.log(receipt);
})
.on('error', console.error);
```

There's more...

Web3.js v1.x.x allows the user to estimate the required gas directly from the contract
instance. This can be done with the help of the `estimateGas` method. Consider the fact
that the estimation can differ from the actual utilization due to the varying state:

```
// Method syntax
myContractInstance.methods
    .myMethod([param1[, param2[, ...]]])
    .estimateGas(options [, callback])

// Example
helloWorldInstance.methods
    .changeText("Greetings!")
    .estimateGas({
        from: "0xce5C2D181f6DD99091351f6E6056c333A969AEC9"
    }, function(error, gasAmount){
        console.log(gasAmount);
    });
```

You can also use the promise returned from the function:

```
// Promise
helloWorldInstance.methods
    .changeText("Greetings!")
```

```
.estimateGas({
    from: "0xce5C2D181f6DD99091351f6E6056c333A969AEC9"
})
.then(function(gasAmount){
    ...
})
.catch(function(error){
    ...
});
```

Watching events from your DApp

Events allow you to access the EVM logging facility, which can be used to keep state change information or to execute callbacks in the DApps. In this recipe, you will learn how to listen for new events raised in the contract and retrieve data stored in the transaction logs.

Getting ready

You need to have web3.js installed in your application to use these methods. Ensure that you have a geth- or Ganache-based Ethereum network to connect and test these methods.

How to do it...

We can watch events from DApp using the following steps:

1. Consider the following contract, which emits events for each state changing operation. There is a dedicated *Essential events–EVM Logger* recipe in the previous chapter, which describes the process of writing events in solidity:

```
pragma solidity ^0.4.22;

contract eventEmitter {
    event simpleEvent(address _sender);
    event indexedEvent(address indexed _sender, uint _id);
    function simpleEmit() public {
        // do something
        emit simpleEvent(msg.sender);
    }
    function indexedEmit(uint _id) public {
        // do something
```

```
            emit indexedEvent(msg.sender, _id);
    }
}
```

2. Watch an emitted event from a decentralized application using the following method. The syntax may be slightly different for various versions of web3.js:

```
// For v0.2x.x
contractInstance.MyEvent([options]).watch([callback]);

// For v1.x.x
contractInstance.events.MyEvent([options][, callback])
```

3. If you are using the existing version of web3.js (0.2x.x), use the watch method to execute a callback for each event. The following snippet listens to the simpleEvent emitted from the sample contract:

```
// For web3.js v0.2x.x
var eventContract = web3.eth.contract(abi);
var eventContractInstance = eventContract.at(address);

// Create an event instance
var simpleEventInstance = myContractInstance.simpleEvent({}, {
    fromBlock: 0,
    toBlock: 'latest'
});

// Start watching the event
simpleEventInstance.watch(function(error, result){
    console.log(result);
});
```

The preceding listener executes callbacks passed to it for events emitted starting from the 0th block. It keeps listening for each new block mined until we ask it to stop listening. You can use the stopWatching method to do that:

```
// Stops watching the event
simpleEventInstance.stopWatching();
```

4. If you are using a newer version of web3.js (1.x.x), use the implementation given here to watch an event:

```
// For web3.js v1.x.x
eventContractInstance.events.simpleEvent({
    filter: {},
    fromBlock: 0
```

```
}, function(error, event) {
    console.log(event);
})
```

You can listen to the following events that are emitted from the event listener:

- `data`: Fired on each event emitted with the event object as an argument
- `changed`: Fired on each event that was removed from the blockchain
- `error`: Fired when an exception occurs:

```
// For web3.js v1.x.x
eventContractInstance.events.simpleEvent({
    filter: {},
    fromBlock: 0
})
.on('data', function(event){
    console.log(event);
})
.on('changed', function(event){
    console.log(event);
})
.on('error', console.error);
```

5. Filter the events further with the help of indexed arguments:

```
// For web3.js 0.2x.x
var indexedEventInstance = eventContractInstance.indexedEvent({
    _sender: '0xce5C2D181f6DD99091351f6E6056c333A969AEC9'
}, {
    fromBlock: 0,
    toBlock: 'latest'
});
// Logs event emitted from a specific address
simpleEventInstance.watch(function(error, result){
    console.log(result);
});

// For web3.js 1.x.x
eventContractInstance.events.indexedEvent({
    filter: {
        _sender: [
            '0xce5C2D181f6DD99091351f6E6056c333A969AEC9',
            '0xD0D18F4A02beb7E528cE010742Db1Cc992070135'
        ] // Use an array for OR condition
    },
    fromBlock: 0
```

```
})
.on('data', function(event){
    console.log(event);
})
.on('error', console.error);
```

 Using web3.js v1.x.x, you can subscribe to an event and unsubscribe from it immediately after the event or error. This can be done using `eventContractInstance.once(event[, options], callback)`. This will only fire for a single event.

6. Try querying all the past logs from the blockchain using web3.js:

```
// For web3.js 0.2x.x
var simpleEventInstance = eventContractInstance
    .simpleEvent({}, {
        fromBlock: 0,
        toBlock: 'latest'
    });

// All past logs
var eventResults = simpleEventInstance
    .get(function(error, logs){
        console.log(logs);
    });
```

7. For the newer version of web3.js, retrieve past logs with the help of the `getPastEvents` method:

```
// For web3.js 1.x.x - Syntax
contractInstance.getPastEvents(event[, options][, callback])

// Example
eventContractInstance.getPastEvents('simpleEvent', {
    filter: { },
    fromBlock: 0,
    toBlock: 'latest'
}, function(error, events) {
    console.log(events);
})
.then(function(events){
    console.log(events) // same result as the callback
});
```

8. Listen to all the events that are raised from a contract with the `allEvents` method:

```
// For web3.js 0.2x.x
var events = eventContractInstance.allEvents({
    fromBlock: 0,
    toBlock: 'latest'
});
events.watch(function(error, result){ ... });
events.get(function(error, logs){ ... });

// For web3.js 1.x.x
eventContractInstance.getPastEvents({
    filter: {},
    fromBlock: 0
})
.on('data', function(event){
    console.log(event);
})
.on('error', console.error);
```

Sending a raw transaction

You can get more control over the transaction and data sent to the Ethereum blockchain. Usually, we send a transaction with send transaction methods. You can also sign a transaction with the private key and send it directly. You will learn various ways to do this in this recipe.

Getting ready

You need to have web3.js installed on your application to use these methods. Some methods may need additional libraries, which are explained along with the respective methods. Ensure that you have a geth- or Ganache-based Ethereum network to connect and test these methods.

How to do it...

We will now learn how we can send raw transactions:

1. You need to sign your transaction before broadcasting it to an Ethereum network. If you are using the existing version of web3.js (0.2x.x), this operation is not built in. Install `ethereumjs-tx` via npm to sign transactions easily:

    ```
    $ npm install ethereumjs-tx --save
    ```

2. Once it is installed, import it into your project and create the transaction object to sign:

```
// For web3.js 0.2x.x
var Tx = require("ethereumjs-tx");

var rawTx = {
  nonce: "0x00",
  gasPrice: "0x09184e72a000",
  gasLimit: "0x2710",
  to: "0x0000000000000000000000000000000000000000",
  value: "0x00",
  data:
  "0x3f926344987500000000000000000000000000000000000000000000000000000000
  00000009"
}

var tx = new Tx(rawTx);
```

Use the following parameters to build the transaction object:

*   `nonce` (optional): The nonce to use while signing the transaction. The default is `web3.eth.getTransactionCount()`.
*   `to` (optional): The address of the transaction receiver. Can be empty when deploying a contract.
*   `data` (optional): The call data for this transaction. Can be empty for value transfers.
*   `value` (optional): The amount to transfer in Wei.
*   `gasPrice` (optional): The gas price set by this transaction. The default is `web3.eth.gasPrice()`.
*   `gas`: The gas provided by the transaction.

3. Sign the transaction object using your private key:

```
// Import your private key as a buffer
var privateKey = new Buffer('<privateKey>', 'hex');
// Sign the transaction with the private key
tx.sign(privateKey);
// Serialize the transaction
var serializedTx = tx.serialize();
```

4. Finally, broadcast the transaction to the network using `sendRawTransaction`:

```
web3.eth.sendRawTransaction('0x' + serializedTx.toString('hex'),
    function(err, hash) {
```

```
      if (!err)
          console.log(hash);
});
```

5. This functionality is available out of the box starting from web3.js v1.x.x. Use the `signTransaction` method to sign a transaction using the private key:

```
web3.eth.accounts.signTransaction({
  nonce: "0x00",
  gasPrice: "0x09184e72a000",
  gasLimit: "0x2710",
  to: "0x0000000000000000000000000000000000000000",
  value: "0x00",
  data:
"0x3f9263449875000000000000000000000000000000000000000000000000000000000
00000009"
}, '<privateKey>')
.then(function(result) {
    console.log(result);
});
```

This method returns an object with the following values:

- `messageHash`: The hash of the given message
- `r`: First 32 bytes of the signature
- `s`: Next 32 bytes of the signature
- `v`: Recovery value +27
- `rawTransaction`: The RLP encoded transaction, which is broadcast to the network

6. Use the `web3.eth.sendSignedTransaction` method to send the `rawTransaction` value:

```
web3.eth.sendSignedTransaction("<rawTransaction>")
    .on('receipt', function(receipt) {
        console.log(receipt);
    });
```

7. To sign data from a specific account without using a private key, use the `eth.sign` method. Make sure that you have unlocked the account before signing the transaction:

```
// For web3.js 0.2x.x
web3.eth.sign(address, dataToSign, [, callback])
```

```
var result = web3.eth.sign(
    "0x11f4d0A3c12e86B4b5F39B213F7E19D048276DAe",
    web3.sha3("Hello World!")
)
console.log(result);

// For web3.js 1.x.x
web3.eth.sign(dataToSign, address [, callback])

web3.eth.sign(
    "Hello world",
    "0x11f4d0A3c12e86B4b5F39B213F7E19D048276DAe"
).then(function (result) {
    console.log(result);
});
```

8. web3.js v1.x.x supports signing arbitrary data using your private key. This can be done with the `eth.accounts.sign` method. This returns an object with the `message`, `messageHash`, r, s, and v values:

```
web3.eth.accounts.sign("Hello World", "<privateKey>");
```

There's more...

Starting from web3.js v1.x.x, there is an option to extract/recover the address from the signed transaction data. This allows us to verify the origin of the transaction:

```
web3.eth.accounts.recoverTransaction(rawTransaction)
```

This method accepts the raw transaction as an input and returns the address used to sign the transaction:

```
var result = web3.eth.accounts.recoverTransaction("0x0...");
console.log(result);
```

You can also recover the address from signed data using the `accounts.recover()` method:

```
web3.eth.accounts.recover(signatureObject);
web3.eth.accounts.recover(message, signature [, preFixed]);
web3.eth.accounts.recover(message, v, r, s [, preFixed]);
```

This method can accept various types of input to recover the data:

```
web3.eth.accounts.recover({
    messageHash: '0x0..',
```

```
        v:  '0x0..',
        r:  '0x0..',
        s:  '0x0..'
})

web3.eth.accounts.recover('0x0..', '0x0..');

web3.eth.accounts.recover('0x0x..', '0x0x..', '0x0..', '0x0..');
```

Batch requests using web3.js

web3.js supports batch requests, which allows for the queuing up of multiple requests and processing them all at once. Batch requests are not exponentially faster. They are mainly used to ensure serial processing of requests, and sometimes can be faster as requests are processed asynchronously.

In this recipe, you will learn to create and process batch requests using web3.js.

Getting ready

You need to have web3.js installed in your application to use these methods. Ensure that you have a geth- or Ganache-based Ethereum network to connect and test these methods.

How to do it...

Here are the steps that must be followed to batch requests using web3.js:

1. Creating and executing batch requests is different between versions of web3.js. If you are using web3.js v0.2x.x, use the following method to create a batch:

```
var batch = web3.createBatch();
```

2. Now, add as many requests as you want to the queue:

```
var balance = web3.eth.getBalance.request(
    web3.eth.accounts[1],
    'latest',
    callback
);
var contract = web3.eth.Contract(abi)
    .at(address)
    .balance
```

```
            .request(web3.eth.accounts[0], callback2)

    batch.add(balance);
    batch.add(contract);
```

3. Once all requests are queued up, start executing them with the `execute` method:

```
    batch.execute();
```

4. The execution of batches works slightly different in the upcoming version of web3.js (1.x.x). You can also find options to create batch requests in all the child modules:

```
    new web3.BatchRequest()
    new web3.eth.BatchRequest()
    new web3.shh.BatchRequest()
    new web3.bzz.BatchRequest()
```

5. Create and add requests to the batch queue and start the execution to run the tasks:

```
    var balance = web3.eth.getBalance.request(
        web3.eth.accounts[1],
        'latest',
        callback
    );
    var contract = new web3.eth.Contract(abi, address)
        .methods.balance("<address>")
        .call.request({
            from: "<address>"
    }, callback2)

    var batch = new web3.BatchRequest();
    batch.add(balance);
    batch.add(contract);
    batch.execute();
```

Interacting with Ethereum using JSON-RPC

You can completely avoid using web3.js and interact with your Ethereum node using JSON-RPC. It is a stateless, lightweight RPC protocol. Etherum JSON-RPC exposes various APIs that can be used within the same process, over sockets, over HTTP, or in various message passing environments.

These APIs are commonly used to interact with blockchain where JavaScript is not supported. In this recipe, you will learn to communicate with Ethereum using various JSON-RPC commands.

Getting ready

You need to have a fully functioning Ethereum node to test these APIs. By default, both geth and Parity expose port 8545 for JSON-RPC. Some examples are given in JavaScript, but you can use any programming language that supports HTTPS requests.

Make sure that you are starting your geth node with enough `--rpcapi` permissions:

```
$ geth --rpc --rpcapi "web3,eth,personal"
```

We will focus on a few important APIs here and you can always find the complete list for reference at `github.com/ethereum/wiki/wiki/JSON-RPC`.

How to do it...

We will now learn how to use JSON-RPC to interact with Ethereum:

1. Build a basic JSON-RPC body with four parameters. The parameters are version, method, parameters, and ID:

```
{
    "jsonrpc":"2.0",
    "method":"", // method identifier
    "params":[], // list of parameters
    "id":0 // id
}
```

2. Use the `net_peerCount` method to return the number of peers connected to a node:

```
curl -X POST
    --data
'{"jsonrpc":"2.0","method":"net_peerCount","params":[],"id":74}'
    http://localhost:8545
```

3. You will get a response like this for all the requests you make. Some requests will return a hex value instead of a decimal/string. You may have to convert it to the required format manually:

```
{
    "id":74,
    "jsonrpc": "2.0",
    "result": "0x2" // 2
}
```

4. Create the same request in Node.js to get the peer count:

```
var request = require('request');

request({
        url: 'http://localhost:8545',
        method: 'POST',
        body:
'{"jsonrpc":"2.0","method":"net_peerCount","params":[],"id":74}'
}, function(error, response, body) {
        if (!error && response.statusCode == 200) {
                console.log(body);
        }
});
```

5. Use this in Python:

```
import requests
data =
'{"jsonrpc":"2.0","method":"net_peerCount","params":[],"id":74}'
response = requests.post('http://localhost:8545/', data=data)
```

6. And use this in Go:

```
body :=
strings.NewReader(`{"jsonrpc":"2.0","method":"net_peerCount","params":[],"id":74}`)

req, err := http.NewRequest("POST", "http://localhost:8545", body)
if err != nil {
    // handle err
}

req.Header.Set("Content-Type", "application/x-www-form-urlencoded")
resp, err := http.DefaultClient.Do(req)
if err != nil {
    // handle err
}
```

```
defer resp.Body.Close()
```

7. Use any programming language that can make HTTP requests for interacting through JSON-RPC.

   Let's look into a few more important examples.

8. To get the current Ether base of the connected node, use `eth_coinbase`:

```
// Request
curl -X POST
    --data
'{"jsonrpc":"2.0","method":"eth_coinbase","params":[],"id":64}'
    http://localhost;8545

// Response
{
  "id":64,
  "jsonrpc": "2.0",
  "result": "0x824e470cCac64CC5fa4Abe953e64FA360EA11366"
}
```

9. To view the list of accounts in the node, use `eth_accounts`:

```
// Request
curl -X POST
    --data
'{"jsonrpc":"2.0","method":"eth_accounts","params":[],"id":1}'
    http://localhost:8545

// Response
{
  "id":1,
  "jsonrpc": "2.0",
  "result": ["0x824e470cCac64CC5fa4Abe953e64FA360EA11366"]
}
```

10. To get the current block height, use `eth_blockNumber`:

```
// Request
curl -X POST
    --data
'{"jsonrpc":"2.0","method":"eth_blockNumber","params":[],"id":83}'
    http://localhost:8545

// Response
{
  "id":83,
  "jsonrpc": "2.0",
```

```
        "result": "0x53D390" // 5493648
    }
```

11. To get the balance of an account in the network, use `eth_getBalance` along with parameters:

```
// Request
curl -X POST
    --data '{"jsonrpc":"2.0",
            "method":"eth_getBalance",
"params":["0x824e470cCac64CC5fa4Abe953e64FA360EA11366", "latest"],
            "id":1
            }'
    http://localhost:8545

// Response
{
  "id":1,
  "jsonrpc": "2.0",
  "result": "0x5AF3107A4000" // 100000000000000
}
```

12. To send a transaction from an account, use `eth_sendTransaction`:

```
// Request
curl -X POST
    --data '{
            "jsonrpc":"2.0",
            "method":"eth_sendTransaction",
            "params": <Trnsaction_Object>,
            "id":1
            }'
    http://localhost:8545

// Response
{
  "id":1,
  "jsonrpc": "2.0",
  "result":
"0xf456c56efe41db20f32853ccc4cbea3d2ab011b2c11082150f29c36212345dbd
"
}
```

13. To get the transaction receipt, use `eth_getTransactionReceipt`:

```
// Request
curl -X POST
    --data '{
                "jsonrpc":"2.0",
                "method":"eth_getTransactionReceipt",
                "params":["<TransactionHash>"],
                "id":1
            }'
    http://localhost:8545

// Result
{ "id":1, "jsonrpc":"2.0", "result": <Receipt> }
```

Other ways to interact with your contract

Web3JS is a great library to use in your decentralized application. You can also use the JSON-RPC API to directly interact with the blockchain. Since the ecosystem is open source, there are some well-maintained libraries built around Ethereum, and you can use them in your application to interact with the network.

In this recipe, you will learn about some alternatives to web3.js that can be used to interact with Ethereum.

Getting ready

You need to have a fully functioning Ethereum node to test these APIs. You can use geth, Parity, or event Ganache to test your code. You may find other dependencies to install as you progress through this recipe.

How to do it...

There are several alternatives to `web3.js`, and we will mainly focus on Nethereum and Web3J.

Nethereum

Nethereum is a .NET library for Ethereum, which allows interaction with Ethereum nodes, both public and permission-based, in a similar way to geth, Parity, or Quorum.

1. Install Nethereum in Windows using the NuGet package manager:

```
PM > Install-Package Nethereum.Web3
// OR
PM > Install-Package Nethereum.Portable
```

2. Mac or Linux users can use the `dotnet` core CLI to install the library:

```
dotnet add package Nethereum.Web3
// OR
dotnet add package Nethereum.Portable
```

3. To initialize the object, use the following methods:

```
// Will connect to default node
var web3 = new Nethereum.Web3.Web3();
// Custom node address
var web3 = new Nethereum.Web3.Web3("https://localhost:7545");
// IPC Connection
var ipcClient = new Nethereum.JsonRpc.IpcClient("./geth.ipc");
var web3 = new Nethereum.Web3.Web3(ipcClient);
```

More information is available from the official documentation at `https://nethereum.readthedocs.io/en/latest/`.

Web3J

1. Web3J is a Java and Android library for interacting with nodes and smart contracts on the Ethereum network.

2. Add the following dependencies to Maven to start using Web3J:

```
// Java 8
<dependency>
  <groupId>org.web3j</groupId>
  <artifactId>core</artifactId>
  <version>3.3.1</version>
</dependency>

// Android
<dependency>
```

```
<groupId>org.web3j</groupId>
<artifactId>core</artifactId>
<version>3.3.1-android</version>
</dependency>
```

3. If you are using Gradle, then use the following methods:

```
// Java 8
compile ('org.web3j:core:3.3.1')

// Android
compile ('org.web3j:core:3.3.1-android')
```

4. To connect to a node and initialize an object, use `Web3J.build`. It defaults to `localhost:8545` and can be changed:

```
Web3j web3 = Web3j.build(new HttpService());
```

5. To send a synchronous request using Web3J, use the following method:

```
Web3ClientVersion web3ClientVersion =
web3.web3ClientVersion().send();
String clientVersion = web3ClientVersion.getWeb3ClientVersion();
```

6. To make it asynchronous, use the following method:

```
Web3ClientVersion web3ClientVersion =
web3.web3ClientVersion().sendAsync().get();
String clientVersion = web3ClientVersion.getWeb3ClientVersion();
```

More information about using this library is available in the official documentation at `https://github.com/web3j/web3j`.

The Truffle Suite 4

In this chapter, we will cover the following recipes:

- Installing and configuring the Truffle framework
- Making use of Truffle boxes
- Compiling smart contracts
- Advanced Truffle configuration
- Migration and deployment in Truffle
- Interacting with your contracts
- Debugging a smart contract using Truffle
- Writing tests for smart contracts
- Building DApps and APIs using Truffle
- Package management in Truffle
- Getting started with Drizzle
- Using HD wallet in Truffle

Introduction

Truffle is a very popular development framework for Ethereum. It provides built-in smart contract compilation, a scriptable deployment framework, and a rich, automated contract testing platform. Truffle also provides an interactive console with the Ethereum network for direct contract communication. Truffle is completely based on JavaScript and is very modular. This allows you to use Truffle as a development platform or integrate it into your toolset to take advantage of its features.

Truffle is suited for anyone who wants a framework for Ethereum development so they can better organize their DApp and not have to worry about manually setting up a test environment.

Installing and configuring the Truffle framework

To develop and test smart contracts for Ethereum, you need to have the Truffle framework installed on your machine. Installing and starting a project in Truffle is relatively easy and you can do it in a few steps. Most of the tasks in Truffle are carried out through a command-line interface, and you will learn more about configuring the framework in this recipe.

Getting ready

The Truffle framework is based on JavaScript and is distributed via npm. You need to have Node.js (5.0+) installed on your machine to set up and work with Truffle.

Also, Truffle requires a working Ethereum network with the Remote Procedure Call (RPC) port exposed for the testing and deployment of smart contracts. You can use geth, Parity, or Ganache (previously TestRPC) as the Ethereum client. For more information, refer to the first chapter of this book.

Node Package Manager (**npm**) is an online repository for the publishing of open source Node.js projects. It is also used as a command-line utility for interacting with the said repository to help in package installation, version management, and dependency management.

How to do it...

1. Install the Truffle package globally using npm. You might want to use the sudo command as follows if you face any permissions issues:

   ```
   npm install -g truffle
   ```

2. Once the package is installed, you can access it through the command line. Create an empty truffle_project folder for your Truffle project using the following command:

   ```
   mkdir truffle_project
   cd truffle_project
   ```

3. Use the init command to initialize your project with the default contracts and migrations:

```
truffle init
```

4. The preceding command will create a basic template that you can use to start your project. The template will have the following file structure:
   - `./contracts` to store your Solidity smart contract files
   - `./tests` to store smart contracts and application test scripts
   - `./migrations` to store deployment and migration scripts
   - `./truffle.js` file to keep the application and network configuration

5. After creating the contract and related scripts, run the following commands to compile, migrate, and test your Truffle project:

   - `truffle compile` to compile your smart contracts
   - `truffle migrate` to run the migration scripts
   - `truffle test` to run the test cases

Windows users may face issues with running truffle commands from the command prompt. This is because of the `truffle.js` file present in the root directory. The command precedence property of the command prompt executes the `.js` file rather than the truffle.cmd executable on the path. To resolve this issue, either call the executable with the `.cmd` extension (`truffle.cmd compile`) or use Git bash or PowerShell terminals to run the scripts.

6. Edit the `truffle.js` configuration file to change the project configuration and change properties such as network, account, gas, and so on. The following is the basic structure of the file:

```
module.exports = {
    networks: {
        development: {
            host: "localhost",
            port: 8545,
            network_id: "*" // Match any network id
        }
    }
};
```

Making use of Truffle boxes

Truffle provides helpful boilerplates known as Truffle boxes. Every box comes with different Solidity contracts, libraries, frontend and backend modules, user interface views, and related documentation. This can help you build your app in a much more efficient and simpler way.

In this recipe, you will learn about various boxes (react, uport, webpack, and so on) that can make your development workflow easier.

Getting ready

You need to have a working installation of Truffle on your system to try this recipe. Also, connection to a working Ethereum client is needed for testing and deployment.

How to do it...

1. Use the `unbox` command to download and use a box. Boxes are directly integrated into the Truffle command line:

```
truffle unbox <box_name>
```

2. Each box downloads related files and libraries for you to work with. Let's start with a very basic example, MetaCoin:

```
truffle unbox metacoin
```

This contains a basic MetaCoin contract along with related migration and test scripts. You can use compile, test, and migrate scripts to do the respective tasks.

Earlier versions of Truffle used MetaCoin as the template during the truffle init command. Now, has been moved to a dedicated box and the init command creates a more basic template. It is recommended to use the MetaCoin box for creating a new project.

3. Use the react box to create a barebones React app and related smart contracts. It also includes jest and webpack for testing and other tasks:

```
truffle unbox react
```

You can start the application using the npm start script. This will serve your application frontend on `http://localhost:3000` with hot reloading. Make sure to compile and migrate your contract manually after each modification:

```
npm run start
```

Smart contract and application tests can be executed using the `truffle` and `jest` commands:

```
// Smart contract tests
truffle test

// Application tests using jest
npm run test
```

You can build your application for production using webpack. You can find the output in the `build_webpack` folder:

```
npm run build
```

4. Use the webpack box if you need a box with the basic build setup of webpack:

```
truffle unbox webpack
```

5. Use the `react-auth` box to create an app with redux, react-router, and a smart contract-based authentication wrapper along with webpack and react:

```
truffle unbox react-auth
```

It includes a basic authentication smart contract, which stores the user details of those who signed up. You can customize the contract and the router to add features required for your application.

You can test, build, and run this box just like you did the previous one:

```
// Serves the application on localhost:3000
npm run start
// To run the smart contract test scripts
truffle test
// To run the jest based application tests
npm run test
// To build the application for production
npm run build
```

6. If you need a UPort implementation, use the `react-uport` box, which is an extension of the `react-auth` box. UPort is an identity and authentication system for Ethereum. UPort allows users to register their own identity on Ethereum, send and request credentials, sign transactions, and securely manage keys and data:

```
truffle unbox react-uport
```

7. Truffle also supports boxes built by the community, and there are some good options available for you to choose from. You can find examples that use AngularJS, ExpressJS, Vue.js, and many more. The complete list of boxes supported by Truffle is available at `https://truffleframework.com/boxes`.

There's more...

You can build your own box for Truffle. You can either start your project from scratch or add the necessary configuration files required to convert your project to a box. Follow these steps to create and upload your box to the Truffle repository:

1. Download the blueprint box to get started. It contains the basic files and configuration to make your life easier.

2. Every box includes a configuration file, `truffle-config.js`, which include the hooks, commands, and ignore attributes.

3. The ignore array contains the list of files that should be ignored while unboxing. Common examples are the readme and gitignore files:

```
ignore: [ 'README.md' ]
```

4. hooks is an object that contains a list of tasks to perform after unboxing. A common example would be npm install:

```
hooks: {
    'post-unpack': 'npm install'
}
```

5. To give the user an idea about the list of commands supported by your box, you can use the commands object. It contains the list of commands the user can use and will be shown in the console after unboxing:

```
commands: {
    "Compile contracts": "truffle compile",
```

```
    "Migrate contracts": "truffle migrate",
    "Test Contracts": "truffle test",
    "Test DApp": "npm test",
    "Start development server": "npm run start",
    "Build": "npm run build"
}
```

6. To list your box in the Truffle portal, you may need to upload it to a published GitHub repository. You can also add your custom images (512px square with 32px padding and a 735px x 100px image with 32px left padding) to personalize it even more.

7. The Truffle team verifies the quality and compatibility of each box. You may need to send an email to the Truffle team to list your box in the official Truffle portal.

Compiling smart contracts

This recipe focuses on compiling smart contracts for a Truffle project. You will also learn about compiling multiple contracts and locating the output to use with your project.

Getting ready

You need to have a working installation of Truffle in your system to try this recipe. Truffle uses `solc-js` to compile your smart contracts, and it will be installed along with Truffle. Ensure that you have the latest version of both using the `version` command:

```
truffle version
```

How to do it...

1. Smart contracts for a Truffle project are located in the `./contracts` directory. Since solidity is the language of choice for smart contracts, the source code files will have the `.sol` extension.

2. There may be one or more contract files in a project. Use the `compile` command to compile the smart contracts present in the directory. Make sure that you are at the root of the project:

```
truffle compile
```

3. If you are running the command for the first time, then it will compile all the contracts present in the folder. You can see the status on your console, as shown in the following screenshot:

```
$ truffle compile
Compiling ./contracts/Migrations.sol...
Compiling ./contracts/SimpleStorage.sol...
Writing artifacts to ./build/contracts
```

4. For subsequent runs, only the contracts that have been modified since the last compile will be compiled by Truffle. If you want to compile all contracts again, use the `--all` option:

```
truffle compile --all
```

5. Compiler output is saved in individual JSON files. It is available in the `./build/contracts` directory. The output file may have the following artifacts:

```
{
    "contractName": "",
    "abi": [],
    "bytecode": "",
    "deployedBytecode": "",
    "sourceMap": "",
    "deployedSourceMap": "",
    "source": "",
    "sourcePath": "",
    "ast": {},
    "legacyAST": {},
    "compiler": {
        "name": "",
        "version": ""
    },
    "networks": {},
    "schemaVersion": "",
    "updatedAt": ""
}
```

6. It is recommended not to edit these files as they will be overwritten by subsequent compilation and deployment processes.

7. Multiple contracts can be linked together for compilation. This is handled in solidity, and you can use the import statement to do the same:

```
import "<path_to_the_contract.sol>";
```

8. Truffle supports package managers such as EthPM and npm, and you can import downloaded contracts by referring to the package as follows:

```
import "packageName/contract.sol";
```

Here, packageName refers to the downloaded package and contract.sol refers to the smart contract source.

9. Truffle gives priority to the packages downloaded through EthPM and then to npm. If there is a naming conflict, Truffle will consider the package downloaded through EthPM.

Advanced Truffle configuration

Configurations in Truffle are stored as a JavaScript file in the root of the project. This helps in configuring various aspects of the project including network, accounts, cost, and so on. In this recipe, you will learn about the various configuration options available in Truffle.

Getting ready

You need to have Truffle installed on your machine to step through this recipe. Verify the installation using the truffle version command.

How to do it...

1. Create a configuration file called `truffle.js` at the root of your project. It should be a JavaScript file that exports the configuration as an object in the required format.

2. If you are using Windows, rename the configuration file to something like `truffle-config.js` to avoid any naming conflicts with the truffle command.

3. Include the network object in the configuration file, which contains the network endpoint for deployment. It will connect the application to an environment running on localhost:8545 for migration and testing:

```
module.exports = {
    networks: {
        development: {
            host: "localhost",
            port: 8545,
            network_id: "*" // Match any network id
        }
    }
};
```

4. Include the list of available networks for the migration process in the networks object. During the migration process for a specific network, deployment artifacts will be saved in the build directory for later use. This helps in managing multiple network deployments, and for each network the related artifact is fetched based on the network identifier.

5. Specify a name for each network to help Truffle to identify them, as follows:

```
networks: {
    development: {
        host: "127.0.0.1",
        port: 8545,
        network_id: "*" // match any network
    },
    test: {
        host: "55.55.55.55",
        port: 8545,
        network_id: 1, // Ethereum main network
    }
}
```

6. During the migration process, select the network using the --network parameter:

```
truffle migrate --network test
```

7. The provider will be set automatically using host and port. You can also specify the network using the provider tag. Use the format new `Web3.providers.HttpProvider("http://<host>:<port>")`:

```
networks: {
    ropsten: {
        provider: new HDWalletProvider(mnemonic,
                        "https://ropsten.infura.io/"),
```

```
            network_id: "3"
    },
    development: {
        provider: new HDWalletProvider(mnemonic,
                    "http://localhost:8545/"),
        network_id: "*"
    }
}
```

You cannot use both host/port and provider together to specify the network. It is recommended to use host and port if you are connecting to an HTTP provider. If you are using a custom provider such as HD Wallet, use provider.

8. Generally, a minimal network connection will be opened to every host specified using the provider. To avoid this, wrap the provider value with a function. In this way, Truffle will ignore the network providers until called explicitly:

```
networks: {
    ropsten: {
        provider: function() {
            return new HDWalletProvider(mnemonic,
                "https://ropsten.infura.io/");
        },
        network_id: "3"
    },
    test: {
        provider: function() {
            return new HDWalletProvider(mnemonic,
                "http://localhost:8545/");
        },
        network_id: "*"
    }
}
```

9. For each network, certain fields can be customized using the configuration file:
    - **from**: The from address to use during the migration process. If not specified, it will use the first account (`web3.eth.accounts[0]`) as the default.
    - **gas**: Gas limit for the migration process. The default is 4712388.
    - **gasPrice**: Gas price for the transaction. The default value is 100000000000.

10. The following is a example of a customized configuration file:

```
networks: {
    development: {
        provider: function() {
            return new HDWalletProvider(mnemonic,
                        "http://localhost:8545/");
        },
        port: 8545,
        network_id: 1208,
        from: "0xB0108b70A181eD91cb1D8d8c822419F0e439f724",
        gas: 560000
    },
    test: {
        host: "55.55.55.55",
        port: 8545,
        network_id: 1,
        gas: 470000,
        gasPrice: 20000000000
    }
}
```

11. The default output directory for compiler output is ./build/contracts. To change this, use the contracts_build_directory attribute:

```
module.exports = {
    contracts_build_directory: "./build_output",
    networks: {
        development: {
            host: "localhost",
            port: 8545,
            network_id: "*"
        }
    }
};
```

You can even target a folder that is outside the Truffle directory. This can be useful if Truffle is part of a collection of projects:

```
module.exports = {
    contracts_build_directory: "../../build_output",
};
```

Absolute paths will also work with this attribute. If you are on Windows, use the double backslash (\\) to specify the path, as follows:

```
module.exports = {
    contracts_build_directory: "C:\\Users\\username\\build_output",
};
```

12. Add compiler configurations to the file using the `solc` key. It works with the default set of settings allowed in the Solidity compiler:

```
solc: {
    optimizer: {
        enabled: true,
        runs: 200
    }
}
```

13. Configure the MochJS test configurations using the mocha attribute as follows:

```
mocha: {
    useColors: true,
    ui: 'tdd',
    reporter: 'list'
}
```

Migration and deployment in Truffle

Migration scripts in Truffle are used for deploying your contracts to an Ethereum network. Scripts are written in JavaScript and you can create new migration scripts throughout the development process. You will learn about creating and running these scripts from this recipe.

Getting ready

You need to have Truffle installed on your machine to try this recipe. Ensure that you have a working Ethereum network to connect and test these scripts.

How to do it...

1. Create and store migration scripts in the `./mirations` directory. You can find the directory at the root of your project.
2. Each file follows a naming convention that includes a number and description. The number denotes the order of execution and is used to record the status of migration. The suffix includes a human-readable description of the scripts:

```
2_token_migration.js
```

3. In the migration script file, include the required import statements followed by the deployment steps:

```
// Import statement
var contract = artifacts.require("contract");

module.exports = function(deployer) {
    // Deployment statement
    deployer.deploy(contract);
};
```

4. Reference the contract using `artifacts.require()`. It is similar to require and import in JavaScript, but returns the contract abstraction with related properties and methods.

5. Contracts are imported using their names. Do not use file paths because each file can contain more than one contract. Consider the following utility contract file:

```
// utility.sol
contract Ownable {
    ...
}

contract Pausable {
    ...
}
```

This file contains two contracts. While importing these contracts, reference them by their names:

```
var ownable = artifacts.require("Ownable");
var pausable = artifacts.require("Pausable");
```

6. The migrations file should export the migration steps as a function using `module.exports`. The function should have at least one parameter called deployer, which can assist in the deployment and to keep the artifacts:

```
module.exports = function(deployer) {
    deployer.deploy(contractInstance);
};
```

7. Deploy more than one contract by calling the deployer method multiple times. It will deploy them in the order you dictated:

```
deployer.deploy(ownable);
deployer.deploy(pausable);
```

Deployer will also return a promise, which can be used to queue up the process. This can help you do tasks that may depend on the previous deployment:

```
deployer.deploy(ownable).then(function() {
    return deployer.deploy(pausable, ownable.address);
});
```

8. If your contract accepts constructor parameters, specify them as part of the deploy method:

```
deployer.deploy(<contract>, parameter1, parameter2, ...);
```

9. If you don't want your contract to be overwritten again, specify it with the overwrite parameter. This will not deploy the contract if it has already been deployed:

```
deployer.deploy(ownable, {
    overwrite: false
});
```

10. The last parameter can also include values such as gas and from. This allows us to specify the values individually for each deployment:

```
deployer.deploy(A, {
    gas: 4612388,
    from: "0x7f1E4A1DC3eB8233B49Bb8E208cC6aAa8B39C77F"
});
```

11. Multiple contract deployments can be part of a single deploy statement. You can do this by passing each contract and its constructor arguments as arrays:

```
deployer.deploy([
    [ownable],
```

```
        [pausable, parameter1, parameter2],
        ...
    ]);
```

12. The deployer method also supports linking libraries and contracts. You can link an already deployed library to another contract before deploying it. The target for linking can be a single contract or an array of contracts. If the target contract does not use the library, the contract will be ignored:

```
// To link a deployed library to another contract
deployer.deploy(<Library>);
deployer.link(<Library>, <Contract>);

// To link a deployed library to multiple contracts
deployer.deploy(<Library>);
deployer.link(<Library>, [<Contract1>, <Contract2>]);
```

13. In addition to deployer, the exportable function also supports two more optional parameters: network and accounts. The network parameter allows you to run the deployment steps based on the current network:

```
module.exports = function(deployer, network) {
    if (network == "development") {
        // Do something
    } else {
        // Do something else
    }
}
```

14. Use the accounts parameter to get the list of accounts on the current network. This value is similar to web3.eth.accounts:

```
module.exports = function(deployer, network, accounts) {
    ...
}
```

15. Include the migrations contract, which is required for the migration's functionality. It follows a predefined interface, but you can edit it to add more features. The default Truffle template comes with the following migration contract:

```
pragma solidity ^0.4.8;

contract Migrations {

    address public owner;
```

```
        // A getter function with the signature
`last_completed_migration()` is required.
        // It should return an uint
        uint public last_completed_migration;
        modifier restricted() {
            if (msg.sender == owner)
            _;
        }

        function Migrations() {
            owner = msg.sender;
        }

        // A function with the signature `setCompleted(uint)` is
required.
        function setCompleted(uint completed) restricted {
            last_completed_migration = completed;
        }

        function upgrade(address new_address) restricted {
            Migrations upgraded = Migrations(new_address);
            upgraded.setCompleted(last_completed_migration);
        }
    }
```

This contract will be deployed initially as the first migration and won't be updated later. You have to include the contract as part of the initial migration script:

```
// ./migrations/1_intial_migration.js
var Migrations = artifacts.require("Migrations");

module.exports = function(deployer) {
    // Initial migration deploys only the migration contract
    deployer.deploy(Migrations);
};
```

16. Once you have configured your contracts and migration scripts, run them using the migrate command:

```
truffle migrate
```

If everything goes right and the migrations are successful, you can see the following output:

```
$ truffle migrate
Using network 'development'.

Running migration: 1_initial_migration.js
  Deploying Migrations...
  ... 0x1f95327bad5ab1cbd706dc6807e88ffc1d0f492ec24591ec4fbd243d4988e091
  Migrations: 0x8cdaf0cd259887258bc13a92c0a6da92698644c0
Saving successful migration to network...
  ... 0xd7bc86d31bee32fa3988f1c1eabce403a1b5d570340a3a9cdba53a472ee8c956
Saving artifacts...
Running migration: 2_deploy_contracts.js
  Deploying SimpleStorage...
  ... 0xca52ac7a96212780cbb1c41ab8b9f189e2c0accae6bb30649a8a05bbcbdc646f
  SimpleStorage: 0x345ca3e014aaf5dca488057592ee47305d9b3e10
Saving successful migration to network...
  ... 0xf36163615f41ef7ed8f4a8f192149a0bf633fe1a2398ce001bf44c43dc7bdda0
Saving artifacts...
```

Interacting with your contract

Truffle provides a rich interface for interacting with your contract. You can either write data to the network or read from it using contract abstractions provided by Truffle. This makes interacting with your contract a breeze.

Writing data to the contract is called a transaction. A transaction can be anything from sending Ether, deploying a smart contract, or executing a state changing function in the contract. You need to pay a certain fee to perform a transaction, known as gas. You can see the result of a transaction only after a miner confirms it. Thus, you cannot receive any return value from the function you are executing.

Reading data from smart contracts is known as a call. This can be used to execute smart contract code, but cannot change any values. Since no state is modified, calls are free to run and you can receive the return value immediately.

This recipe focuses on making transactions or calls using contract abstractions in Truffle.

Getting ready

You need to have Truffle installed on your machine to try this recipe. For deployment and testing, Truffle will try to connect to an Ethereum network. Make sure that you have specified the provider in the config file.

The following scripts can be executed using Truffle's interactive console. Start the console using the following command:

```
truffle console
```

The Truffle console will look for a network called development in the Truffle configuration file and will connect to it. You can manually point to other networks using --network <network_name>. This will allow your contract to interact with your network of choice. The Truffle console also provides the option to use a specific mnemonic or account list.

How to do it...

1. Consider the following contract as an example for this recipe. This is a simple token contract with a feature to transfer tokens and check the balance of each address. The contract is only for illustration purposes, so don't use it in your production application:

```solidity
pragma solidity ^0.4.23;

contract TokenContract {
    mapping (address => uint) balances;

    event Transfer(address indexed _from, address indexed _to,
uint256 _value);

    constructor() public {
        balances[msg.sender] = 100000;
    }

    function sendToken(address receiver, uint amount) public
returns(bool) {
        require(balances[msg.sender] < amount);
        balances[msg.sender] -= amount;
        balances[receiver] += amount;
        emit Transfer(msg.sender, receiver, amount);
        return true;
    }

    function getBalance(address addr) public view returns(uint) {
        return balances[addr];
    }
}
```

2. This contract contains a constructor, a state changing method called sendToken, and a read-only method, getBalance. The constructor will be executed during the contract deployment and other functions have to be called with either a transaction or a call.

3. Truffle will create a JavaScript object for the contract. Use the deployed() function to interact with the deployed version of the contract:

```
TokenContract.deployed().then(function(instance) {
    console.log(instance);
});
```

Make sure that you have migrated your contract before trying to interact with them. If you are using truffle console, use truffle migrate from the root of your project.

4. The sendToken function will try to send some tokens from one account to another. This results in a state change, and we need to use a transaction for this.

5. Call the function directly and it will result in a transaction by default, instead of a call:

```
TokenContract.sendToken();
```

6. Pass the parameters that are required to execute the function. Use an object as the optional last parameter that lets you configure specific details about the transaction, such as from address, value, gas, and so on:

```
var from_address = "0xa...";
var to_address = "0xb...";

TokenContract.sendToken(to_address, 500, {
    from: from_address
});
```

7. Use the promise functionality to fire callbacks on success and failure. With this, you don't have to check the status of the transaction yourself:

```
TokenContract.sendToken(to_address, 500, {
    from: from_address
}).then(function(result) {
    console.log(result);
})
```

8. The whole operation will look something as follows:

```
var from_address = "0xa...";
var to_address = "0xb...";

var tokenContract;

TokenContract.deployed().then(function(instance) {
    tokenContract = instance;
    return tokenContract.sendToken(to_address, 500, {
        from: from_address
    });
}).then(function(result) {
    // Transaction successful!
    console.log(result);
}).catch(function(e) {
    // Transaction failed
    console.log(e);
})
```

9. The getBalance function is used for reading the balance of a specific address. Note that this does not modify any state. So, execute the function using the call method:

```
var account = "0xa...";
tokenContract.getBalance.call(account);
```

10. Use the promise method to read data immediately from the execution. It will return the result instead of the transaction hash. It will also return a BigNumber object, which you may need to convert:

```
var account = "0xf17f52151EbEF6C7334FAD080c5704D77216b732";

TokenContract.deployed().then(function(instance) {
    return instance.getBalance.call(account);
}).then(function(result) {
    // Returns result
    console.log(result.toNumber())
}).catch(function(e) {
    // Exception
    console.log(e);
});
```

11. Now, you know how to make a transaction and a call. Let's look deep into the various things you can do with the transaction result.

12. The transaction returns an object with the transaction hash, receipt, and array of events logged during the transaction:

```
var from_address = "0xa...";
var to_address = "0xb...";

var tokenContract;

TokenContract.deployed().then(function(instance) {
    tokenContract = instance;
    return tokenContract.sendToken(to_address, 500, {
        from: from_address
    });
}).then(function(result) {
    console.log(result.tx); // Transaction hash
    console.log(result.logs); // Event logs
    console.log(result.receipt); // Transaction receipt
})
```

13. Use the logs array to locate any event and then perform tasks based on that. Try catching the Transfer event during token transfer:

```
var from_address = "0xa...";
var to_address = "0xb...";

var tokenContract;

TokenContract.deployed().then(function(instance) {
    tokenContract = instance;
    return tokenContract.sendToken(to_address, 500, {
        from: from_address
    });
}).then(function(result) {
    for(var i = 0; i < result.logs.length; i++) {
        if(result.logs[i].event == "Transfer") {
            console.log("Event raised!");
        }
    }
})
```

14. Send Ether directly to a contract to trigger the fallback function. The contractInstance provides the `sendTransaction` method, which accepts the standard transaction object for this operation:

```
contractInstance.sendTransaction({
    from: "0x..",
    value: 10000 // in wei
```

```
    }).then(function(result) {
        // Transaction obj
        console.log(result);
    });
```

There's more...

All the preceding examples use the already deployed contract abstraction. We can deploy a different version to the network using the new() method:

```
TokenContract.new().then(function(instance) {
    // New contract instance
    console.log(instance.address);
}).catch(function(err) {
    // Exception
});
```

Truffle also provides an option to create an instance from any deployed address. The instance can be created using the at() method:

```
var instance = TokenContract.at("0x...");
```

Debugging a smart contract using Truffle

Truffle provides a rich debugging interface, which allows you to debug the transactions against your contract. This is very similar to existing command-line debuggers for other development environments. The following features are supported by the Truffle debugger:

- Code stepping: Over, into, out, next, instruction, and so on
- Variable inspection: Stack, memory, and storage
- Breakpoints
- Watch expressions
- Custom expression evaluation
- Current code location, including the address of the running contract

Unlike other tools and methods, while debugging an Ethereum transaction, you are not running the code in real time. While debugging a contract, you are stepping through the historical execution of a transaction. In this recipe, you will learn how to debug a transaction using Truffle's debugging tool.

Getting ready

You need to have Truffle (>= 4) installed on your system to try this recipe. If you are new to Truffle, you can install it using the following command; you may have to use sudo if you are using Linux/Mac:

```
npm install -g truffle
```

If you already have an older version of Truffle installed, run the following commands to get the latest version:

```
npm uninstall -g truffle
npm install -g truffle
```

How to do it...

1. Consider the following token contract as an example for debugging. This contract is for illustration purposes only. Never use it in your application:

```
pragma solidity ^0.4.23;

contract TokenContract {
  mapping (address => uint) balances;

  event Transfer(address indexed _from, address indexed _to,
uint256 _value);

  constructor() public {
    balances[msg.sender] = 100000;
  }

  function sendToken(address receiver, uint amount) public
returns(bool) {
    require(balances[msg.sender] < amount);
    balances[msg.sender] -= amount;
    balances[receiver] += amount;
    emit Transfer(msg.sender, receiver, amount);
    return true;
  }

  function getBalance(address addr) public view returns(uint) {
    return balances[addr];
  }
}
```

2. Let's try to debug the sendToken function. You need to have received the transaction hash while making a call to that function. Use the truffle debug command to start the debugging process:

```
truffle debug
0x4e3bbf1f5097357f8a4e3d42a3377520c409a2804236eeda89173739a46c7a55
```

3. Starting a debugger will open an interface with a list of addresses that have been affected during the transaction, commands available for debugging, and a contract source code file and preview:

```
$ truffle debug 0x4e3bbf1f5097357f8a4e3d42a3377520c409a2804236eeda89173739a46c7a55

Gathering transaction data...

Addresses affected:
 0x8cd918cee8f93989e334bc0107bb33a9586d05c0 - TokenContract

Commands:
(enter) last command entered (step next)
(o) step over, (i) step into, (u) step out, (n) step next
(;) step instruction, (p) print instruction, (h) print this help, (q) quit
(b) toggle breakpoint, (c) continue until breakpoint
(+) add watch expression (`+:<expr>`), (-) remove watch expression (-:<expr>)
(?) list existing watch expressions
(v) print variables and values, (:) evaluate expression - see `v`


TokenContract.sol:

1: pragma solidity ^0.4.23;
2:
3: contract TokenContract {
   ^^^^^^^^^^^^^^^^^^^^^^^^^^

debug(development:0x4e3bbf1f...)> 
```

You can press the **Enter** key to rerun the last command entered, or enter one of the available commands to analyze the transaction in more detail. When the debugger starts, the default value for the Enter key will be to step through the transaction.

4. To step to the next logical statement or expression in the source code, use the step next (n) command. This helps in evaluating sub-expressions before the virtual machine can evaluate the full expression. Use this command if you'd like to analyze each logical item the virtual machine evaluates:

```
debug(development:0x4e3bbf1f...)> n

TokenContract.sol:

12:    function sendToken(address receiver, uint amount) public returns(bool) {
13:        require(balances[msg.sender] >= amount);
14:        balances[msg.sender] -= amount;
                ^^^^^^
```

5. To step over the current line, relative to the position of the statement or expression currently being evaluated, use the step over (o) command. It is very helpful if you'd like to quickly jump to a specific point in the Solidity file, or if you don't want to step into a function call or contract creation on the current line.

6. To step into the function call or contract creation currently being evaluated, use the step into (i) command. This is useful to jump into the function and quickly start debugging the code that exists there.

7. To step out of the currently running function, use the step out (u) command. This can be used to quickly get back to the calling function, or end the execution of the transaction if this was the entry point of the transaction.

8. To print the current instruction and stack data, use the print instructions (p) command. Use this when you'd like to see the current instruction and stack data to verify the result after debugging through the transaction. It does not step to the next instruction:

```
debug(development:0x0fc3c301...)> p

TokenContract.sol:

(64) DUP2
  00000000000000000000000000000000000000000000000000000000412664ae
  000000000000000000000000000000000000000000000000000000000000009c
  000000000000000000000000f17f52151ebef6c7334fad080c5704d77216b732
  000000000000000000000000000000000000000000000000000000000000000a
  0000000000000000000000000000000000000000000000000000000000000000 (top)

11:
12:    function sendToken(address receiver, uint amount) public returns(bool) {
13:        require(balances[msg.sender] >= amount);
                ^^^^^^
```

9. To step through each individual instruction evaluated by the virtual machine, use the step instructions (;) command. This is useful if you're interested in understanding the low-level bytecode created by the Solidity source code. When you use this command, the debugger will also print out the stack data at the time the instruction was evaluated.

10. You can add variables to the watch list using the + command and remove them from the list using the - command. These can be used to glance at the variables during each debugging step. To view the complete list of variables in the watchlist, use the ? command:

```
debug(development:0x4e3bbf1f...)> +:amount
10

debug(development:0x4e3bbf1f...)> n

TokenContract.sol:

13:        require(balances[msg.sender] >= amount);
14:        balances[msg.sender] -= amount;
15:        balances[receiver] += amount;
                               ^^^^^^

:amount
   10

debug(development:0x4e3bbf1f...)> -:amount
```

11. Use v to print variables and values, and use : to evaluate the expressions:

```
debug(development:0x4e3bbf1f...)> v

 receiver:  '0xf17f52151ebef6c7334fad080c5704d77216b732'
   amount: 10
        : true
 balances: null

debug(development:0x4e3bbf1f...)> :amount
10
```

If you are stuck during the debugging process, use the help (h) command. This will print the set of commands supported by the debugger. You can find the same list when you started the debugging console.

12. The console will be exited automatically once you have reached the end of a transaction. To exit manually during debugging, use the quit (q) command.

Writing tests for smart contracts

Truffle provides a solid test framework, which allows you to write test cases in both JavaScript and Solidity. Tests in a Truffle project should exist in the ./test directory. Tests can have either a .js or .sol extension, based on the language they are written in. In this recipe, you will learn to write test cases for your smart contract in both JavaScript and Solidity.

Getting ready

You need to have Truffle installed on your machine to step through this recipe. You also need to have a working Ethereum network to enable Truffle to run tests on the contracts.

How to do it...

Truffle allows test cases written in both JavaScript and Solidity. JavaScript tests follow Mocha as a testing framework and Chai for assertions. For Solidity-based test cases, Truffle provides a default assertion library for you to use. Let's look into each method and write some test cases.

Writing tests in JavaScript

1. The structure of a JavaScript-based test is very similar to a Mocha-based test. The difference lies in the fact that Truffle has an extra contract() function. This method works like describe() in Mocha, except it creates a new instance of the contract:

```
contract('TokenContract', function() {
    // Write tests
});
```

Truffle uses the clean room feature while running tests. This feature redeploys the contract before executing the contract() method in tests. This ensures that you have a fresh set of contracts to test against. You can still use describe() to run tests without the clean room feature.

2. The contract() function also provides the list of accounts in the Ethereum client, which you can use to write tests:

```
contract('TokenContract', function(accounts) {
    // Write tests
});
```

3. Reference any contract using the artifacts.require() method. It works the same way as using it within the migrations:

```
var TokenContract = artifacts.require("TokenContract.sol");
```

4. Use contract abstractions to interact with the deployed contract. Use them to make sure your contracts are working properly:

```
var TokenContract = artifacts.require("TokenContract.sol");

contract('TokenContract', function(accounts) {
    it("Contract test template", function() {
        return TokenContract.deployed().then(function(instance) {
            console.log(instance);
        });
    });
});
```

5. Make use of the contract instance to execute each function in the contract and then use Chai to assess these results. Consider the following simple example of checking the balance after deploying:

```
var TokenContract = artifacts.require("TokenContract.sol");

contract('TokenContract', function(accounts) {

    it("should allocate 10000 Token to the owner account",
    function() {
        return TokenContract.deployed().then(function(instance) {
            return instance.getBalance.call(accounts[0]);
        }).then(function(balance) {
            assert.equal(balance.valueOf(), 100000,
                "100000 wasn't in the first account");
        });
    });

})
```

6. Write more complex tests that include multiple transactions and calls. Promise returns allow you to chain multiple transactions together, which helps in evaluating lengthy control flows:

```
var TokenContract = artifacts.require("TokenContract.sol");

contract('TokenContract', function(accounts) {

    it("should transfer tokens correctly", function() {
        var token;
        var account_one_starting_balance;
        var account_two_starting_balance;
        var account_one_ending_balance;
        var account_two_ending_balance;
        var amount = 10;

        return TokenContract.deployed().then(function(instance) {
            token = instance;
            return token.getBalance.call(accounts[0]);
        }).then(function(balance) {
            account_one_starting_balance = balance.toNumber();
            return token.getBalance.call(accounts[1]);
        }).then(function(balance) {
            account_two_starting_balance = balance.toNumber();
            return token.sendToken(accounts[1], amount, {
                from: accounts[0]
            });
        }).then(function(tx) {
            return token.getBalance.call(accounts[0]);
        }).then(function(balance) {
            account_one_ending_balance = balance.toNumber();
            return token.getBalance.call(accounts[1]);
        }).then(function(balance) {
            account_two_ending_balance = balance.toNumber();

            assert.equal(account_one_ending_balance,
                account_one_starting_balance - amount,
                "Amount wasn't correctly taken from the sender");
            assert.equal(account_two_ending_balance,
                account_two_starting_balance + amount,
                "Amount wasn't correctly sent to the receiver");
        });
    });

});
```

7. Javascript tests also support async/await notation. Here is the same test case after replacing then() statements:

```javascript
var TokenContract = artifacts.require("TokenContract.sol");

contract('TokenContract', function(accounts) {

    it("should transfer tokens correctly", async () => {

        let amount = 10;

        let token = await TokenContract.deployed();

        let balance = await token.getBalance.call(accounts[0]);
        let account_one_starting_balance = balance.toNumber();

        balance = await token.getBalance.call(accounts[1]);
        let account_two_starting_balance = balance.toNumber();

        await token.sendToken(accounts[1], amount, {
            from: accounts[0]
        });

        balance = await token.getBalance.call(accounts[0]);
        let account_one_ending_balance = balance.toNumber();

        balance = await token.getBalance.call(accounts[1]);
        let account_two_ending_balance = balance.toNumber();

        assert.equal(account_one_ending_balance,
            account_one_starting_balance - amount,
            "Amount wasn't correctly taken from the sender");
        assert.equal(account_two_ending_balance,
            account_two_starting_balance + amount,
            "Amount wasn't correctly sent to the receiver");
    });

});
```

8. Run the tests using the truffle test command. The tests described here will produce the following output:

```
$ truffle test
Using network 'development'.


  Contract: TokenContract
    ✓ should put 10000 Token in the first account
    ✓ should send coin correctly (79ms)


  2 passing (111ms)
```

9. Run a specific test script by explicitly specifying its name:

```
truffle test ./test/TokenContract.js
```

Truffle includes a web3 instance in each test file. It is configured to use the correct provider specified on the network. You can use all supported APIs, such as web3.eth.accounts, from the test file.

Writing tests in Solidity

1. You should write tests just like a contract, and the contract name should start with Test, using an uppercase T. It uses the clean room environment just like the JavaScript test cases:

```
contract TestContract {
    ...
}
```

2. Write individual functions to represent each test case that must start with test, using a lowercase t. Each function is executed by a single transaction in the same order as the declaration:

```
contract TestContract {
    testCase1() { ... }
    testCase2() { ... }
}
```

3. Use the Assert.sol library provided by Truffle to handle the assertions. Import it from truffle/Assert.sol. You can replace the library with your custom made one, but it should follow the exact signature of Assert.sol:

```
import "truffle/Assert.sol";
```

4. Assertion functions emit events that the test framework evaluates to determine the result of the test. These functions return a Boolean value, which represents the outcome of the assertion.

5. Consider the following test example, which checks for the balance of an account:

```
import "truffle/Assert.sol";
import "truffle/DeployedAddresses.sol";
import "../contracts/TokenContract.sol";

contract TestTokenContract {

    function testInitialBalance() {
        TokenContract token =
            TokenContract(DeployedAddresses.TokenContract());

        uint expected = 100000;

        Assert.equal(token.getBalance(msg.sender),
            expected,
            "Owner should have 100000 TokenContract initially");
    }

}
```

6. Solidity test cases also include various hook functions, similar to Mocha. These hooks are beforeAll, beforeEach, afterAll, and afterEach. Use these hooks to perform actions before and after each test case or test suit.

7. You can even write the same hook multiple times, each with an additional suffix. This will help you to write a complex setup process that might use a lot of gas:

```
import "truffle/Assert.sol";

contract TestHooks {

    uint value;
    function beforeEach() {
        value = 1;
    }
```

```
function beforeEachIncrement() {
    value++;
}

function testSomeValue() {
    uint expected = 2;

    Assert.equal(value, expected, "value should be 2");
}
}
```

8. Execute the tests with the truffle test command. It will display the result similar to JavaScript test cases in the console.

Building DApps and APIs using Truffle

Truffle provides a contract abstract that can be used in Node.js and in a browser. This allows us to create distributed applications right from the Truffle project. This abstract provides some additional features such as promises, default values, and returning logs and receipts from each transaction. In this recipe, you will learn how to create apps using Truffle.

Getting ready

To try this recipe, you need to have Truffle installed on your system. Your application needs to connect to a running Ethereum network to perform read and write operations. So, ensure you have a working Ethereum client in place.

How to do it...

1. Truffle provides a truffle-contract module, which creates the smart contract abstract. It is distributed via npm; run the following command to install it:

```
npm install truffle-contract
```

2. Import the browser module provided by Truffle for your frontend application:

```
<script type="text/javascript" src="web3.js"></script>
<script type="text/javascript" src="./dist/truffle-
contract.min.js"></script>
```

3. To use the library in your Node.js application, import it using the module name. Don't forget to set a web3 provider instance before importing it:

```
var provider = new
Web3.providers.HttpProvider("http://localhost:8545");
var contract = require("truffle-contract");

var MyContract = contract({
    // Optional. Defaults to "Contract"
    contract_name: "MyContract",
    // Required. Application binary interface.
    abi: ...,
    // Optional. Binary without resolve library links.
    unlinked_binary: "...",
    // Optional. Deployed address of contract.
    address: "...",
    // Optional. ID of network being saved within abstraction.
    network_id: "...",
    // Optional. ID of default network this
    default_network: "..."
});

MyContract.setProvider(provider);
```

If you are using the browser module, truffle-contract will be available through TruffleContract:

```
var MyContract = TruffleContract({
    ...
});
```

4. If you have already deployed the contract by any other means, then use the at method() to create an instance with that address.

5. To deploy a completely new version of the contract to the network, use the new() method.

6. To create an instance with the default address, use deployed(). Each instance supports promises and you can use them to perform synchronized transactions:

```
var contractInstance;

MyContract.deployed().then(function(instance) {
    var contractInstance = instance;
    return contractInstance.contractFunction();
}).then(function(result) {
    // Do something
```

```
        });
```

7. Let's use the TokenContract example discussed previously in this chapter and make transfer tokens between accounts:

```
var provider = new
Web3.providers.HttpProvider("http://localhost:8545");
var contract = require("truffle-contract");

var TokenContract = contract({
    contract_name: "TokenContract",
    abi: [...],
    unlinked_binary: "...",
    address: "..."
});

TokenContract.setProvider(provider);

var account_one = "0x1...";
var account_two = "0x2...";
var contract_address = "0xC...";
var token;

TokenContract.at(contract_address).then(function (instance) {
    token = instance;
    return token.sendTokens(account_two, 100, {
        from: account_one
    });
}).then(function (result) {
    return token.getBalance.call(account_two);
}).then(function (balance_of_account_two) {
    console.log("Account two:" + balance_of_account_two);
    return token.sendTokens(account_one, 50, {
        from: account_two
    });
}).then(function (result) {
    return token.getBalance.call(account_two)
}).then(function (balance_of_account_two) {
    console.log("Account two: " + balance_of_account_two);
}).catch(function (err) {
    console.log(err);
});
```

8. Create the contract abstract using the truffle-artifactor library. Use npm to install artifactor:

```
npm install truffle-artifactor
```

9. Generate a `.sol.js` file that can be used to import, as a contract, abstract in truffle-contract:

```
var artifactor = require("truffle-artifactor");

var contract_data = {
    contract_name: "TokenContract",
    abi: [],
    unlinked_binary: "...",
    address: "...",
    network_id: "...",
    default_network: "..."
};

artifactor.save(contract_data, "./TokenContract.sol.js")
    .then(function () {
        // Success
    });
```

10. Import the generated file in truffle-contract as an abstract using the require method:

```
var TokenContract = require("./TokenContract.sol.js");

TokenContract.setProvider(provider);
```

Package management in Truffle

With a growing number of reusable modules and libraries, it is important to have a package management mechanism for every development environment. Truffle supports both npm and EthPM. This recipe focuses mainly on installing, using, and publishing packages to various registries that are available with Truffle.

Getting ready

You need to have Truffle installed on your machine to download and run packages. Also, ensure that you have a stable version of npm available.

How to do it...

Truffle comes with two package managers: EthPM and npm. EthPM is the new package registry for Ethereum. It follows certain community-supported specifications for publishing and consuming smart contract packages. npm is the traditional package manager for Node.js, and Truffle provides support for using those packages.

EthPM

1. To install a package from EthPM, use the truffle install command. You can also specify the version number exactly like you do with npm:

```
truffle install <package_name>

truffle install <package_name>@<version>
```

2. Create an ethpm.json file to save your project-specific dependencies and versions. To install all dependencies listed in the file, run the following command:

```
truffle install
```

3. EthPM will create a directory called installed_contracts within your root folder to save the dependencies. This is exactly like a node_modules folder.

4. To import a dependency into your contract, use Solidity's import statement with the package and filename:

```
pragma solidity ^0.4.23;

import "owned/ownable.sol";

contract MyContract is ownable {
    ...
}
```

5. To import the dependency into your migration script, you can use the regular artifacts.require() statement:

```
var MyPackage = artifacts.require("package/contract");
var MyContract = artifacts.require("MyContract");

module.exports = function(deployer) {
    deployer.deploy(MyPackage).then(function() {
        return deployer.deploy(MyContract, MyPackage.address);
```

```
        });
    };
```

npm

1. Installing a package is very straightforward, and is like the normal npm installation:

   ```
   npm install <package>
   ```

2. The most important directories in a Truffle package are the `./contracts` and `./build` directories.

3. To import a package into your contract, use Solidity's import statement. Specify the downloaded package name and the filename to import it:

   ```
   import "npm-library/contracts/contract.sol";
   ```

4. To interact with the contracts from JavaScript, refer to the package's build files. Using them with truffle-contract will convert them into their respective contract abstractions:

   ```
   var contract = require("truffle-contract");
   ]var data = require("npm-library/build/contracts/contract.json");

   var SimpleNameRegistry = contract(data);
   ```

There's more...

You can publish your own packages to either EthPM or npm. Publishing a contract with npm is exactly similar to publishing any other module. You can follow the same steps to deploy a Truffle package as well.

To publish your package to the EthPM registry, it is important to have a separate configuration file called ethpm.json at the root of the project:

```
{
    "package_name": "test",
    "version": "0.0.3",
    "description": "Test contract to check EthPM",
    "authors": [ "Manoj <email>" ],
    "keywords": [
        "ethereum", "test", "ethpm"
```

```
    ],
    "dependencies": {
        "ownable": "^0.1.3"
    },
    "license": "MIT"
}
```

The EthPM registry still exists in the Ropsten network and you need to publish your package to the Ropsten network. So, add the necessary network options to enable your application to interact with Ropsten. You can either use INFURA or set up your own Ropsten node.

Finally, run the publish command to publish your package to the registry:

```
truffle publish
```

Getting started with Drizzle

Drizzle is a collection of frontend libraries based on the Redux store to make writing DApps easier. You have complete access to various development tools that are provided by Redux. Drizzle provides fully reactive contract data, including state, events, and transactions. In this recipe, you will learn about installing and using Drizzle in your application.

Getting ready

Drizzle is distributed via npm, and you need to have Node.js installed on your machine to get it. You also need to have a working Ethereum network for testing and deployment purposes.

How to do it...

1. Drizzle is based on JavaScript and is distributed via npm. Use the npm install command to get the library:

    ```
    npm install --save drizzle
    ```

If you are already using React, you can get the react flavored drizzle to use with your application. Use the npm install --save drizzle-react command to get the library. If you are starting from scratch, it is recommended to get the drizzle box using truffle unbox drizzle. It includes a complete example of using drizzle-react in your DApp.

2. Include providers from Drizzle by using the import statement:

```
import { Drizzle, generateStore } from 'drizzle';
```

3. Create an options object with the necessary contract artifacts:

```
const options = {
    contracts,
    events: {
        contractName: [
            eventName
        ]
    },
    polls: {
        accounts: interval,
        blocks: interval
    },
    web3: {
        fallback: {
            type
            url
        }
    }
}
```

The following are the guidelines to fill each option:

- **contracts**: Provides an array of contract artifact files.
- **events**: It is an object that includes contract names with an array of strings of event names that you would like to listen to.
- **polls**: It is an object that contains the values to poll and the interval (in milliseconds) between each poll. For example, you can pool accounts or blocks.
- **web3**: It contains the fallback web3 provider if there is no injected provider such as MetaMask. It includes a type with the ws value as the only possibility and a URL to provide the web3 provider with (ws://127.0.0.1:8545).

4. Use the object created to instantiate Drizzle:

```
import TokenContract from './../build/contracts/TokenContract.json'

const options = {
    contracts: [ TokenContract ]
}

const drizzleStore = generateStore(this.props.options)
const drizzle = new Drizzle(this.props.options, drizzleStore)
```

5. Use the `cacheCall()` function on a contract to execute the desired call and return the corresponding key so that the data can be retrieved from the store. The store updates itself whenever it finds a transaction that modifies our contract:

```
var state = drizzle.store.getState()

// Continue if Drizzle is initialized.
if (state.drizzleStatus.initialized) {

    // Call which is cached and synchronized.
    // We'll receive the store key for recall.
    const key = drizzle.contracts.TokenContract
                    .methods.getOwner.cacheCall()

    // Use the dataKey to display data from the store.
    return state.contracts.TokenContract
                    .methods.getOwner[key].value
}

// Display a loading message if Drizzle isn't initialized.
return 'Loading...'
```

6. Use the `cacheSend()` function on a contract to send a transaction and return a corresponding transaction hash so that the status can be retrieved from the store. It accepts an object as the final argument, which contains the typical transaction data:

```
var state = drizzle.store.getState()

// Continue if Drizzle is initialized.
if (state.drizzleStatus.initialized) {

    // Declare this transaction to be observed.
    // We'll receive the stackId for reference.
    const stackId = drizzle.contracts.TokenContract
                    .methods.transferTokens
```

```
        .cacheSend("0x2", 100, {
            from: '0x1...'
    })

// Use the dataKey to display the transaction status.
if (state.transactionStack[stackId]) {
    const txHash = state.transactionStack[stackId]
    return state.transactions[txHash].status
}
}

// Display a loading message if Drizzle isn't initialized.
return 'Loading...'
```

7. The Drizzle state keeps all the data related to your DApp so that you can always get access to the latest state. Here is the complete list of state objects you can read from the Redux store:

```
{
    accounts,
    accountBalances: {}
    contracts: {
        contractName: {
            initialized,
            synced,
            events,
            callerFunctionName: { }
        }
    },
    transactions: { txHash: { } },
    transactionStack
    drizzleStatus: { }
    web3: { }
}
```

The following list contains a description of each object:

- **accounts**: An array of account addresses available on the network.
- **accountBalances**: An object containing an address as the key and its balance as the value.
- **contracts**: Contains the contract state objects. It includes events, initialization status (initialized), synchronization status (synced), and the list of callerFunctionNames.

- **transactions**: A series of transaction objects.
- **transactionStack**: An array to keep track of malformed transactions.
- **drizzleStatus**: An object to keep track of Drizzle status.
- **initialized**: A boolean value to indicate whether a web3 instance was found or not.
- **web3**: An object containing initializing, initialized, and failed statuses.

There's more...

Drizzle-react also provides a set of reusable components for common UI elements. You can get them using npm:

```
npm install --save drizzle-react-components
```

This includes the following components:

- **Loading container**: This component wraps your entire app and will show a loading screen until Drizzle is initialized. You can configure the loadingComp and errorComp properties to do this.
- **Contract data**: It contains contract, method, methodArgs, hideIndicator, toUtf8, and toAscii.
- **Contract form**: It includes contract, method, and labels.

Using HD wallet in Truffle

Truffle provides an HD wallet-enabled web3 provider. You can use it to sign transactions for addresses derived from a 12-word mnemonic. In this recipe, you will learn how to use the HD wallet in your Truffle application.

Getting ready

You need to have Truffle installed on your machine to try this recipe. Sending a transaction requires connection to an Ethereum network. You can use Ganache, geth, Parity, or even INFURA as the network.

How to do it...

1. Truffle distributes HD wallet through npm. Use the regular install command to get it:

   ```
   npm install truffle-hdwallet-provider
   ```

2. This provider supports non-Truffle projects. Use it wherever a web3 provider is needed. Import the package using the require statement:

   ```
   var HDWalletProvider = require("truffle-hdwallet-provider");
   ```

3. Use the mnemonic phrase and an Ethereum endpoint to create a provider:

   ```
   // 12 word mneminic to create randomness
   var mnemonic = "cat oreo water ...";

   var provider = new HDWalletProvider(mnemonic,
   "http://localhost:8545");
   ```

4. The HD wallet uses the first address that's generated. You have the option to pass in a specific index and it will use that address instead:

   ```
   var addressIndex = 7;
   var provider = new HDWalletProvider(mnemonic,
   "http://localhost:8545", addressIndex);
   ```

5. Use the providers generated by the HD wallet, and the Truffle configuration will accept them:

```
var HDWalletProvider = require("truffle-hdwallet-provider");

var mnemonic = "cat oreo water ...";

module.exports = {
    networks: {
        development: {
            host: "localhost",
            port: 8545,
            network_id: "*"
        },
        ropsten: {
            provider: new HDWalletProvider(mnemonic,
"https://ropsten.infura.io/"),
            network_id: 3
        }
    }
};
```

5
Tokens and ICOs

In this chapter, you will learn the following recipes:

- Creating a basic ERC20 token in Ethereum
- Transferring tokens between accounts
- Delegating other accounts to spend your token
- Creating a token that can be minted
- Creating a token that can be burnt
- Creating an ERC223 token
- Building your own Initial Coin Offering
- Adding features to the ICO contract
- Providing bonus tokens to the investors
- Whitelisting users for the crowdsale
- Accepting other crypto payments for the crowdsale
- Creating a wallet that supports all ERC20 tokens

Introduction

Tokens in Ethereum represent a financial value or exist as a digital asset. These tokens can be either fungible or non-fungible, based on the requirement. They can represent anything ranging from a currency to a virtual cat that can be traded. Using an Ethereum-based token allows you to make use of Ethereum's existing infrastructure rather than building a blockchain from scratch.

A fungible token is one that is not unique and is perfectly interchangeable with other identical tokens. For example, the US dollar can be compared with fungible tokens. It is perfectly exchangeable with any other US dollar. **Non-Fungible Tokens** (**NFTs**) are unique in nature and can be distinguished from one another. For example, a collectible card can be considered as an NFT, and each card has different characteristics that make it stand out.

The Ethereum community has some standards defined for various token types. These standards can be used to create a variety of use case-based tokens such as a custom cryptocurrency or assets. These coins, tokens, or assets are often distributed to the public through a process called **Initial Coin/Initial Token Offering (ICO/ITO)**.

> The terms ICO and ITO are used interchangeably throughout the book. They represent the process of distributing assets/coins/tokens using Ethereum.

In this chapter, you will learn to create tokens based on standards accepted by the Ethereum community. You will also learn to create a crowdsale/ICO, which distributes these tokens efficiently to the general public. Furthermore, there are distinct recipes that explain the way to accept payments and create wallets for your tokens.

> One of the most common bugs in a token contract is integer overflow or underflow. This occurs when the number you are assigning to a data type is outside the memory boundary. To avoid this, we need to perform strict validation after each arithmetic operation. We will be using OpenZeppelin's `SafeMath` library throughout this chapter to perform arithmetic operations. It is a well-tested and widely used library to avoid integer over or underflows.

Creating a basic ERC20 token in Ethereum

One of the most well-known and widely used token standards within the Ethereum community is ERC20. ERC20 makes the assets more easily interchangeable and ensures they can work with the various distributed applications that follows the same standard.

In this recipe, you will learn to create an ERC20 token and learn about various properties of it.

Getting ready

Since you will be creating a smart contract in Ethereum, you need to have a development environment that supports solidity programming and an Ethereum network to deploy and test your code.

The most commonly used IDE for solidity is Remix and it has a built-in Ethereum test environment. You can access it from `https://remix.ethereum.org/`.

How to do it...

1. To create an ERC20-based token in Ethereum, you need to follow a certain standard. The contract should include the following functions:

   - `totalSupply()`
   - `balanceOf(address _owner)`
   - `transfer(address _to, uint256 _value)`
   - `transferFrom(address _from, address _to, uint256 _value)`
   - `approve(address _spender, uint256 _value)`
   - `allowance(address _owner, address _spender)`

   It should also include these events:

   - `transfer(address indexed _from, address indexed _to, uint256 _value)`
   - `approval(address indexed _owner, address indexed _spender, uint256 _value)`

   We will discuss each function and event in detail throughout this chapter.

2. Create a contract with the target compiler version and a name:

```
pragma solidity ^0.4.23;

contract ERC20 {
    ..
}
```

3. Associate openzeppelin's `SafeMath` library to all unsigned integers. It includes functions for all basic arithmetic operations such as addition, subtraction, multiplication, and division. Download the library from `https://github.com/OpenZeppelin/openzeppelin-solidity/tree/master/contracts/math`:

```
pragma solidity ^0.4.23;
import "./math/SafeMath.sol";

contract ERC20 {
    using SafeMath for uint256;
}
```

4. The ERC20 standard needs to store the total number of tokens in existence. We need to create a `state` variable to keep the value. This should be an unsigned integer of type `uint256`:

```
// Total number of tokens in existence
uint256 totalSupply_;
```

5. A `getter` function to read the value should be defined with the name `totalSupply`:

```
pragma solidity ^0.4.23;
import "./math/SafeMath.sol";

contract ERC20 {
    using SafeMath for uint256;

    // The total number of tokens in existence
    uint256 totalSupply_;

    function totalSupply() public view returns (uint256) {
        return totalSupply_;
    }
}
```

6. The token balance of each account/address is maintained using a mapping in solidity. The address is saved as the key and the token amount is saved as the value:

```
mapping(address => uint256) balances;
```

7. A function to get the balance of a specified address should be defined. The function will accept an address as the input and should return a value of type `uint256`:

```
pragma solidity ^0.4.23;
import "./math/SafeMath.sol";

contract ERC20 {
    using SafeMath for uint256;

    mapping(address => uint256) balances;

    /**
    * @dev To get the balance of the specified address.
    * @param _owner The address to query the the balance of.
    * @return An uint256 representing the amount owned by the
    passed address.
```

```
*/
function balanceOf(address _owner) public view
    returns (uint256) {
    return balances[_owner];
}
}
```

8. The constructor function can be used to initialize the values, such as total supply and balance of initial users:

```
pragma solidity ^0.4.23;
import "./math/SafeMath.sol";

contract ERC20 {
    using SafeMath for uint256;

    mapping(address => uint256) balances;
    uint256 totalSupply_;

    constructor(uint _totalSupply) {
        totalSupply_ = _totalSupply;
        // Assigns all tokens to the owner
        balances[msg.sender] = _totalSupply;
    }

    /**
    * @dev An uint256 representing the total number of tokens.
    */
    function totalSupply() public view returns (uint256) {
        return totalSupply_;
    }

    /**
    * @dev Gets the balance of the specified address.
    * @param _owner The address to query the the balance of.
    * @return An uint256 representing the amount owned by
    * the passed address.
    */
    function balanceOf(address _owner) public view
        returns (uint256) {
        return balances[_owner];
    }
}
```

9. Mark read-only functions such as `balanceOf()` and `totalSupply()` with the view modifier so that it will ensure no state is modified and there is no gas cost.

10. This contract is not fully ERC20 compliant since we only implemented balance and total supply properties. We will implement the remaining functions in the next two recipes.

There's more...

The **ERC** in **ERC20** stands for **Ethereum Request for Comment**. This is similar to the **Request For Comments (RFC)** concept used by the Internet Engineering Task Force. In Ethereum, ERC is derived from **Ethereum Improvement Proposal (EIP)**. The EIPs describe standards for the Ethereum platform, including core protocol specifications, client APIs, and contract standards.

The proposals are categorized into three types: standard track, informational, and meta. The standard track proposals describe any change that affects most or all Ethereum implementations, such as a change to the network protocol, a change in block or transaction validity rules, or changes to proposed application standards/conventions. Informational proposals describe an Ethereum design issue, or provide general guidelines or information to the Ethereum community, but do not propose a new feature. Meta proposals describe a process surrounding Ethereum or propose a change to (or an event in) a process.

ERCs comes under the standard track EIP. You can find the complete list of EIPs at `https:/ /eips.ethereum.org/`.

Transferring tokens between accounts

Tokens can be transferred between multiple accounts. This allows you to trade tokens in exchange for services. To achieve this functionality, ERC20 provides a standard function definition. You will learn to implement basic transfer function with this recipe.

Getting ready

You need to have a development environment that supports solidity programming and an Ethereum network to deploy and test your code.

How to do it...

1. ERC20 defines a `transfer` function to transfer tokens between accounts. Create the function to implement the feature:

```
function transfer() { }
```

2. Modify the function to accept two parameters: to address the amount to transfer. It should return a result of type `boolean` to indicate success or failure:

```
function transfer(address _to, uint256 _value)
    public returns (bool) { }
```

3. Use the `msg.sender` property to determine the from address. You don't have to explicitly pass the from address. The function considers the address of the transaction sender as the from account.

4. For each transfer, deduct the amount from the sender account and add it to the target account. Make sure to use the `SafeMath` library to perform arithmetic operations or check the integer over or underflows manually:

```
// Subtract amount from sender account
balances[msg.sender] = balances[msg.sender].sub(_value);

// Add the amount to target account
balances[_to] = balances[_to].add(_value);
```

5. It is important to perform validations such as checking for enough balance in the sender account. Validate it before transferring the amount from one account to another:

```
// Will throw if sender has insufficient balance
require(_value <= balances[msg.sender]);
```

6. A user may accidentally transfer an amount to invalid addresses such as a null address. Since the token transfer process is irreversible, it is recommended to verify the target account before any actual token transfer:

```
require(_to != address(0));
```

7. Emit an event for each token transfer to create logs. This will notify any application that might be listening to the transfer. The token standard requires you to have a `Transfer` event emitted for every token transfer:

```
// Event declaration
event Transfer(address indexed from, address indexed to, uint256
```

```
value);

// Emitting the event
emit Transfer(msg.sender, _to, _value);
```

8. Return a `boolean` value from the function after completing the transfer process:

```
return true;
```

9. The token `transfer` function should look like this after following the previous steps:

```
/**
 * @dev transfer token for a specified address
 * @param _to The address of target account.
 * @param _value The amount to transfer.
 */
function transfer(address _to, uint256 _value) public
    returns (bool) {
    require(_to != address(0));
    require(_value <= balances[msg.sender]);

    balances[msg.sender] = balances[msg.sender].sub(_value);
    balances[_to] = balances[_to].add(_value);
    emit Transfer(msg.sender, _to, _value);

    return true;
}
```

10. The `transfer` function along with the total supply and `balance` functions can be used to create a basic variant of an ERC20 token:

```
pragma solidity ^0.4.23;
import "./math/SafeMath.sol";

contract ERC20 {
    using SafeMath for uint256;

    mapping(address => uint256) balances;
    uint256 totalSupply_;

    function totalSupply() public view returns (uint256) {
        return totalSupply_;
    }

    function transfer(address _to, uint256 _value) public
        returns (bool) {
        require(_to != address(0));
```

```
        require(_value <= balances[msg.sender]);

        balances[msg.sender] = balances[msg.sender].sub(_value);
        balances[_to] = balances[_to].add(_value);
        emit Transfer(msg.sender, _to, _value);

        return true;
    }

    function balanceOf(address _owner) public view
        returns (uint256) {
        return balances[_owner];
    }
}
```

There's more...

ERC2o is a problem that has already been solved and you don't have to create a contract from scratch every time you need a token. There are well-tested and widely used libraries such as openzeppelin that include contracts for the ERC20 standard. Since these are used by many ICOs and products, they can have zero vulnerabilities.

The library is very modularized and you can use the components as per your requirements. It even includes interfaces that you can use with other contracts.

You can get the complete ERC20 implementation from `https://github.com/OpenZeppelin/openzeppelin-solidity/tree/master/contracts/token/ERC20` or install it via npm with the `npm install -E openzeppelin-solidity` command.

Delegating other accounts to spend your token

In addition to the regular transfer function, ERC20 provides an option to allow other accounts to spend on your behalf. This is made possible by allocating an amount they can spend from your account. This recipe focuses on implementing such approval methods from the token standard.

Getting ready

You need to have a development environment that supports solidity programming and an Ethereum network to deploy and test your code.

How to do it...

1. ERC20 includes a few functions that enable a user to transfer on behalf of someone else. You can allocate the tokens using the `approve` function and transfers can be carried out using the `transferFrom` function.

2. Use a nested mapping to track allocations. Use the first key to denote the actual owner of the tokens and use the second key to store the address that has permission to spend those tokens. Use the final value to store the amount allocated. Create a mapping that follows this structure:

```
mapping (address => mapping (address => uint256)) internal allowed;
```

3. Use the `approve` function to set allowance for each address. It accepts a `spender` address and a value to allocate. On successful allocation, the function should return a `boolean` value indicating success:

```
function approve(address _spender, uint256 _value) public
    returns (bool) { }
```

4. Save the allocation directly to the mapping with `msg.value` and the `spender` address as keys:

```
allowed[msg.sender][_spender] = _value;
```

5. Emit an event called `Approval` to log each allocation process:

```
// Event declaration
event Approval();

// Raise the event
emit Approval(msg.sender, _spender, _value);
```

6. To check the approved amount for each account, the ERC20 standard includes a read-only function. Create a function called `allowance` and set it to accept an approver and a `spender` address. It should return a unit that represents the allowed amount:

```
function allowance(address _owner, address _spender) public view
    returns (uint256) {
    return allowed[_owner][_spender];
}
```

7. Create a `transferFrom` function to perform any actual transfer. Its workings are mostly similar to the `transfer` function but it transfers the balance from another account and includes an additional `allowed` mapping.

8. Include an initial validation check to ensure that enough token transfers are approved by the origin account. This is in addition to the null address check and balance check that already exist in the regular transfer function:

```
require(_to != address(0));
require(_value <= balances[_from]);
require(_value <= allowed[_from][msg.sender]);
```

9. For each transfer, reduce the amount transferred from the allowed token transfers. It will ensure that the spender is not spending more token than is initially allowed:

```
allowed[_from][msg.sender] =
allowed[_from][msg.sender].sub(_value);
```

10. Deduct the balance from the source account and then add it to the target account to ensure the token transfer occurs:

```
balances[_from] = balances[_from].sub(_value);
balances[_to] = balances[_to].add(_value);
```

11. Emit the `Transfer` event with the required details and return a `Boolean` value indicating the successful completion of the process. It is similar to the regular transfer function:

```
emit Transfer(_from, _to, _value);
return true;
```

12. The combined contract is given here. It includes `approval` and `transferFrom` functions to allocate and spend tokens:

```solidity
pragma solidity ^0.4.23;

import "./math/SafeMath.sol"

contract ERC20 {

    mapping (address => mapping (address => uint256))
        internal allowed;

    /**
     * @dev Transfer tokens from one address to another
     * @param _from address Address which you want to send
     * tokens from
     * @param _to address Address which you want to transfer to
     * @param _value uint256 Amount of tokens to be transferred
     */
    function transferFrom(address _from, address _to,
        uint256 _value)
        public returns (bool) {
        require(_to != address(0));
        require(_value <= balances[_from]);
        require(_value <= allowed[_from][msg.sender]);

        balances[_from] = balances[_from].sub(_value);
        balances[_to] = balances[_to].add(_value);
        allowed[_from][msg.sender] =
            allowed[_from][msg.sender].sub(_value);
        emit Transfer(_from, _to, _value);
        return true;
    }

    /**
     * @dev Approve the passed address to spend the passed
     * tokens on behalf of msg.sender.
     * @param _spender The address which will spend the funds.
     * @param _value The amount of tokens to be spent.
     */
    function approve(address _spender, uint256 _value) public
        returns (bool) {
        allowed[msg.sender][_spender] = _value;
        emit Approval(msg.sender, _spender, _value);
        return true;
    }

    /**
```

```
 * @dev Function to check the amount of tokens that an
 * owner allowed to a spender.
 * @param _owner address The address which owns the funds.
 * @param _spender address The address which will spend
 * the funds.
 * @return A uint256 specifying the amount of tokens still
 * available for the spender.
 */
function allowance(address _owner, address _spender)
    public view returns (uint256) {
    return allowed[_owner][_spender];
}
}
```

There's more...

The `approve` method in ERC20 is susceptible to the **Transaction Ordering Dependence (TOD)** attack. A malicious spender can wait for the approver to change the allowance from *x* to *y* and include a transaction to spend *x* tokens. If the spender's transaction will be executed before the approver's transaction, then the spender will successfully transfer *x* tokens and will gain the ability to transfer another *y* tokens.

One possible solution to resolve this condition is to first reduce the spender's allowance to *0* and set the desired value afterwards. The recent standards also include increase and decrease approval methods to safely change the approval limit. These functions avoid the need to call the approve function twice and wait until the first transaction is confirmed for safe allowance.

The `increaseApproval` method increases the number of tokens allocated to a spender:

```
/**
 * @dev Increase the amount of tokens allowed.
 * @param _spender Address which will spend the funds.
 * @param _addedValue Amount of tokens to increase.
 */
function increaseApproval(address _spender, uint _addedValue)
    public returns (bool) {
    allowed[msg.sender][_spender] =
        (allowed[msg.sender][_spender].add(_addedValue));
    emit Approval(msg.sender, _spender, allowed[msg.sender][_spender]);
    return true;
}
```

The `decreaseApproval` method works in the same way to reduce the number of tokens allocated to a spender:

```
/**
 * @dev Decrease the amount of tokens allowed.
 * @param _spender Address which will spend the funds.
 * @param _subtractedValue Amount of tokens to decrease.
 */
function decreaseApproval(address _spender, uint _subtractedValue)
    public returns (bool) {
    uint oldValue = allowed[msg.sender][_spender];

    if (_subtractedValue > oldValue) {
        allowed[msg.sender][_spender] = 0;
    } else {
        allowed[msg.sender][_spender] = oldValue.sub(_subtractedValue);
    }

    emit Approval(msg.sender, _spender, allowed[msg.sender][_spender]);
    return true;
}
```

Creating a token that can be minted

We can always add a few more functionalities to our token contract. One of the widely used custom properties is to mint tokens as per the requirement. This will create new tokens dynamically as per the requirement, and is very useful when the total supply is not known at the beginning.

In this recipe, you will learn to create a token that can be minted as per the requirement.

Getting ready

You need to have a development environment that supports solidity programming and an Ethereum network to deploy and test your code.

This contract extends the ERC20 contract explained in the first three recipes of this chapter. If you don't know what ERC20 is, then it is recommended to try the previous recipes before stepping through this one.

How to do it...

1. Create a new token contract that extends the default ERC20 contract created from the first three recipes. You can also include the following functions as part of the ERC20 contract itself, but it is recommended to modularize the code for better reusability:

```
pragma solidity ^0.4.23;

import "./ERC20.sol";

contract Mintable is ERC20 {
    ...
}
```

2. Create a `mint` function that will accept the target address and token amount as inputs. It should return a `boolean` value just like the `transfer` function:

```
function mint(address _to, uint amount) public
        returns (bool) { }
```

3. Use this function to create new tokens and allocate them to a target user account. It is also important to add the newly created token count to the total supply function:

```
totalSupply_ = totalSupply_.add(_amount);
balances[_to] = balances[_to].add(_amount);
```

4. Emit an event for each `mint` transaction. It can help to keep track of newly created tokens. Also, emit the `transfer` event to indicate a new token transfer:

```
// Event declaration
event Mint(address indexed to, uint256 amount);

// Events emitted
emit Mint(_to, _amount);
emit Transfer(address(0), _to, _amount);
```

5. Unlimited minting is not a good idea and it should be restricted. Use a status flag to impose this restriction. Allow the owner to change the status to finished, once all the required tokens are minted:

```
//Status flag
bool public mintingFinished = false;

// Status change event
```

```
event MintFinished();

// Function to change the status
function finishMinting() onlyOwner public returns (bool) {
    mintingFinished = true;
    emit MintFinished();
    return true;
}
```

6. Create a `modifier` using the status flag so that restrictions can be imposed on other functions:

```
modifier canMint() {
    require(!mintingFinished);
    _;
}
```

7. The final contract will look like this:

```
pragma solidity ^0.4.23;

import "./ERC20.sol";

contract Mintable is ERC20 {
    event Mint(address indexed to, uint256 amount);
    event MintFinished();

    bool public mintingFinished = false;
    address owner;

    modifier canMint() {
        require(!mintingFinished);
        _;
    }

    modifier onlyOwner() {
        require(msg.sender == owner);
        _;
    }

    constructor() {
        owner = msg.sender;
    }

    /**
     * @dev Function to mint tokens
     * @param _to Address that will receive the minted tokens.
     * @param _amount Amount of tokens to mint.
```

```
         * @return Boolean that indicates if the operation was
     successful.
         */
        function mint(address _to, uint256 _amount) onlyOwner canMint
            public returns (bool) {
            totalSupply_ = totalSupply_.add(_amount);
            balances[_to] = balances[_to].add(_amount);
            emit Mint(_to, _amount);
            emit Transfer(address(0), _to, _amount);
            return true;
        }

        /**
         * @dev Function to stop minting new tokens.
         * @return True if the operation was successful.
         */
        function finishMinting() onlyOwner canMint public
            returns (bool) {
            mintingFinished = true;
            emit MintFinished();
            return true;
        }
    }
}
```

Creating a token that can be burnt

If new tokens can be created as per requirement, then we can also have a functionality that will delete the tokens from the network. In simple terms, burnt tokens cannot be spent anymore. In reality, decreasing the total supply can increase the value of each token in addition to other benefits.

In this recipe, you will learn a method to delete tokens permanently from the contract.

Getting ready

You need to have a development environment that supports solidity programming and an Ethereum network to deploy and test your code.

This contract extends the ERC20 contract explained in the first three recipes of this chapter. If you don't know what ERC20 is, then it is recommended to try the previous recipes before stepping through this one.

How to do it...

1. Extend the ERC20 contract to create a new burnable token contract:

```
pragma solidity ^0.4.23;

import "./ERC20.sol";

contract Burnable is ERC20 {
    ...
}
```

2. Create a function that can be called by the user to burn some tokens:

```
function burn(uint256 _value) public { }
```

3. Verify whether the sender has enough balance to burn:

```
require(_value <= balances[msg.sender]);
```

4. While burning tokens, subtract the number of tokens burnt from the balance of the current holder and from total supply:

```
balances[_who] = balances[_who].sub(_value);
totalSupply_ = totalSupply_.sub(_value);
```

5. Emit an event for every token burning transaction. Create a burn event with the sender address and value as parameters:

```
// Event declaration
event Burn(address indexed burner, uint256 value);

// Emit the event during burning process
emit Burn(msg.sender, _value);
```

6. It is also recommended to emit the transfer function that marks a transfer to the null address. Transferring a token to the null address makes it unusable:

```
emit Transfer(msg.sender, address(0), _value);
```

7. Modify the contract further by creating an internal function that allows other contracts to burn tokens for users. This can improve the reusability of the function:

```
pragma solidity ^0.4.23;

import "./ERC20.sol";
```

```
contract BurnableToken is BasicToken {

    event Burn(address indexed burner, uint256 value);

    /**
     * @dev Burns a specific amount of tokens.
     * @param _value The amount of token to be burned.
     */
    function burn(uint256 _value) public {
        _burn(msg.sender, _value);
    }

    /**
     * @dev Internal function for burning tokens.
     * @param _user Address to burn the tokens from.
     * @param _value Amount of token to be burned.
     */
    function _burn(address _user, uint256 _value) internal {
        require(_value <= balances[_user]);

        balances[_user] = balances[_user].sub(_value);
        totalSupply_ = totalSupply_.sub(_value);

        emit Burn(_user, _value);
        emit Transfer(_user, address(0), _value);
    }
}
```

There's more...

In addition to the minting and burning functionality, you can think of any useful feature to include in the token contract. The following contracts are some of the examples you can include in your token:

1. You can add a functionality to pause the token transfer for a certain period. Use a state variable for the status and modifier to include the restriction in the transfer function.
2. The total mintable value can be restricted with a cap. This will check for the token cap for each minting and will reject it if it exceeds the limit.
3. Tokens can be transferred with a time lock on them. This will restrict the receiver to using those tokens only after a set time period.

Creating an ERC223 token

ERC20 is a widely used token standard but it comes with some issues. Transferring ERC20 standard tokens to a non-supported address such as a contract address can make them unusable. ERC223 tries to solve this problem by recommending some modifications to the existing standard.

In this recipe, you will understand the difference between these two standards and will learn to implement an ERC223-based contract.

Getting ready

You need to have a development environment that supports solidity programming and an Ethereum network to deploy and test your code.

How to do it...

1. The standard handles the token transfers to a contract address. Follow this standard to create a function that will reject the transaction if the receiving contract does not support such functionality.

2. The standard modifies the transfer function to include an additional data field. It also keeps the regular transfer function for backward compatibility. Use the following interface to implement a minimal ERC223 standard token:

    ```solidity
    pragma solidity ^0.4.23;

    contract ERC223Interface {
        uint public totalSupply;
        function balanceOf(address who) view returns (uint);
        function transfer(address to, uint value) public;
        function transfer(address to, uint value, bytes data) public;
        event Transfer(address indexed from, address indexed to,
            uint value, bytes data);
    }
    ```

3. Follow the ERC223 standard for all receiving contracts. It includes a function called tokenFallback to validate the compatibility with the standard:

    ```solidity
    pragma solidity ^0.4.23;

    contract ERC223Receiver {
        function tokenFallback(address _from, uint _value, bytes
    ```

```
    _data);
    }
```

4. During the token transfer, check whether the target address is a contract or an externally owned account. This is done by retrieving the size of the code stored in the target address:

```
uint codeLength;
assembly {
    codeLength := extcodesize(_to)
}
```

5. If the external code size is greater than zero, the address belongs to a contract:

```
if (codeLength > 0) {
    // Contract
} else {
    // Externally owned account
}
```

6. If the target address is a contract, then validate the support with the help of the receiver interface:

```
if (codeLength > 0) {
    // Require proper transaction handling.
    ERC223Receiver receiver = ERC223Receiver(_to);
    receiver.tokenFallback(msg.sender, _value, _data);
}
```

7. The transfer function for ERC223 will look like the following example:

```
function transfer(address to, uint value, bytes data) {
    uint codeLength;
    assembly {
        codeLength := extcodesize(_to)
    }

    balances[msg.sender] = balances[msg.sender].sub(_value);
    balances[_to] = balances[_to].add(_value);

    if (codeLength > 0) {
        ERC223Receiver receiver = ERC223Receiver(_to);
        receiver.tokenFallback(msg.sender, _value, _data);
    }
}
```

8. Also, include the regular transfer function in the contract for backward compatibility:

```
function transfer(address _to, uint256 _value) public
    returns (bool) {
    balances[msg.sender] = balances[msg.sender].sub(_value);
    balances[_to] = balances[_to].add(_value);
    emit Transfer(msg.sender, _to, _value);
    return true;
}
```

 ERC223 can definitely help resolve the loss associated with accidental Ether transfers to an account. But it is still not as popular and well tested as the ERC20 standard. This can bring up unknown vulnerabilities in the future. It is up to you to choose a suitable standard for your requirement.

Building your own Initial Coin Offering

An **Initial Coin Offering** (**ICO**) is a method of crowdfunding through cryptocurrencies and blockchain. In general, the ICO provides tokens for investors in exchange for legal tender or other cryptocurrencies such as Bitcoin or Ethereum. ICOs provide a means by which startups can get funding for their projects. This can also help avoid the costs of intermediaries, such as venture capitalists, banks, and stock exchanges.

This recipe focuses on creating an ICO contract in Ethereum.

Getting ready

You need to have a development environment that supports solidity programming and an Ethereum network to deploy and test your code.

If your ICO distributes tokens to the investors in exchange for their investment, then you should have a token contract implemented with a widely accepted standard such as ERC20. Refer to the first three recipes of this chapter to create an ERC20 token.

How to do it...

1. Create a crowdsale contract that can be used for the Initial Coin/Token Offering process. Import `SafeMath` for arithmetic operations:

```
pragma solidity ^0.4.23;

import "./math/SafeMath.sol";

contract CrowdSale {
    // ..
}
```

2. If you are distributing tokens to investors, then import the token contract and create a state variable to keep the address of the distributable token contract:

```
pragma solidity ^0.4.23;

import "./math/SafeMath.sol";
import "./ERC20.sol";

contract CrowdSale {
    // The token sold through the ICO
    ERC20 public token;
}
```

3. Tokens sold for each purchase are calculated at a rate; create a state variable to store it in the contract. The rate parameter stores the number of tokens the buyer gets for a `Wei`:

```
uint256 public rate;
```

4. The funds collected should be transferred to the project or company address. Create a variable to save the wallet address:

```
address public wallet;
```

5. To keep track of funds raised, create a state variable:

```
uint256 public weiRaised;
```

6. Rate, wallet, and token values should be initialized first. Use `constructor` to enforce initialization during contract creation. Make sure to add enough validations for each input value:

```
constructor(uint256 _rate, address _wallet, ERC20 _token) public {
    require(_rate > 0);
    require(_wallet != address(0));
    require(_token != address(0));

    rate = _rate;
    wallet = _wallet;
    token = _token;
}
```

7. Create a function to calculate the tokens for each input amount. Creating a function for this operation can allow other contracts to make use of the functionality:

```
function calculateToken(uint256 _weiAmount) public view
    returns (uint256) {
    return _weiAmount.mul(rate);
}
```

8. Create a payable function to allow the investor to purchase tokens:

```
function buyTokens(address _investor) public payable {
    // ..
}
```

9. Include enough validations for ensuring proper inputs to the function. The inputted amount and investor address can be validated using `require()`:

```
require(_investor != address(0));
require(msg.value != 0);
```

10. On successful validation, add the amount to the total `Wei` raised:

```
weiRaised = weiRaised.add(msg.value);
```

11. Calculate the number of tokens that can be purchased and transfer them to the user through the token's `transfer` function:

```
// Calculate the token amount
uint256 tokens = calculateTokens(msg.value);

// Transfer them to the investor address
token.transfer(_investor, tokens);
```

12. Create an `event` to log the token selling process:

```
// Event declaration
event TokenPurchase(
    address indexed purchaser,
    address indexed beneficiary,
    uint256 value,
    uint256 amount
);

// Event emit
emit TokenPurchase(msg.sender, _investor, msg.value, tokens);
```

13. Once the token purchase is completed, transfer the collected Ether to the wallet for safe keeping:

```
wallet.transfer(msg.value);
```

14. To improve usability for the token purchase process, add a payable `call back` function to accept Ether without needing to call a specific function:

```
function () external payable {
    buyTokens(msg.sender);
}
```

15. Including all these properties will result in the following `crowdsale` contract:

```
pragma solidity ^0.4.23;
import "./SafeMath.sol";
import "./ERC20.sol";

contract CrowdSale {
    using SafeMath for uint256;

    // The token being sold
    ERC20 public token;

    // Address where funds are collected
    address public wallet;

    // How many token units a buyer gets per wei
    uint256 public rate;

    // Amount of wei raised
    uint256 public weiRaised;

    /**
    * Event for token purchase logging
```

```
*/
event TokenPurchase(
    address indexed purchaser,
    address indexed beneficiary,
    uint256 value,
    uint256 amount
);

/**
* @param _rate Number of token units a buyer gets per wei
* @param _wallet Address where collected funds will be
* forwarded to
* @param _token Address of the token being sold
*/
constructor(uint256 _rate, address _wallet, ERC20 _token)
    public {
    require(_rate > 0);
    require(_wallet != address(0));
    require(_token != address(0));

    rate = _rate;
    wallet = _wallet;
    token = _token;
}

function () external payable {
    buyTokens(msg.sender);
}

function buyTokens(address _investor) public payable {
    uint256 weiAmount = msg.value;

    require(_investor != address(0));
    require(weiAmount != 0);

    weiRaised = weiRaised.add(weiAmount);

    uint256 tokens = calculateToken(weiAmount);
    token.transfer(_investor, tokens);
    emit TokenPurchase(
        msg.sender, _investor,
        weiAmount, tokens
    );

    wallet.transfer(msg.value);
}

function calculateToken(uint256 _weiAmount)
```

```
        internal view returns (uint256) {
            return _weiAmount.mul(rate);
    }
}
```

Adding features to the ICO contract

So far, we have talked about creating a basic ICO contract. The crowdsale contract can also have additional features such as a sale duration or limiting the number of tokens sold. This helps in further automating the crowdsale process for efficient distribution.

In this recipe, you will learn to limit the tokens sold and the time in which a sale can happen. We will extend the `crowdsale` contract created in the previous recipe to add these features.

Getting ready

You need to have a development environment that supports solidity programming and an Ethereum network to deploy and test your code.

Since the contract extends the `crowdSale` contract created in the previous recipe, it is recommended to finish it before stepping through this recipe.

How to do it...

1. Contracts can have a cap to restrict the amount that can be raised through the crowdsale. Create a variable to store the `cap` restriction:

   ```
   uint256 public cap;
   ```

2. The value is assigned through the `constructor`. Add the initialization to the constructor along with the rate, wallet, and token:

   ```
   constructor(uint256 _cap, ....)
       public {
       // Other validations and assignment

       require(_cap > 0);
       cap = _cap;
   }
   ```

3. During the token purchase operation, add an additional condition to verify the `cap`:

```
function buyTokens(address _investor) public payable {
    require(weiRaised.add(_weiAmount) <= cap);
    //..
}
```

4. Create a read-only function that can be used to check whether the `cap` has been reached. It returns `true` or `false`:

```
function capReached() public view
    returns (bool) {
    return weiRaised >= cap;
}
```

5. A similar procedure can be followed to restrict the sale with a time duration. Create state variables to hold the start and end times. Time in solidity is generally calculated with a UNIX timestamp:

```
uint256 public openingTime;
uint256 public closingTime;
```

6. Initialize the time duration using the `constructor`:

```
constructor(uint256 _openingTime, uint256 _closingTime) public {
    require(_openingTime >= block.timestamp);
    require(_closingTime >= _openingTime);

    openingTime = _openingTime;
    closingTime = _closingTime;
}
```

7. Create a `modifier` to verify the time duration. The functions that use this modifier cannot be executed after a certain period of time:

```
modifier onlyWhileOpen {
    require(block.timestamp >= openingTime
        && block.timestamp <= closingTime);
    _;
}
```

8. Use this `modifier` in the buy tokens function to prevent someone from buying the tokens once the sale period has ended or when it has not yet started:

```
function buyTokens(address _investor) public payable
    onlyWhileOpen {
```

```
    //...
}
```

9. Include a read-only function for anyone who wants to verify the status of the
    sale:

```
function hasClosed() public view returns (bool) {
    return block.timestamp > closingTime;
}
```

10. The contract will look something like this code example:

```
contract additionalFeatues {
    uint256 public openingTime;
    uint256 public closingTime;
    uint256 public cap;

    /**
     * @dev Reverts if not in crowdsale time range.
     */
    modifier onlyWhileOpen {
        require(block.timestamp >= openingTime
            && block.timestamp <= closingTime);
        _;
    }

    /**
     * @dev Constructor, takes crowdsale opening and closing times.
     * @param _openingTime Crowdsale opening time
     * @param _closingTime Crowdsale closing time
     */
    constructor(uint256 _openingTime, uint256 _closingTime,
        uint256 _cap) public {
        require(_openingTime >= block.timestamp);
        require(_closingTime >= _openingTime);
        require(_cap > 0);

        cap = _cap;
        openingTime = _openingTime;
        closingTime = _closingTime;
    }

    /**
     * @dev Checks whether the period in which the crowdsale is
     8 open has already elapsed.
     * @return Whether crowdsale period has elapsed
     */
```

```
function hasClosed() public view returns (bool) {
    return block.timestamp > closingTime;
}

/**
 * @dev Checks whether the cap has been reached.
 * @return Whether the cap was reached
 */
function capReached() public view returns (bool) {
    return weiRaised >= cap;
}

function buyTokens(address _investor, address spender)
    onlyWhileOpen {
    // ...
}
}
```

There's more...

Cap restrictions can be added to each individual also, and this allows the owner to have more control. To do this, create a mapping that stores the address as the key and cap as the value. Creating a mapping for contributions is also required:

```
mapping(address => uint256) public contributions;
mapping(address => uint256) public caps;
```

Verify the individual cap for every token purchase to restrict users:

```
require(contributions[_beneficiary].add(_weiAmount) <= caps[_beneficiary]);
```

Create read-only methods for reading both the contributions and caps of an individual user:

```
function getUserCap(address _beneficiary) public
    view returns (uint256) {
    return caps[_beneficiary];
}

function getUserContribution(address _beneficiary) public
    view returns (uint256) {
    return contributions[_beneficiary];
}
```

Create `setter` functions for creating user restrictions. You can also create a `batch` function, which accepts multiple addresses and caps for easier assignment:

```
function setUserCap(address _beneficiary, uint256 _cap)
    external onlyOwner {
    caps[_beneficiary] = _cap;
}

function setGroupCap( address[] _beneficiaries, uint256 _cap )
    external onlyOwner {
    for (uint256 i = 0; i < _beneficiaries.length; i++) {
        caps[_beneficiaries[i]] = _cap;
    }
}
```

Providing bonus tokens to investors

To increase the interest of investors in your ICO, you can provide an attractive bonus to investors based on certain conditions. For example, you can give early investors 10 percent more tokens than someone who invests at a later stage, as a bonus.

In this recipe, you will learn to include this bonus feature in your crowdsale contract.

Getting ready

You need to have a development environment that supports solidity programming and an Ethereum network to deploy and test your code.

Since the contract extends the `crowdSale` contract created in the *Building your own Initial Coin Offering* recipe, it is recommended to finish that before stepping through this recipe.

The contracts are for illustration purposes only, are not well optimized, and may contain bugs. DO NOT USE THEM in your end product.

How to do it...

1. You can set your own time duration for providing the bonus. In this recipe, we will provide a 20% bonus to those investors who buy within the first 24 hours of the sale starting.

2. Create constant state variables to store the bonus percentage and time duration:

```
uint public bonusPercent = 20;
uint public bonusDuration = 1 days;
```

3. Create a different function to calculate the bonus. It should return the number of bonus tokens, if any, and zero if not applicable:

```
function calculateBonus(uint _toknes) public view
    returns (uint bonusTokens) {
    // calculate bonus
}
```

4. Add a condition to check whether the buyer buys a token on the first day:

```
function calculateBonus(uint _toknes) public view
    returns (uint bonusTokens) {
    if(block.timestamp <= openingTime + bonusDuration) {
        // Token purchased during bonus duration
    } else {
        // Bonus duration finished
    }
}
```

5. Calculate the number of bonus tokens based on the time. Return `zero` if the tokens are bought after the bonus duration:

```
function calculateBonus(uint _toknes) public view
    returns (uint bonusTokens) {
    if(block.timestamp <= openingTime + bonusDuration) {
        bonusTokens = _tokens.mul(bonusPercent).div(100);
    } else {
        bonusTokens = 0;
    }
}
```

6. The final contract with the bonus feature will look like this. The function to calculate the bonus should be invoked for every token purchase:

```
contract BonusContract {
    using SafeMath for uint;
```

```
// Percentage of bonus tokens to allocate
uint public bonusPercent = 20;
// Bonus duration
uint public bonusDuration = 1 days;

/**
 * @dev Calculate the bonus tokens for each purchase
 * @param _tokens Number of tokens purchased
 * @return Amount of bonus tokens
 */
function calculateBonus(uint _toknes) public view
    returns (uint bonusTokens) {
    if(block.timestamp <= openingTime + bonusDuration) {
        // Token purchased during bonus duration
        bonusTokens = _toknes.mul(bonusPercent).div(100);
    } else {
        // Bonus duration finished
        bonusTokens = 0;
    }
}
}
}
```

There's more...

1. You can have multiple bonus levels in your contract to provide a bonus based on different time durations, for example, 30% for the first day, 15% for the second day, and 5% for the third day.

2. A `struct` can be used to save the bonus duration for each day:

```
// Custom data type to store bonus parameter
struct Bonus {
    uint startTime;
    uint endTime;
    uint bonusPercent
}

// Array of fixed length to store 3 bonus levels
Bonus[3] bonus;
```

3. The values can be initialized through the `constructor`. Based on the bonus logic, you can either use an iteration or assign values individually. For simplicity, we are assigning each bonus duration individually:

```
constructor() {
    bonus[0].startTime = openingTime;
```

```
        bonus[0].endTime = openingTime + 1 days;
        bonus[0].bonusPercent = 30;

        bonus[1].startTime = openingTime + 1 days;
        bonus[1].endTime = openingTime + 2 days;
        bonus[1].bonusPercent = 15;

        ...
    }
```

4. The calculate bonus function can be modified to work with the multiple bonus structures. The modified contract will look like this:

```
contract BonusContract {
    using SafeMath for uint;

    // Custom data type to store bonus parameter
    struct Bonus {
        uint startTime;
        uint endTime;
        uint bonusPercent;
    }

    // Array of fixed length to store 3 bonus levels
    Bonus[3] bonus;

    constructor() public {
        bonus[0].startTime = openingTime;
        bonus[0].endTime = openingTime + 1 days;
        bonus[0].bonusPercent = 30;

        bonus[1].startTime = openingTime + 1 days;
        bonus[1].endTime = openingTime + 2 days;
        bonus[1].bonusPercent = 15;

        bonus[2].startTime = openingTime + 2 days;
        bonus[2].endTime = openingTime + 3 days;
        bonus[2].bonusPercent = 5;
    }

    /**
    * @dev Calculate bonus tokens
    * @param _toknes Tokens purchased
    * @return Number of bonus tokens
    */
    function calculateBonus(uint _toknes) public view
        returns (uint bonusTokens) {
```

```
// Default bonus amount
bonusTokens = 0;

if(block.timestamp >= bonus[0].startTime
    && block.timestamp < bonus[0].endTime) {

    bonusTokens =
        _toknes.mul(bonus[0].bonusPercent).div(100);

} else if(block.timestamp >= bonus[1].startTime
    && block.timestamp < bonus[1].endTime) {

    bonusTokens =
        _toknes.mul(bonus[1].bonusPercent).div(100);

} else if(block.timestamp >= bonus[2].startTime
    && block.timestamp < bonus[2].endTime) {

    bonusTokens =
        _toknes.mul(bonus[2].bonusPercent).div(100);
    }
  }
}
```

Whitelisting users for the crowdsale

Sometimes, you may want your sale to be private or you need to provide an increased bonus to a set of users. For these situations, a whitelisting contract is created to keep track of a certain set of users. This allows you to restrict operations between them to provide a more personalized approach.

In this recipe, you will learn to create a whitelisting function that can be used along with the `crowdsale` contract.

Getting ready

You need to have a development environment that supports solidity programming and an Ethereum network to deploy and test your code.

Since the contract extends the `crowdSale` contract created in the *Building your own Initial Coin Offering* recipe, it is recommended to finish that before stepping through this recipe.

The contracts are for illustration purposes only, are not well optimized, and may contain bugs. DO NOT USE THEM in your end product.

How to do it...

1. Create a `mapping` variable to store the address as a key and whitelisting status as the value. Marking the mapping as a `public` variable will create a `getter` function that can be used to verify the `whitelist` status:

```
mapping(address => bool) public whitelist;
```

2. Create a function to add users to the whitelisting contract. This function should be restricted to the owner or admin:

```
function addToWhitelist(address _investor) external
    onlyOwner {
    whitelist[_investor] = true;
}
```

3. For easy whitelisting, you can have another function that accepts an array of addresses:

```
function addMultipleToWhitelist(address[] _investors)
    external onlyOwner {
        for (uint256 i = 0; i < _investors.length; i++) {
            whitelist[_investors[i]] = true;
        }
}
```

4. Create a function to remove a user from the whitelist. It can come in handy if an address is added by mistake, or the user is no longer invited to the function:

```
function removeFromWhitelist(address _beneficiary) external
    onlyOwner {
    whitelist[_beneficiary] = false;
}
```

5. Create a `modifier` to prevent non-whitelisted users from accessing the functions:

```
modifier isWhitelisted(address _investor) {
    require(whitelist[_investor]);
    _;
}
```

6. Apply the modifier to the token buying function. It will allow only whitelisted users to buy tokens through this `crowdsale`. The final contract should look like the following example:

```
contract WhitelistContract {

    mapping(address => bool) public whitelist;

    /**
    * @dev Check if investor is whitelisted.
    */
    modifier isWhitelisted(address _investor) {
        require(whitelist[_investor]);
        _;
    }

    /**
    * @dev Adds an address to whitelist.
    * @param _investor Address to whitelist
    */
    function addToWhitelist(address _investor) external
        onlyOwner {
        whitelist[_investor] = true;
    }

    /**
    * @dev Adds list of addresses to whitelist.
    * @param _investors Addresses to be added to the whitelist
    */
    function addManyToWhitelist(address[] _investors) external
        onlyOwner {
        for (uint256 i = 0; i < _investors.length; i++) {
            whitelist[_investors[i]] = true;
        }
    }

    /**
    * @dev Removes single address from whitelist.
    * @param _investor Address to be removed to the whitelist
    */
    function removeFromWhitelist(address _investor) external
        onlyOwner {
        whitelist[_investor] = false;
    }

    // Add isWhitelisted modifier to token buying function
    function buyTokens(address _investor, uint256 _weiAmount)
        public isWhitelisted(_investor) {
```

```
                        // ..
            }

        }
```

There's more...

There are a lot of implementations for `crowdsale` contracts and you can always choose the features based on your requirements. It is strongly recommended to test and audit your smart contract before publishing it to the main network. Any bug found is irreversible and you may lose all your raised funds. You can include fail-safe methods such as pausing the smart contract to reduce the impact, but it is better to strictly check for bugs before going with the final implementation.

OpenZeppelin provides well-tested implementations of the `crowdsale` contract with most commonly used functionalities. It is written in an extendable manner so that you can add your own features to it. The open source library includes contracts for basic crowdsale, capped crowdsale, timed crowdsale, whitelisting process, refundable contract, and so on.

You can download the `openzeppelin` library from here: `https://github.com/ OpenZeppelin/openzeppelin-solidity`.

Accepting crypto payments for the crowdsale

Tokens from an ICO are generally purchased by sending Ether to the contract. The examples given in the current chapter use a `fallback` function to accept direct Ether payments. This allows anyone to send Ether to the contract address through a transaction to purchase tokens.

If the user does not have Ether, they can either purchase it from an exchange or convert other cryptocurrencies to Ether using services such as Shapeshift. Also, you can make use of BTCRelay to accept Bitcoin transactions from Ethereum.

In this recipe, you will learn various options for accepting cryptocurrency payments in your ICO.

Getting ready

You need to have a crowdsale contract set up in Ethereum before stepping through this recipe. Refer to other recipes in this chapter to understand more about creating a token and crowdsale.

How to do it...

MetaMask is the easiest way to buy tokens if you, the user, are trying to purchase tokens directly by using Ether. You can get Ether from a cryptocurrency exchange or by using Shapeshift. You can also use BTCRelay to accept Bitcoin directly. Let's look into each option individually.

MetaMask

1. Download MetaMask from `https://metamask.io`. It currently supports the Chrome, Firefox, Opera, and Brave browsers.
2. Create an account in MetaMask or import an existing account using the private key or seed phrase. If you are new to MetaMask, refer to the related recipe from the first chapter.
3. If you do not have enough Ether in your MetaMask account, buy some from a cryptocurrency exchange. For testing purposes, it is recommended to use a private or test Ethereum network.

 Do not send Ether directly from an exchange to an ICO. Most exchanges do not support buying tokens through a crowdsale and you won't be able to recover the tokens. It is recommended to use your own wallet.

4. Use the **SEND** button to transfer Ether to the `crowdsale` contract. Enter the `crowdsale` address in the recipient column and Ether to invest in the amount column. Click **NEXT** to sign the transaction.

5. The users will be asked to enter values for the gas limit and gas price, along with options to accept and reject the transaction. Make sure to provide a high enough enough gas limit so that the transaction does not run out of gas during execution. Click **SUBMIT** to send the transaction:

6. Once the transaction is mined and execution was successful, the sender's account will be credited with the ICO tokens. Some ICOs may not distribute tokens immediately, and you won't be able to transfer them immediately

7. MetaMask also provides an option to watch tokens from its interface. Select the **TOKENS** tab and add tokens to view their status:

Shapeshift

Shapeshift allows anyone to trade cryptocurrencies easily. It is one of the best ways to swap cryptocurrencies in a safe and easy manner. The service requires no emails or passwords and it does not ask you to bid. Shapeshift does not ask you to send your money to be held in a centralized exchange.

Let's look into the steps in detail:

1. Navigate to the Shapeshift portal from `https://shapeshift.io`.
2. Choose the assets to trade from the home page. It supports all the major altcoins and blockchain tokens. You can also select from either *quick* or *precise* trading.
3. Quick trading will match approximate orders to complete your request faster, but you may not get the best value for trading. The precise option will provide you with the best trade value, but it will take some time to find a match.
4. Let's assume you have **Bitcoin** and you want **Ether**. Select **Bitcoin** as the input and Ether as the output:

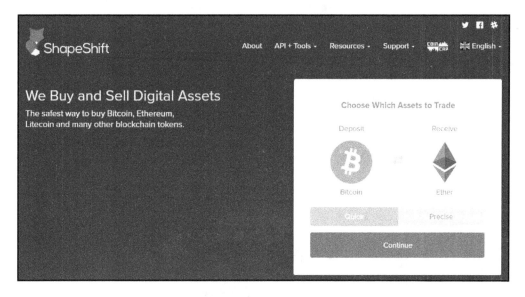

5. Provide the target Ethereum address from your wallet in the destination address field. You will also be asked to input a refund address if something goes wrong. Provide your bitcoin address in the refund address field. Click on **I agree to Terms**, and then click the **Start Transaction** button:

6. On the third screen, ShapeShift will generate an address for you to deposit Bitcoins from your wallet. Before sending your bitcoin to this generated address, make sure that the amount is no more than *Deposit Max* or less than *Deposit Min*:

7. Your account will be credit with Ether as soon as it gets confirmed. If your order fails, Shapeshift will auto-return your funds to the refund address and deduct the minor fee from your returned transaction.

 Shapeshift also provides various tools and APIs offering crypto swap services. You can make use of them in your application to improve the customer experience.

BTC Relay

To read bitcoin transactions from Ethereum, you can use the service provided by BTC Relay. It is a smart contract in Ethereum that stores Bitcoin block headers. BTC Relay uses this block header data to build a miniature version of the Bitcoin blockchain in Ethereum. You can use this information to verify a Bitcoin transaction from your Ethereum contract. Follow these steps to understand more about the service:

1. BTC relay is available as a service in the Ethereum main network and you can achieve the following functionalities with it:

   - Storing Bitcoin block header data
   - Relaying Bitcoin transactions to an Ethereum contract
   - Verifying a Bitcoin transaction

2. To verify a Bitcoin transaction, you can use the `verifyTx` function included in the BTC Relay contract:

   ```
   verifyTx(raw_transaction, transaction_index, merkle_sibling,
   block_hash);
   ```

   You need to pass the following parameters to verify a transaction:

   - `raw_transaction`: The transaction bytes in raw format
   - `transaction_index`: Index of the transactions in the block
   - `merkle_sibiling`: Array of hashes present in the Merkel proof
   - `block_hash`: Hash of the block

3. For each call, it returns the hash if the transaction is verified. You will receive *0* if the transaction has failed or the `rawTransaction` has a length of 64 bytes.

4. To relay a transaction, you can use the `relayTx` function. Use the same parameters as `verifyTx` with an additional contract address:

```
relayTx(raw_transaction, transaction_index, merkle_sibling,
block_hash, contract_address);
```

The function relays the verified transaction to the specified contract address. The smart contract at the contract address should implement a function called `processTransaction`. This what will be invoked by `relayTx` if the transaction passes verification:

```
processTransaction(bytes rawTransaction, uint256 transactionHash)
returns (int256)
```

5. The contract also includes APIs for various other tasks, such as setting and getting block headers, reading block hashes, and so on. You can find the complete list of APIs from their official repository at `https://github.com/ethereum/btcrelay`.

6. New block headers are submitted to BTC Relay by relayers. This process can be incentivized, which increases the interest of the community in being relayers. This allows BTC Relay to be autonomous and up to date with the Bitcoin blockchain. The relayer will get the fee for the block they submit when any transactions in that block are verified or the header is retrieved.

Creating a wallet that supports all ERC20 tokens

One of the important advantages of following a standard during token creation is the support for wallets. The wallets created for one token can support all the other tokens that follow the same standard. In this recipe, you will learn to create a wallet that can send tokens, check token balance, approve transfers, and other ERC20 functions.

Getting ready

You need to have an ERC20 token set up and deployed for testing your wallet. If you are not familiar with creating a token in Ethereum, it is recommended to step through the first few recipes of this chapter.

The examples given in this recipe use web3js v1.x. Older versions may have different syntax and you can find more information in `Chapter 3`, *Interacting with the Contract*.

How to do it...

1. Every ERC20 contract will have the same ABI structure, which is predefined by the standard. Create an application that makes use of this ABI to support all the tokens created using the standard.

2. A basic ERC20 token specification will have the following functions:
   - `totalSupply()`: Returns uint
   - `balanceOf(address tokenOwner)`: Returns uint balance
   - `allowance(address tokenOwner, address spender)`: Returns remaining uint
   - `transfer(address to, uint tokens)`: Returns bool success
   - `approve(address spender, uint tokens)`: Returns bool success
   - `transferFrom(address from, address to, uint tokens)`: Returns bool success

3. From your application, create an instance using the ABI and address of the token contract. This will allow you to interact with the token contract:

```
var abi = [...]; // Contract interface
var address = "0x0..."; // Deployed ERC20 contract address

var tokenContract = new web3.eth.Contract(abi, address);
```

 Since all ERC2o contracts follow the same function layout, you don't have to change the ABI to support multiple tokens. Make the address variable dynamic so that it is easy to switch between multiple tokens implemented using the ERC2o standard.

4. The contract instance will have all the functions related to your token contract and use them to interact with your application.

5. For example, use the `getBalance` function to retrieve the balance of a particular account:

```
var userAddress = "0x0..."; // Address of the user

tokenContract.methods.getBalance(userAddress)
    .call()
    .then(function(result) {
        console.log(result);
    })
```

6. Invoke state-changing methods, such as transfer, using a transaction. Make sure to sign the transaction using the sender's address:

```
var fromAddress = "0x1.."; // Address of the sender
var toAddress = "0x2.."; // Address of the receiver
var amount = 10; // Amount to transfer

tokenContract.methods.transder(toAddress, amount)
    .send({
        from: fromAddress;
    })
    .then(function(receipt){
        console.log(receipt);
    });
```

7. Follow a similar structure for other functions in the ERC20 standard. An application that implements all these functions will support every ERC20 token.

There's more...

In addition to the previously mentioned functions, ERC20 also implements some events for logging:

```
event Transfer(address indexed from, address indexed to, uint tokens);
event Approval(address indexed tokenOwner, address indexed spender, uint tokens);
```

These events can be listened to from your application to provide a seamless UI for the user. This can help notify the users of tokens received or approved:

```
tokenContract.events.Transfer({
    filter: { },
    fromBlock: 0
})
.on('data', function(event){
    // ...
})
.on('changed', function(event){
    // ...
})
.on('error',function(event){
    // ...
});
```

6
Games and DAOs

In this chapter, you will learn the following recipes:

- Creating a non-fungible token
- Asset tracking and movement
- Creating a basic game on Ethereum
- Building a decentralized lottery on Ethereum
- Selecting a winner based on the ticket number
- Sharing dividends among investors
- Affiliating a program to attract more users

Introduction

In the last chapter, we discussed creating tokens and ICOs. Every ERC20 token will have the same value as every other token in the same contract. This class of identical fungible tokens may not be suited for all needs. For non-identical and unique tokens in Ethereum blockchain, ERC-721 defines the standard. It defines the interface that describes how to build non-fungible tokens.

One of the popular examples of non-identical tokens is CryptoKitties. It is a game that allows the users to buy, sell, trade, and breed digital cats. The uniqueness of each kitty cannot be represented by ERC-20 tokens. This chapter also covers the topics needed for creating an extremely collectable token such as CryptoKitties.

In this recipe, you will learn how to create non-fungible ERC-721 tokens. You will also learn how to create games and decentralized organizations in Ethereum blockchain.

Creating a non-fungible token

Non-fungible is something of such a nature that one part or quantity cannot be replaced by another equal part or quantity in paying a debt or settling an account. The Ethereum community defines ERC-721 as the standard for creating and managing non-fungible tokens or **Non-fungible tokens** (NFTs). These tokens can be used to represent a physical or virtual asset. Some examples are land, artwork, and virtual collectables. NFTs are also suitable to represent assets such as loans that have negative values. ERC-721 is inspired by ERC-20 and adds additional features to make each token unique. In this recipe, you will learn the basics of creating such assets.

Getting ready

You need to have a working installation of Ethereum (`geth`, `Parity`, `ganache`, and so on) or the Remix IDE to test this recipe.

It would be great if you know how the ERC-20 standard works before stepping through this recipe. Go through `Chapter 5`, *Tokens and ICO*, to learn more about this.

How to do it...

1. To check the balance of tokens in each address, the usual `balanceOf` function from ERC-20 is present in the standard. It accepts an address as input and returns the number of non-fungible tokens owned by the address. Create the same function to store the balances:

```
function balanceOf(address _owner) external view returns (uint256);
```

2. Create a mapping with the address as the key and count as the value to store the number of tokens:

```
mapping (address => uint256) internal ownedTokensCount;
```

3. Modify the `balanceOf` function to read the value from the mapping:

```
function balanceOf(address _owner) public view returns (uint256) {
    require(_owner != address(0));
    return ownedTokensCount[_owner];
}
```

4. Since the ownership of each token can be different, create a function called `ownerOf` to find the owner of an NFT. It should accept an ID of a token and return the address of the owner. The individual token ownership and parameters are the key features that differentiate ERC721 NFT from the ERC20 token standard:

```
function ownerOf(uint256 _tokenId) external view returns (address);
```

5. Create a mapping similar to `ownedTokensCount` for maintaining token ownership:

```
mapping (uint256 => address) internal tokenOwner;
```

6. Modify the `ownerOf` function to read the owner address of each token:

```
function ownerOf(uint256 _tokenId) public view returns (address) {
    address owner = tokenOwner[_tokenId];
    require(owner != address(0));
    return owner;
}
```

7. Verify token existence by checking whether a token has a valid owner or not. Add an additional function called `exists`, which makes use of the `tokenOwner` mapping:

```
function exists(uint256 _tokenId) public view returns (bool) {
    address owner = tokenOwner[_tokenId];
    return owner != address(0);
}
```

8. It is always a good idea to keep a modifier for validation purposes. To verify the token owner, create a modifier called `onlyOwnerOf`. This will accept the token ID as a parameter and will verify it against the `ownerOf` function:

```
modifier onlyOwnerOf(uint256 _tokenId) {
    require(ownerOf(_tokenId) == msg.sender);
    _;
}
```

9. With all these methods and properties, we have a basic NFT contract (given next), which can store the tokens and their identities. This can be modified further to enable token transfers, which we will discuss in the next recipe:

```
pragma solidity ^0.4.23;

import "./SafeMath.sol";
```

```
contract BasicERC721 {
    using SafeMath for uint256;

    // Mapping from token ID to owner
    mapping (uint256 => address) internal tokenOwner;

    // Mapping from owner to number of owned token
    mapping (address => uint256) internal ownedTokensCount;

    /**
     * @dev Guarantees msg.sender is owner of the given token
     * @param _tokenId uint256 ID of the token
     */
    modifier onlyOwnerOf(uint256 _tokenId) {
        require(ownerOf(_tokenId) == msg.sender);
        _;
    }

    /**
     * @dev Gets the balance of the specified address
     * @param _owner address to query the balance of
     * @return uint256 represents the amount owned
     */
    function balanceOf(address _owner) public view
        returns (uint256) {
        require(_owner != address(0));
        return ownedTokensCount[_owner];
    }

    /**
     * @dev Gets the owner of the specified token ID
     * @param _tokenId uint256 ID of the token to query the owner
     * @return owner address currently marked as the owner
     */
    function ownerOf(uint256 _tokenId) public view
        returns (address) {
        address owner = tokenOwner[_tokenId];
        require(owner != address(0));
        return owner;
    }

    /**
     * @dev Returns whether the specified token exists
     * @param _tokenId uint256 ID of the token to query
     * @return whether the token exists
     */
    function exists(uint256 _tokenId) public view returns (bool) {
        address owner = tokenOwner[_tokenId];
```

```
                  return owner != address(0);
              }

      /**
        * @dev Function to add a token ID
        * @param _to address of the new owner
        * @param _tokenId uint256 ID of the token to be added
        */
        function addTokenTo(address _to, uint256 _tokenId) internal {
              require(tokenOwner[_tokenId] == address(0));
              tokenOwner[_tokenId] = _to;
              ownedTokensCount[_to] = ownedTokensCount[_to].add(1);
        }

      /**
        * @dev Function to remove a token ID
        * @param _from address of the previous owner
        * @param _tokenId uint256 ID of the token to be removed
        */
        function removeTokenFrom(address _from, uint256 _tokenId)
    internal {
              require(ownerOf(_tokenId) == _from);
              ownedTokensCount[_from] = ownedTokensCount[_from].sub(1);
              tokenOwner[_tokenId] = address(0);
        }
    }
```

10. The basic contract can be further modified to include other properties such as the name and symbol. You can use the `constructor` to set values for these parameters:

```
string internal name_;
string internal symbol_;

constructor(string _name, string _symbol) public {
    name_ = _name;
    symbol_ = _symbol;
}

function name() public view returns (string) {
    return name_;
}

function symbol() public view returns (string) {
    return symbol_;
}
```

11. For listing all the tokens owned by an address, store them in a mapping. The key will be the owner address and the value will be the array of token IDs:

```
mapping(address => uint256[]) internal ownedTokens;
```

12. Since finding an item from the array is an expensive task, it is a good idea to maintain a different mapping to store the array index:

```
mapping(uint256 => uint256) internal ownedTokensIndex;
```

13. While adding and removing the tokens, make sure to update the ownedTokens and ownedTokensIndex values:

```
function addTokenTo(address _to, uint256 _tokenId) internal {
    // call the previous addToken method here
    uint256 length = ownedTokens[_to].length;
    ownedTokens[_to].push(_tokenId);
    ownedTokensIndex[_tokenId] = length;
}

function removeTokenFrom(address _from, uint256 _tokenId) internal
{
    // call the previous removeToken method here
    uint256 tokenIndex = ownedTokensIndex[_tokenId];
    uint256 lastTokenIndex = ownedTokens[_from].length.sub(1);
    uint256 lastToken = ownedTokens[_from][lastTokenIndex];

    ownedTokens[_from][tokenIndex] = lastToken;
    ownedTokens[_from][lastTokenIndex] = 0;

    ownedTokens[_from].length--;
    ownedTokensIndex[_tokenId] = 0;
    ownedTokensIndex[lastToken] = tokenIndex;
}
```

14. For iteration, create an array with all the tokens that exist in the contract. Also, maintain a mapping to store each token index:

```
uint256[] internal allTokens;

mapping(uint256 => uint256) internal allTokensIndex;
```

15. The `allTokens` array can also be used to calculate the total supply. Declare a function to read the total token supply:

```
function totalSupply() public view returns (uint256) {
    return allTokens.length;
}
```

16. The final contract with the additional properties will look like this:

```
pragma solidity ^0.4.23;
import "./BasicERC721.sol";

contract ERC721Token is BasicERC721 {
    // Token name
    string internal name_;

    // Token symbol
    string internal symbol_;

    // Mapping from owner to list of owned token IDs
    mapping(address => uint256[]) internal ownedTokens;

    // Mapping from token ID to index of the owner tokens list
    mapping(uint256 => uint256) internal ownedTokensIndex;

    // Array with all token ids
    uint256[] internal allTokens;

    // Mapping from token id to position in the allTokens array
    mapping(uint256 => uint256) internal allTokensIndex;

    constructor(string _name, string _symbol) public {
        name_ = _name;
        symbol_ = _symbol;
    }

    /**
    * @dev Gets the token name
    * @return string representing the token name
    */
    function name() public view returns (string) {
        return name_;
    }

    /**
    * @dev Gets the token symbol
    * @return string representing the token symbol
    */
```

```
function symbol() public view returns (string) {
    return symbol_;
}

/**
 * @dev Gets the token ID at a given index
 * @param _owner address owning the tokens list
 * @param _index uint256 representing the index
 * @return uint256 token ID at the given index of the tokens
 */
function tokenOfOwnerByIndex(address _owner, uint256 _index)
    public view returns (uint256) {
    require(_index < balanceOf(_owner));
    return ownedTokens[_owner][_index];
}

/**
 * @dev Gets the total amount of tokens
 * @return uint256 representing the total amount
 */
function totalSupply() public view returns (uint256) {
    return allTokens.length;
}

/**
 * @dev Gets the token ID at a given index
 * @param _index uint256 representing the index
 * @return uint256 token ID at the given index
 */
function tokenByIndex(uint256 _index) public view
    returns (uint256) {
    require(_index < totalSupply());
    return allTokens[_index];
}

/**
 * @dev Function to add a token ID
 * @param _to address representing the new owner
 * @param _tokenId uint256 ID of the token to be added
 */
function addTokenTo(address _to, uint256 _tokenId) internal {
    super.addTokenTo(_to, _tokenId);
    uint256 length = ownedTokens[_to].length;
    ownedTokens[_to].push(_tokenId);
    ownedTokensIndex[_tokenId] = length;
}

/**
```

```
 * @dev Function to remove a token ID
 * @param _from address of the previous owner
 * @param _tokenId uint256 ID of the token to be removed
 */
function removeTokenFrom(address _from, uint256 _tokenId)
    internal {
    super.removeTokenFrom(_from, _tokenId);

    uint256 tokenIndex = ownedTokensIndex[_tokenId];
    uint256 lastTokenIndex = ownedTokens[_from].length.sub(1);
    uint256 lastToken = ownedTokens[_from][lastTokenIndex];

    ownedTokens[_from][tokenIndex] = lastToken;
    ownedTokens[_from][lastTokenIndex] = 0;
    ownedTokens[_from].length--;
    ownedTokensIndex[_tokenId] = 0;
    ownedTokensIndex[lastToken] = tokenIndex;
  }
}
```

There's more...

All the contracts we have created so far only stores and manages the token ID. A token will have a lot more data depending on the use case. One quick way to store the details is by using a string of characters designed for unambiguous identification. The **Uniform Resource Identifier** (URI) scheme is one such implementation that uses the type string:

```
mapping(uint256 => string) internal tokenURIs;
```

This allows any data to be stored as a token. Read and write is performed with the help of dedicated functions:

```
/**
 * @dev Returns an URI for a given token ID
 * @dev Throws if the token ID does not exist. May return an empty string.
 * @param _tokenId uint256 ID of the token to query
 */
function tokenURI(uint256 _tokenId) public view returns (string) {
    require(exists(_tokenId));
    return tokenURIs[_tokenId];
}

/**
 * @dev Internal function to set the token URI for a given token
 * @dev Reverts if the token ID does not exist
 * @param _tokenId uint256 ID of the token to set its URI
```

```
    * @param _uri string URI to assign
    */
function _setTokenURI(uint256 _tokenId, string _uri) internal {
    require(exists(_tokenId));
    tokenURIs[_tokenId] = _uri;
}
```

Asset tracking and movement

NFTs can be transferred just like regular ERC-20 tokens. The standard provides modified `transfer` and `approve` functions for token transfer and delegation tasks. It also includes the standard event logging facility so that asset tracking can be made easier.

In this recipe, you will learn how to implement asset movement and tracking functionality in the ERC-721 token created in the previous recipe. Token transfer functionality can be achieved by modifying the standard transfer method and asset tracking can be implemented with event filtering.

Getting ready

You need to have a working installation of Ethereum (`geth`, `Parity`, `ganache`, and so on) or the Remix IDE to test this recipe.

The contracts explained in this recipe extend the basic ERC-721 token created in the previous recipe. It is recommended to read through it before stepping through this recipe.

How to do it...

1. Create a new contract that inherits the `BasicERC721` contract created in the previous recipe. This removes the need to declare the token and ownership properties:

    ```
    pragma solidity ^0.4.23;
    import "./BasicERC721.sol";

    contract ERC721Token {
        //...
    }
    ```

2. A token can be transferred by the owner or by the approved person. The approval can be of two types. The user can set approval for one specific token or all the tokens owned by an address. Create two different mappings to maintain this:

```
// Mapping from token ID to approved address
mapping (uint256 => address) internal tokenApprovals;

// Mapping from owner to operator approvals
mapping (address => mapping (address => bool)) internal
operatorApprovals;
```

3. Declare dedicated functions to verify the approval status of each address:

```
function getApproved(uint256 _tokenId) public view
    returns (address) {
    return tokenApprovals[_tokenId];
}

function isApprovedForAll(address _owner, address _operator)
    public view returns (bool) {
    return operatorApprovals[_owner][_operator];
}
```

4. Define events that will be emitted whenever a token transfer or approval task occurs:

```
// Transfer event
event Transfer(address indexed _from,
    address indexed _to, uint256 _tokenId);
// Approval event for a specific token
event Approval(address indexed _owner,
    address indexed _approved, uint256 _tokenId);
// Approval event for all tokens
event ApprovalForAll(address indexed _owner,
    address indexed _operator, bool _approved);
```

5. Use the `approve` function to approve someone to transfer a specific token on your behalf:

```
function approve(address _to, uint256 _tokenId) public {
    address owner = ownerOf(_tokenId);
    require(_to != owner);
    require(msg.sender == owner ||
        isApprovedForAll(owner, msg.sender));

    if (getApproved(_tokenId) != address(0) || _to != address(0)) {
```

```
        tokenApprovals[_tokenId] = _to;
        emit Approval(owner, _to, _tokenId);
    }
}
```

6. Use the `setApprovalForAll` function to set the approval status for all the tokens owned by a user:

```
function setApprovalForAll(address _to, bool _approved) public {
    require(_to != msg.sender);
    operatorApprovals[msg.sender][_to] = _approved;
    emit ApprovalForAll(msg.sender, _to, _approved);
}
```

7. Authorization for all token transfers can be revoked by using the same function. But, for individual tokens, create a different function to remove permissions:

```
function clearApproval(address _owner, uint256 _tokenId) internal {
    require(ownerOf(_tokenId) == _owner);
    if (tokenApprovals[_tokenId] != address(0)) {
        tokenApprovals[_tokenId] = address(0);
        emit Approval(_owner, address(0), _tokenId);
    }
}
```

8. Any approved user, or the owner, can transfer tokens to other addresses. To restrict unauthorized transfers, create a `modifier` that verifies the same:

```
modifier canTransfer(uint256 _tokenId) {
    require(isApprovedOrOwner(msg.sender, _tokenId));
    _;
}

function isApprovedOrOwner(address _spender, uint256 _tokenId)
    internal view returns (bool) {
    address owner = ownerOf(_tokenId);
    return (
        _spender == owner ||
        getApproved(_tokenId) == _spender ||
        isApprovedForAll(owner, _spender)
    );
}
```

9. The actual transfer of ownership is performed using the `transferFrom` function.
   Use the `canTransfer` modifier for authorization:

```
function transferFrom(address _from, address _to, uint256 _tokenId)
    public canTransfer(_tokenId) {
    require(_from != address(0));
    require(_to != address(0));

    clearApproval(_from, _tokenId);
    removeTokenFrom(_from, _tokenId); // From BasicERC721.sol
    addTokenTo(_to, _tokenId); // From BasicERC721.sol
    emit Transfer(_from, _to, _tokenId);
}
```

10. Use the safe transfer mechanism, which verifies whether the receiving address
    supports tokens or not. This avoids accidental token transfers to contract
    addresses:

```
function checkAndCallSafeTransfer(address _from, address _to,
    uint256 _tokenId, bytes _data) internal returns (bool) {
    uint256 size;
    assembly { size := extcodesize(_to) }
    if (size == 0) {
        return true;
    }

    bytes4 retval = ERC721Receiver(_to)
        .onERC721Received(_from, _tokenId, _data);
    return (retval == ERC721_RECEIVED);
}

function safeTransferFrom(address _from, address _to,
    uint256 _tokenId, bytes _data)
    public canTransfer(_tokenId) {
    transferFrom(_from, _to, _tokenId);
    require(checkAndCallSafeTransfer(_from, _to, _tokenId, _data));
}
```

11. If the target address is a contract, it must implement the
    `onERC721Received` function. It is called upon safe transfer and should return
    the
    value `bytes4(keccak256("onERC721Received(address,uint256,bytes)"))`;. Otherwise, the transfer is cancelled:

```
contract ERC721Receiver {
    bytes4 constant ERC721_RECEIVED = 0xf0b9e5ba;
```

```
        /**
         * @notice Handle the receipt of an NFT
         * @param _from The sending address
         * @param _tokenId The NFT identifier which is being
    transferred
         * @param _data Additional data with no specified format
         * @return `bytes4(keccak256("onERC721Received(...)"))`
         */
        function onERC721Received(address _from, uint256 _tokenId,
            bytes _data) public returns(bytes4);
    }
```

12. The final transferable token contract will look like this:

```
    pragma solidity ^0.4.23;

    import "./BasicERC721.sol";
    import "./SafeMath.sol";

    contract ERC721Token is BasicERC721 {
        using SafeMath for uint256;

        // Equals to
    `bytes4(keccak256("onERC721Received(address,uint256,bytes)"))`
        // which can be also obtained as
    `ERC721Receiver(0).onERC721Received.selector`
        bytes4 constant ERC721_RECEIVED = 0xf0b9e5ba;

        mapping (uint256 => address) internal tokenApprovals;
        mapping (address => mapping (address => bool))
            internal operatorApprovals;

        modifier canTransfer(uint256 _tokenId) {
            require(isApprovedOrOwner(msg.sender, _tokenId));
            _;
        }

        function approve(address _to, uint256 _tokenId) public {
            address owner = ownerOf(_tokenId);
            require(_to != owner);
            require(msg.sender == owner ||
                    isApprovedForAll(owner, msg.sender));

            if (getApproved(_tokenId) != address(0) ||
                _to != address(0)) {
                tokenApprovals[_tokenId] = _to;
                emit Approval(owner, _to, _tokenId);
            }
```

```
    }

    function getApproved(uint256 _tokenId) public view
        returns (address) {
        return tokenApprovals[_tokenId];
    }

    function setApprovalForAll(address _to, bool _approved)
        public {
        require(_to != msg.sender);
        operatorApprovals[msg.sender][_to] = _approved;
        emit ApprovalForAll(msg.sender, _to, _approved);
    }

    function isApprovedForAll(address _owner, address _operator)
        public view returns (bool) {
        return operatorApprovals[_owner][_operator];
    }

    function transferFrom(address _from, address _to,
        uint256 _tokenId)
        public canTransfer(_tokenId) {
        require(_from != address(0));
        require(_to != address(0));

        clearApproval(_from, _tokenId);
        removeTokenFrom(_from, _tokenId);
        addTokenTo(_to, _tokenId);

        emit Transfer(_from, _to, _tokenId);
    }

    function safeTransferFrom(address _from, address _to,
        uint256 _tokenId, bytes _data)
        public canTransfer(_tokenId) {
        transferFrom(_from, _to, _tokenId);
        require(checkAndCallSafeTransfer(_from, _to,
            _tokenId, _data));
    }

    function isApprovedOrOwner(address _spender, uint256 _tokenId)
        internal view returns (bool) {
        address owner = ownerOf(_tokenId);
        return (_spender == owner ||
            getApproved(_tokenId) == _spender ||
            isApprovedForAll(owner, _spender));
    }
```

```
function clearApproval(address _owner, uint256 _tokenId)
    internal {
    require(ownerOf(_tokenId) == _owner);
    if (tokenApprovals[_tokenId] != address(0)) {
        tokenApprovals[_tokenId] = address(0);
        emit Approval(_owner, address(0), _tokenId);
    }
}

function checkAndCallSafeTransfer(address _from,
    address _to, uint256 _tokenId, bytes _data)
    internal returns (bool) {
    uint256 size;
    assembly { size := extcodesize(_to) }
    if (size == 0) { return true; }
    bytes4 retval = ERC721Receiver(_to)
        .onERC721Received(_from, _tokenId, _data);
    return (retval == ERC721_RECEIVED);
}
}
```

Creating a basic game on Ethereum

Another wonderful use case for a decentralized platform like Ethereum is building games. CryptoKitties is one such popular game, which is built on Ethereum blockchain. There are many options to consider while creating a decentralized game. You can either go with a fully decentralized and transparent game, or partially decentralized, feature-rich game. It depends on your requirements and target players.

In this recipe, you will learn how to create a simple game that allows the player to own heroes and battle against others.

Getting ready

You need to have a working installation of Ethereum (`geth`, `Parity`, `ganache`, and so on) or the Remix IDE to test this recipe.

The contracts given are for illustration purposes only and cannot be used in real-world systems.

How to do it...

1. Create a game contract with a target compiler version. We will use version 0.4.23 for this specific contract. This contract acts as a database to store our hero details and a battle arena where heroes can fight against each other:

```
pragma solidity ^0.4.23;

contract HeroBattle {
    //...
}
```

2. Create a hero data structure with name, DNA, level, win count, and loss count. Each hero will have a DNA number. Just like human DNA, each part of this number denotes different traits of a hero. For example, the first two digit map to the hero's looks, the second two digits maps to the flying ability, and so on. This can be configured in your game UI:

```
struct Hero {
    string name;
    uint dna;
    uint32 level;
    uint16 winCount;
    uint16 lossCount;
}
Hero[] public heroes;
```

3. To identify the owner of each hero, create a mapping with the `heroId` as the key and the owner address as the value:

```
    mapping (uint => address) public heroToOwner;
```

4. This mapping can also be used in a function `modifier` for restricting hero access:

```
modifier ownerOf(uint _heroId) {
    require(msg.sender == heroToOwner[_heroId]);
    _;
}
```

5. Declare a function to create new heroes. The function should accept a name and DNA to create a hero:

```
function _createHero(string _name, uint _dna) external {
    //...
}
```

6. Create a new hero using the input and push it to the heroes array. A `push` operation in solidity will return the new array index. We can use this index as the `heroId` for easy identification. Save the new ID to hero to owner mapping:

```
uint id = heroes.push(Hero(_name, _dna, 0, 0, 0)) - 1;
heroToOwner[id] = msg.sender;
```

7. Emit an event for the hero creation process with the ID and owner address:

```
// Declaration
event NewHero(uint heroId, string name, uint dna);
// Logging
emit NewHero(id, _name, _dna);
```

The `createHero` function allows anyone to create a hero. This can be further restricted by including a fee for each hero or by allowing only the admin to create new heroes. You can impose conditions based on your target audience.

8. This should be enough to create and manage a hero on Ethereum. But, that is not the fun part. Let's include a battle system where one hero can attack another to advance in level. Create another function that can be used to battle. Use the `modifier` to restrict it only to the hero's owner:

```
function attack(uint _heroId, uint _targetId)
    external
    ownerOf(_heroId) {
    //...
}
```

9. Let's design the battle system in such a way that the attacker has a *60%* chance of winning against the target hero. Create a random number from *0* to *100*. We can use the block time, sender address, and a `nonce` to create enough randomness. You can always add or remove parameters, or change the logic completely to accommodate your needs:

```
nonce++;
uint rand = uint(keccak256(now, msg.sender, nonce)) % 100;
```

10. The winner is chosen by comparing the random number and probability of winning. The win/loss count and hero level should be changed based on the result:

```
if (rand <= 60) { // 60%
    myHero.winCount++;
    myHero.level++;
```

```
        enemyHero.lossCount++;
    } else {
        myHero.lossCount++;
        enemyHero.winCount++;
    }
```

11. Finally, `emit` an event to notify the listeners:

```
emit attackWon(_heroId, _targetId, winnerId)
```

12. This contract will allow anyone to start a battle and level up based on the battle result. The final hero battle contract is given here:

```
pragma solidity ^0.4.23;

contract HeroBattle {

    struct Hero {
        string name;
        uint dna;
        uint32 level;
        uint16 winCount;
        uint16 lossCount;
    }

    Hero[] public heroes;

    mapping (uint => address) public heroToOwner;

    uint nonce = 0;
    uint attackerProbability = 75;

    event NewHero(uint heroId, string name, uint dna);
    event attackWon(uint attackerId, uint targetId, uint winnerId);

    modifier ownerOf(uint _heroId) {
        require(msg.sender == heroToOwner[_heroId]);
        _;
    }

    /**
     * @dev Create a new hero
     * @param _name Name of the hero
     * @param _dna DNA of the hero
     */
    function _createHero(string _name, uint _dna) external {
        uint id = heroes.push(Hero(_name, _dna, 0, 0, 0)) - 1;
        heroToOwner[id] = msg.sender;
```

```
            emit NewHero(id, _name, _dna);
    }

    /**
     * @dev Adds single address to whitelist.
     * @param _heroId Attacker hero id
     * @param _targetId Target hero id
     */
    function attack(uint _heroId, uint _targetId)
        external ownerOf(_heroId) {
        Hero storage myHero = heroes[_heroId];
        Hero storage enemyHero = heroes[_targetId];

        uint winnerId;

        nonce++;
        uint rand = uint(keccak256(now, msg.sender, nonce)) % 100;

        if (rand <= attackerProbability) {
          myHero.winCount++;
          myHero.level++;
          enemyHero.lossCount++;
          winnerId = _heroId;
        } else {
          myHero.lossCount++;
          enemyHero.winCount++;
          winnerId = _targetId;
        }

        emit attackWon(_heroId, _targetId, winnerId);
    }

}
```

Building a decentralized lottery on Ethereum

Distributed technologies are some of the most suitable platforms for running decentralized organizations. A **Decentralized Autonomous Organization (DAO)** is an organization that is run through the rules encoded in a smart contract. You can use Ethereum to create your own DAOs with the set of rules hardcoded inside the contract.

In this recipe, you will learn how to create a decentralized organization that runs a lottery system on Ethereum blockchain.

Getting ready

You need to have a working installation of Ethereum (`geth`, `Parity`, `ganache`, and so on) or the Remix IDE to test this recipe.

The contracts given are for illustration purposes only and cannot be used in real-world systems.

How to do it...

1. Let's consider a lottery system that selects the winning numbers based on a future block hash. While buying a ticket, the user is asked to guess a random set of numbers and is validated against some future block. The prize is given based on how accurate the prediction was.

2. Create a contract by specifying the solidity version and a name:

   ```solidity
   pragma solidity ^0.4.17;

   // Decentralized autonomous lottery
   contract DAL {
       // ...
   }
   ```

3. Create a data structure that will store the bet details of each user. Include the bet amount, guessed number, and a future block number to validate the bet against. Also, create a mapping that maps each bet against a user address:

   ```solidity
   struct Bet {
       // Bet amount
       uint256 value;
       // Guessed numbers
       uint32 betHash;
       // Future block to validate the bet
       uint32 validateBlock;
   }

   // Mapping to store bet against an user.
   mapping(address => Bet) bets;
   ```

4. Let's assume the future block number as the third block. For every bet, validate the guess against the fourth future block. This is a very simple example, but you can think of other methods to create more randomness.

5. Create a `play` function that will be used by the user to create a `bet`. The function should accept a guessed number and should be payable:

```
function play(uint _hash) payable public {
    //...
}
```

6. Inside the function, verify whether the user has sent enough value for the bet. Let's assume the minimum value as *0.1 ETH* and the maximum as *1 ETH*:

```
require(msg.value <= 1 ether && msg.value >= 0.1 ether);
```

7. Calculate the `bethash` and future block number based on the input and current state:

```
uint24 bethash = uint24(_hash);

uint256 blockNumber = block.number + 3;
```

8. Save the calculated bet values to the mapping for future reference:

```
bets[msg.sender] = Bet({
    value: msg.value,
    betHash: uint32(bethash),
    validateBlock: uint32(blockNumber)
});
```

9. Finally, `emit` an event for each play so that it is easy to track and update it in any application listening to the event:

```
// Event declaration
event LogBet(
    address indexed player,
    uint256 bethash,
    uint256 blocknumber,
    uint256 betsize
);

// Event log
emit LogBet(
    msg.sender,
    uint(bethash),
    blockNumber,
    msg.value
);
```

10. To improve usability, invoke the `play` function from the `fallback` function of the contract. Create a random input number using the built-in hash functions to help the user:

```
function () payable external {
    play(uint(keccak256(msg.sender, block.number)));
}
```

11. The final contract will look like this:

```
pragma solidity^0.4.23;

contract DAL {

    // Data structure to store the bet details
    struct Bet {
        uint256 value;
        uint32 betHash;
        uint32 validateBlock;
    }

    // Mapping of user and their bet
    mapping(address => Bet) bets;

    // Event to track each bet
    event LogBet(
        address indexed player,
        uint256 bethash,
        uint256 blocknumber,
        uint256 betsize
    );

    /**
     * @dev Function to place a bet
     * @param _hash Number guessed
     */
    function play(uint _hash) payable public {
        require(msg.value <= 1 ether &&
                msg.value >= 0.1 ether);

        uint24 bethash = uint24(_hash);
        uint256 blockNumber = block.number + 3;

        bets[msg.sender] = Bet({
            value: msg.value,
            betHash: uint32(bethash),
            validateBlock: uint32(blockNumber)
        });
```

```
            emit LogBet(
                msg.sender,
                uint(bethash),
                blockNumber,
                msg.value
            );
        }

        /**
         * @dev Fallback function which acts as a shortcut
         * to the token buying process
         */
        function () payable external {
            play(uint(keccak256(msg.sender, block.number)));
        }

    }
```

This is a very basic lottery contract that accepts bets from the user. The mechanism to select a winner is not yet implemented, and we will look into that in the next recipe.

The contract can be further expanded to include dividend and affiliate programs. It allows investors to contribute toward the jackpot amount, and a percentage of ticket sales revenue will be paid as a dividend to the investor. This will accept more investment and interest toward the system.

An affiliate program works like a referral system. The person promoting the system will be paid based on the ticket sale revenue.

Selecting a winner based on the ticket number

In the previous recipe, we learned how to create a basic decentralized token and the procedure to record a bet. A lottery is more interesting when there is a prize involved. The logic for selecting a winner can be something like verifying the guess against some future block hash or number. We can also add a feature to decide the winning amount based on how accurate the prediction was.

In this recipe, you will learn how to select a winner based on logic in the smart contract. You will also learn how to calculate the winning amount and transfer it to the player.

Getting ready

You need to have a working installation of Ethereum (geth, Parity, ganache, and so on) or the Remix IDE to test this recipe. The contract inherits the basic lottery contract created in the previous recipe. It is recommended to step through that before continuing with this recipe.

The contracts given are for illustration purposes only and cannot be used in real-world systems.

How to do it...

1. Inherit the DAL contract created in the previous recipe:

```
pragma solidity^0.4.23;

import "./DAL.sol";

contract WinnableDAL is DAL {
    //...
}
```

2. Let's look into the winning process. Ask the user to select six numbers, each ranging from *0* to *15*. Since the hex value in block hash ranges from 0-15 (0-F), it will be easier to verify the prediction.

3. Once the future block is mined, allow the user to validate the predicted number against the generated block hash. For example, assume that the future block is 501232 and that the predicted number is 314721. After the future block is mined, the number is validated against the last five digits of the block hash.

4. Calculate the winning amount based on how many correct guesses the user has made.

5. Create a function to verify the future block hash. It should accept a bet object and the actual future block hash. The function should return the winning amount. Since it is a read-only function to verify the hash, it can be marked as a pure function:

```
function verifyBet(Bet _bet, uint24 _result) pure
    internal returns(uint)  {
    //..
}
```

6. Calculate the bet hash and the final block hash for verification:

```
uint24 userBet = uint24(_bet.betHash);
uint24 actualValue = userBet ^ _result;
```

7. Verify each individual number and increment the number of correct predictions:

```
uint24 predictions =
    ((actualValue & 0xF)       == 0 ? 1 : 0) +
    ((actualValue & 0xF0)      == 0 ? 1 : 0) +
    ((actualValue & 0xF00)     == 0 ? 1 : 0) +
    ((actualValue & 0xF000)    == 0 ? 1 : 0) +
    ((actualValue & 0xF0000)   == 0 ? 1 : 0);
```

8. For each correct prediction, return the winning amount. The winning amount will be the ticket price times the multiplier for each prediction. If the number of correct predictions is less than two, return *0* as the winning amount:

```
if (predictions == 5)
    return _bet.value * 10000;
if (predictions == 4)
    return _bet.value * 1000;
if (predictions == 3)
    return _bet.value * 100;
if (predictions == 2)
    return _bet.value * 10;
return 0;
```

9. If a user makes correct predictions and wins an amount, send it to the user address:

```
function pay(address _winner, uint _amount) internal {
    // Check if the contract has enough balance
    require(address(this).balance > _amount);

    // Transfer the amount to the user
    _winner.transfer(_amount);
}
```

10. Allow the user to get paid using the `isWon` function. This function will accept a user address and will use the `verifyBet` and `pay` functions to check and transfer the winning amount:

```
function isWon(address _user) public {
    //...
}
```

11. Check whether the future block was mined or not:

```
Bet storage userBet = bets[_user];
require(userBet.validateBlock >= block.number);
```

12. Calculate the `blockhash` of the future block and verify it against the predicted number:

```
uint24 futureHash =
    uint24(blockhash(userBet.validateBlock));

uint prize = verifyBet(userBet, futureHash);
```

13. If the user is lucky and won an amount, transfer it to the user address:

```
if(prize > 0) {
    pay(_user, prize);
}
```

14. Delete the bet to avoid multiple withdrawals:

```
delete bets[_user];
```

15. The final winnable lottery contract will look like this:

```
contract WinnableDAL is DAL {

    /**
     * @dev Function to verify the bet
     * @param _bet bet object
     * @param _result future block hash
     * @returns uint indicating the winning amount
     */
    function verifyBet(Bet _bet, uint24 _result) pure internal
        returns(uint) {
        uint24 userBet = uint24(_bet.betHash);
        uint24 actualValue = userBet ^ _result;

        uint24 predictions =
            ((actualValue & 0xF) == 0 ? 1 : 0) +
            ((actualValue & 0xF0) == 0 ? 1 : 0) +
            ((actualValue & 0xF00) == 0 ? 1 : 0) +
            ((actualValue & 0xF000) == 0 ? 1 : 0) +
            ((actualValue & 0xF0000) == 0 ? 1 : 0);

        if (predictions == 5)
            return _bet.value * 10000;
        if (predictions == 4)
```

```
                return _bet.value * 1000;
        if (predictions == 3)
            return _bet.value * 100;
        if (predictions == 2)
            return _bet.value * 10;
        return 0;
    }

    /**
     * @dev Function to pay an user
     * @param _wiinner Address of the receiver
     * @param _amount Amount to transfer
     */
    function pay(address _winner, uint _amount) internal {
        require(address(this).balance > _amount);
        _winner.transfer(_amount);
    }

    /**
     * @dev Function to check the winning status
     * @param _user Address of the user
     */
    function isWon(address _user) public {
        Bet storage userBet = bets[_user];
        require(userBet.validateBlock >= block.number);

        uint24 futureHash =
            uint24(blockhash(userBet.validateBlock));
        uint prize = verifyBet(userBet, futureHash);

        if(prize > 0) {
            pay(_user, prize);
        }
        delete bets[_user];
    }
}
```

Sharing dividends among investors

To make the system completely run on its own, the profit should be shared among investors. Ticket sales are the source of profit in a lottery system. For each ticket sold, a percentage of the cost can go to the investor. This will increase interest in the platform.

In this recipe, you will learn how to manage the investments and dividends of a decentralized organization.

Getting ready

You need to have a working installation of Ethereum (`geth`, `Parity`, `ganache`, and so on) or the Remix IDE to test this recipe. The contract inherits the winnable lottery contract created in the previous recipe. It is recommended to step through it before continuing with this recipe.

The contracts given are for illustration purposes only and cannot be used in real-world systems. It is also recommended to use `SafeMath` for arithmetic operations.

How to do it...

1. Inherit the winnable DAL contract created in the previous recipe. Since the investments are usually handled using an ERC20 token, import the `StandardToken` contract from the `openzeppelin` library:

```
pragma solidity^0.4.23;

import "./WinnableDAL.sol";
import "./StandardToken.sol";

contract InvestableDAL is WinnableDAL, StandardToken {
    //...
}
```

2. Create an `invest` function, which accepts investments from the user and allocates tokens accordingly:

```
function invest() public {
    //...
}
```

3. For simplicity, assume that each investor gets one token per Ether invested. Use the standard token functions to mint and allocate tokens:

```
address investor = msg.sender;
uint tokens = msg.value;

mint(investor, tokens);
```

4. Create a state variable to store the dividend amount. This will be modified for each ticket purchase:

```
uint dividendAmount = 0;
```

5. For example, allocate 5% of the total ticket sales revenue to the dividend pool. Modify the `play` function to include this functionality:

```
function play(uint _hash) payable public {
    uint dividend = msg.value * (5/100);
    dividendAmount+= dividend;
    uint ticketValue = msg.value - dividend;

    //...
}
```

6. To avoid multiple dividend payouts, create a `mapping` that stores the payout status of each investor:

```
mapping(address => bool) payoutStatus;
```

7. Allow the user to get the payout by calling a `payout` function:

```
function getPayout() {
    require(!payoutStatus[msg.sender]);

    uint percentage = balance[msg.sender]/totalSupply;
    uint dividend = dividendAmount * (percentage/100);

    msg.sender.transfer(dividend);

    payoutStatus[msg.sender] = true;
}
```

8. This function allows the investor to get the dividend only once. It is not an ideal approach, since tokens can be purchased after the dividend. One possible solution is to use multiple dividend payout periods for efficient distribution.

9. The final dividend contract will look something like this:

```
pragma solidity^0.4.23;

import "./WinnableDAL.sol";
import "./StandardToken.sol";

contract InvestableDAL is WinnableDAL, StandardToken {

    uint dividendAmount = 0;

    mapping(address => bool) payoutStatus;

    /**
```

```
    * @dev Function to invest
    */
   function invest() public {
       address investor = msg.sender;
       uint tokens = msg.value;

       mint(investor, tokens);
   }

   /**
    * @dev Modified play function with dividend
    * @param _hash Guessed number
    */
   function play(uint _hash) payable public {
       uint dividend = msg.value * (5/100);
       dividendAmount+= dividend;
       uint ticketValue = msg.value - dividend;

       //...
   }

   /**
    * @dev Function to get payout
    */
   function getPayout() {
       require(!payoutStatus[msg.sender]);

       uint percentage = balances[msg.sender] / totalSupply;
       uint dividend = dividendAmount * (percentage / 100);

       msg.sender.transfer(dividend);

       payoutStatus[msg.sender] = true;
   }
}
```

Affiliating programs to attract more users

Affiliate programs are one of the most widely used methods to attract more users. The program pays a person who helps bring in business. This can also be hardcoded into a smart contract to provide a referral bonus based on various factors.

In this recipe, you will learn how to create an affiliate program that rewards a person for bringing in new business. The referral bonus provided will be a percentage of the coins or tokens involved in the transaction. The logic stays as part of the smart contract to bring trust and transparency to the system.

Getting ready

You need to have a working installation of Ethereum (geth, Parity, ganache, and so on) or the Remix IDE to test this recipe. The contract inherits the investable lottery contract created in the previous recipe. It is recommended to step through that before continuing with this recipe.

The contracts given are for illustration purposes only and cannot be used in real-world systems. It is also recommended to use SafeMath for arithmetic operations.

How to do it...

1. Create a new affiliate contract that inherits the lottery contract created in the previous recipe:

```
pragma solidity^0.4.23;

import "./InvestableDAL.sol";

contract AffiliateDAL is InvestableDAL {
    //...
}
```

2. Create a mapping to store the amount earned by each person with the help of the affiliate program:

```
mapping(address => uint) affiliate;
```

3. Create a function that can be used by someone to claim their affiliate earnings:

```
function getAffiliatePay() public {
    //...
}
```

4. Transfer the amount to the address and empty the affiliate mapping for each payout:

```
uint amount = affiliate[msg.sender];
require(amount > 0);

msg.senser.transfer(amount);
affiliate[msg.sender] = 0;
```

5. Modify the `play` function to accept the affiliate address:

```
function play(uint _hash, address _affiliate)
    payable public {
    //...
}
```

6. Calculate the affiliate amount for each valid address:

```
uint ticketValue = msg.value;

if(_affiliate != address(0)) {
    uint affiliateAmount = msg.value * (1/100);
    affiliate[msg.sender] += affiliateAmount;
    ticketValue = msg.value - affiliateAmount;
}

//...
```

7. The final contract with affiliate functionality will look like this:

```
pragma solidity^0.4.23;

import "./InvestableDAL.sol";

contract AffiliateDAL is InvestableDAL {

    mapping(address => uint) affiliate;

    /**
     * @dev Function to get affiliate payout
     */
    function getAffiliatePay() public {
        uint amount = affiliate[msg.sender];
        require(amount > 0);

        msg.senser.transfer(amount);
        affiliate[msg.sender] = 0;
    }
```

```
/**
 * @dev Modified play function with affiliate
 * @param _hash Guessed number
 * @param _affiliate Address of the affiliate
 */
function play(uint _hash, address _affiliate) payable public {
    uint ticketValue = msg.value;

    if(_affiliate != address(0)) {
        uint affiliateAmount = msg.value * (1/100);
        affiliate[msg.sender] += affiliateAmount;
        ticketValue = msg.value - affiliateAmount;
    }

    //...
}
}
```

7
Advanced Solidity

In this chapter, we will cover the following recipes:

- Handling errors properly in solidity
- Abstract and interface contracts
- Managing contracts from other contracts
- Contract inheritance in solidity
- Creating libraries in solidity
- Mathematical and cryptographic functions in solidity
- Creating upgradable smart contracts
- Fetching data from APIs using solidity
- Function as a type in solidity
- Understanding solidity assembly
- Implementing multisig wallets in solidity

Introduction

We covered some fundamentals of writing smart contracts using solidity in `Chapter 2`, *Smart Contract Development*. There is a lot more to it and we will cover those advanced topics in this chapter.

Handling errors properly in solidity

Error handling is an essential part of every programming language. The general usage includes `try`, `catch`, and `throw` statements, but solidity uses `require`, `revert`, and `assert` methods to handle exceptions in the contract. Since Ethereum is a state machine, the exceptions that occur will revert all changes made to the state in the current call.

In this recipe, you will learn to handle exceptions using the `require`, `revert`, and `assert` methods.

Getting ready

You need to have a working Ethereum installation for deploying and testing the smart contract. You can also use the Remix IDE to write and test the solidity code.

How to do it...

Solidity provides the `require`, `revert`, and `assert` functions for handling exceptions and validations in smart contracts. Let's look into the usecase for each function and how they are handled by the solidity compiler.

require()

1. `require()` is a convenience function used to check conditions and throw an exception if a condition is not met.
2. Earlier versions of solidity (prior to *0.4.13*) used the `throw` pattern to revert the state during an exception. It is deprecated now and will be removed in a future version:

```
// Older and deprecated method
if (msg.sender != owner) {
    throw;
}
```

3. Use the `require()` method to ensure conditions such as inputs are valid, or to validate return values from calls to external contracts:

```
require(toAddress != address(0));
require(targetContract.send(amountInWei));
require(balances[msg.sender] >= amount);
```

4. Return an error message or a number corresponding to an error type using `require()`:

```
require(condition, "Error Message");
```

5. The function will refund the remaining gas to the caller if an exception occurs.
6. `require()` uses the `0xfd` opcode to cause an error condition. The `0xfd` opcode is currently (EIP-140) mapped to the REVERT instruction.

 Ethereum Improvement Proposal (**EIP**) 140 introduces a new opcode called REVERT. The proposal is to create a REVERT opcode that would throw an exception without draining all the gas that is allocated by the caller. You can get more information here: `https://github.com/ethereum/EIPs/issues/140`.

revert()

1. `revert()` works just like the `require()` function, but use it for more complex conditions:

```
if (msg.sender != owner) {
    revert();
}
```

2. `revert` also uses the `0xfd` opcode to raise exceptions, so it supports the return message and gas refund functionalities:

```
if (!condition) {
    revert("Error Message");
}
```

3. If you have complex nested `if-else` control flow statements, use the `revert()` method instead of the `require()` method.
4. Both `require` and `revert` functions should be used more often. They are generally used at the beginning of a function.

assert()

1. Use `assert()` to prevent something bad from happening:

```
assert(condition);
```

2. Use it to check conditions such as integer overflow/underflow:

```
pragma solidity ^0.4.24;

contract TestException {
    function add(uint _a, uint _b) returns (uint) {
        uint x = _a + _b;
        assert(x > _b);
        returns x;
    }
}
```

You should not use `assert()` blindly for checking overflow/underflow. It should be used only if you think that previous `require` or `if` checks would make it impossible.

3. Use it to check invariants in the contract. One example is to verify the contract balance against the total supply:

```
assert(address(this).balance >= totalSupply);
```

4. `assert` is commonly used to validate state after making changes. It helps in preventing conditions that should never be possible. In an ideal scenario, the contract should never reach a failing assert statement. If this happens, there is a bug in your contract that you should fix.

5. Generally, use `assert` towards the end of your function and use it less often.

6. `assert()` uses the `0xfe` opcode to cause an error condition if something fails.

7. The opcode will consume all available gas for the call and revert the state changes made before the exception.

Abstract and interface contracts

Solidity supports both interface and abstract contracts. This can help create base or layout contracts in solidity. In this recipe, you will learn to create the interface and abstract contracts.

Getting ready

You need to have a working Ethereum installation for deploying and testing the smart contract. You can also use the Remix IDE to write and test the solidity code.

It is required to have a basic knowledge of solidity to understand this recipe. Refer to `Chapter 2`, *Smart Contract Development*, for more information.

How to do it...

Interface and abstract contracts are mostly very similar, but they cannot have any functions implemented along with other differences. Let's look into each one in detail.

Abstract contracts

1. Create abstract contracts just like regular contracts, but they have at least one function without an implementation:

```
pragma solidity ^0.4.24;

contract AbstractContrct {
    // Function without declaration
    function f() public returns (uint);

    // Function with declaration
    function c() public returns (uint) {
        return 0;
    }
}
```

2. Abstracted contracts cannot be compiled. Use it as a base contract while inheriting. The inherited contracts will only compile if it implements all non-implemented functions by overriding:

```
pragma solidity ^0.4.24;

// Abstract contract
contract AbstractContrct {
    function f() public returns (uint);
}

// Contract with functions implemented
contract InheritedContract is AbstractContrct {
    function f() public returns (uint) {
        return 11;
    }
}
```

3. Use abstract contracts for decoupling the implementation from the definition of the contract. This provides better extensibility for the contract.

Interface contracts

1. Create an interface contract using the `interface` keyword:

```
interface InterfaceContract {
    // ...
}
```

2. Interface contracts are similar to abstract contracts, but they cannot have any implemented functions:

```
interface ERC20 {

    function transfer(
        address target,
        uint amount) public;

    function transferFrom(
        address source,
        address target,
        uint amount) public;


    ...
}
```

3. Interfaces cannot inherit other contracts or interfaces, but can be inherited by other contracts:

```
interface ERC20 {
    function transfer(address target, uint amount) public;
}

contract Token is ERC20 {
    function transfer(address target, uint amount) public {
        //...
    }
}
```

4. Interface contracts are limited to what the Contract ABI can represent. Use this to create a contract instance using its address:

```
interface ERC20 {
    function transfer(address target, uint amount) public;
}

contract Token {
    constructor(address _token) public {
        ERC20 token = ERC20(_token);
    }
}
```

5. Interface contracts cannot have `constructors`, `variables`, `structs`, or `enums` defined.

> The restrictions currently imposed on interface contracts might be lifted in future releases. It is recommended to use a target compiler version to avoid conflicts from any breaking changes.

Managing contracts from other contracts

Solidity allows communication between smart contracts deployed in the network. It allows both creation of new contracts and interaction with existing contracts. This opens the door for a lot of features as well as security vulnerabilities.

In this recipe, you will learn to manage contracts from other contracts.

Getting ready

You need to have a working Ethereum installation for deploying and testing the smart contract. You can also use the Remix IDE to write and test the solidity code.

It is required to have a basic knowledge of solidity to understand this recipe. Go through Chapter 2, *Smart Contract Development,* for more information.

How to do it...

1. Solidity allows creating contracts from other contracts. This can be done during function execution or while deploying the parent contract.
2. The source code of the newly deploying contract has to be known in advance. This helps in avoiding recursive creation dependencies.
3. Use the new keyword for creating contracts from other contracts:

```
pragma solidity ^0.4.23;

contract Storage {
    ...
}

contract Parent {
    // Creation of new contract
    Address storeAddress = new Storage();
    ...
}
```

4. Creating a new contract will return the address of the newly deployed contract. Convert it into an object of the contract type to access the functions directly:

```
Storage store = new Storage();
```

5. Use this object for interacting with the newly deployed contract. All public functions and state variables can be accessed through this:

```
pragma solidity ^0.4.23;

contract Storage {

    uint public num;

    function changeNum(uint _num) public {
        num = _num;
```

```
        }
    }

    contract Parent {

        Storage store = new Storage();

        function interact() public {
            store.changeNum(10);
        }

    }
```

6. Pass `constructor` **parameters, if any, along with the contract creation process:**

```
    pragma solidity ^0.4.23;

    contract Storage {

        uint public num;

        constructor(uint _num) public {
            num = _num;
        }
    }

    contract Parent {

        Storage store = new Storage(10);

    }
```

7. Try forwarding Ether while creating contracts with the `new` keyword. Limiting the gas usage is not yet supported:

```
    pragma solidity ^0.4.23;

    contract Storage {

        uint public num;

        constructor(uint _num) payable public {
            num = _num;
        }
    }

    contract Parent {
```

```
        function createStore() public payable {
            Storage store = (new Storage).value(msg.value)(10);
        }
    }
```

8. An exception is thrown if the contract creation fails for some reason.

9. Apart from creating new contracts, solidity allows interaction with existing contracts as well. Create an object of the contract using the deployed address:

```
pragma solidity ^0.4.23;

contract Storage {

    uint public num;

    constructor(uint _num) payable public {
        num = _num;
    }
}

contract Parent {

    Storage store;

    function changeStore(address _storeAddress) public payable {
        store = Storage(_storeAddress);
    }
}
```

10. This can be further simplified by accepting the address as a contract in the parameter. This avoids the need for explicit conversion:

```
pragma solidity ^0.4.23;

contract Storage {

    uint public num;

    constructor(uint _num) payable public {
        num = _num;
    }
}

contract Parent {

    Storage store;

    function changeStore(Storage _store) public payable {
```

```
        store = _store;
    }
}
```

11. Call the functions from external contracts with the help of the `call` or `delegatecall` methods included as part of the contract object.

12. The `call` function executes the code of another contract. Use this method to change the state of another contract.

13. Use it by specifying the function signature as the first parameter, followed by arguments to the function:

```
<address>.call(<function_signature>, parameters...);
```

14. While using this function, modify the gas and value according to your needs. This can be done using the `value()` and `gas()` subfunctions:

```
pragma solidity ^0.4.23;

contract Storage {

    uint public num;

    function changeValue(uint _num) payable public {
        num = _num;
    }
}

contract Parent {

    function changeStoreValue(address _store, uint _value)
        public payable {
        _store.call
            .gas(100000)
            .value(1 ether)
            (bytes4(keccak256("changeValue(uint256)")), _value);
    }
}
```

15. Use the `delegatecall` function to modify the state of the current contract with the code of the calling contract.

16. Use it just like the `call` function, and the options to specify gas and value are also present:

```solidity
pragma solidity ^0.4.23;

contract Storage {

    uint public num;

    function changeValue(uint _num) payable public {
        num = _num;
    }
}

contract Parent {
    uint public num;

    function changeStoreValue(address _store, uint _value)
        public payable {
        _store.delegatecall
            .gas(100000)
            (bytes4(keccak256("changeValue(uint256)")), _value);
    }
}
```

17. The `callcode` method was an older implementation of `delegatecall`. It does not preserve information such as `msg.owner` and `msg.value`. This function is deprecated and will be removed soon.

The `low-level` call and `delegatecall` calls will return false if an exception occurs. While using these methods, it is recommended to verify the return type of the call to ensure that no exception has occurred.

There's more...

External contract calls to untrusted contracts can be very harmful. With a method like `delegatecall`, the target contract can modify any state variable and even steal all your money. It is not at all recommended to use a third-party contract that is not trustworthy.

Furthermore, a malicious external contract can throw an exception every time. This will cause the condition in the calling contract to fail. This can lead to some sort of denial-of-service attack and even make your contract permanently useless.

Contract inheritance in solidity

Smart contracts can be inherited to extend the functionality. Solidity also supports multiple inheritance and polymorphism. We will look into each of them in detail with this recipe.

Getting ready

You need to have a working Ethereum installation for deploying and testing the smart contract. You can also use the Remix IDE to write and test the solidity code.

It is required to have a basic knowledge of solidity to understand this recipe. Go through Chapter 2, *Smart Contract Development*, for more information.

How to do it...

1. Inherit contracts using the `is` keyword. The parent contract has to be imported or copied to the same file before inheriting:

```
contract A {
    ...
}

contract B is A {
    ...
}
```

2. When a contract inherits from multiple contracts, only a single contract is created in the blockchain. The other code from all the base contracts is copied into the created contract.

3. In inheritance, the `final` function will be invoked while calling it by name. Call the functions in the parent contract by explicitly specifying their names:

```
pragma solidity ^0.4.23;

contract A {
```

```
    uint public value;

    function changeValue() public {
        value = 1;
    }
}

contract B is A {

    function changeValue() public {
        value = 2;
    }
}
```

4. Access the functions from the base contract using the `super` keyword:

```
pragma solidity ^0.4.23;

/**
 * First parent contract
 */
contract A {

    uint public value;

    function changeValue() public {
        value = 1;
    }
}

/**
 * Second parent contract
 */
contract B {

    uint public value;

    function changeValue() public {
        value = 2;
    }
}

/**
 * Contract which inherits 2 base contracts
 */
contract C is A, B {

    function changeValue() public {
```

```
                value = 3;
                super.changeValue();
            }
    }
```

5. Specify the constructor parameters of the base contract during inheritance or by using the constructor of the inheriting contract. It is recommended to use the first way if the constructor argument is a constant value. The second way has to be used if the constructor arguments of the parent depend on those inputs of the derived contract. If both methods are used simultaneously, the second way takes precedence:

```
pragma solidity ^0.4.23;

/**
 * Parent contract
 */
contract A {
    uint public value;
    constructor(uint _value) public {
        value = _value;
    }
}

/**
 * Constructor parameter is specified during inheritance
 */
contract B is A(1) {
    constructor() public {
        // ...
    }
}

/**
 * Constructor parameter is specified in the constructor
 */
contract C is A {
    constructor() A(10) public {
        // ...
    }
}
```

6. The inheritance order in which the base classes are given is important. It helps in avoiding the *diamond problem*. It is recommended to inherit in the order of most basic to most derived.

The *diamond problem* is an ambiguity that arises when two contracts, *B* and *C*, inherit from *A* and override a method. Contract *D* inherits from both *B* and *C*, and *D* does not override it. So, which version of the method does *D* inherit, *B* or *C*?

Creating libraries in solidity

A library in solidity is a singleton that is deployed once and can be called from any contract. A library in solidity does not have storage and cannot hold Ether. This helps a lot in avoiding duplicate code in the Ethereum blockchain (saves a lot of gas by not deploying the same code again).

In this recipe, you will learn to create, deploy, and interact with libraries using solidity.

Getting ready

You need to have a working Ethereum installation for deploying and testing the smart contract. You can also use the Remix IDE to write and test solidity code.

It is required to have a basic knowledge of solidity to understand this recipe. Go through Chapter 2, *Smart Contract Development*, for more information.

How to do it...

1. Create a library in the same way a contract is defined, but with the `library` keyword:

```
libary libName {
    //....
}
```

2. Consider the following differences while creating a library contract:

   - Libraries cannot have any state variables
   - Libraries cannot inherit nor be inherited
   - Libraries cannot have a fallback or payable functions to receive Ether

3. Invoke the `library` functions like invoking external contract calls:

```
<library>.<function>();
```

4. Calling a function in the library will use the `delegatecall` instruction. This allows the code to execute in the context of the caller:

```
library lib {
    function getBal() returns (uint) {
        return address(this).balance;
    }
}

contract Sample {
    function getBalance() returns (uint) {
        return lib.getBal();
    }

    function() payable {}
}
```

5. Consider the following example, which illustrates the use of the `library` in a contract:

```
pragma solidity ^0.4.23;

/**
 * Calc library for addition and subtraction
 * This library is for illustration purpose only.
 * Do not use it in any contracts.
 */
library calc {

    /**
     * @dev Function to add two numbers
     * @param a first uint to add
     * @param b second uint to add
     */
    function add(uint a, uint b) public
        returns (uint) {
        return a + b;
    }

    /**
     * @dev Function to find difference between two numbers
     * @param a uint value to subtract from
     * @param b uint value to subtract
     */
```

```
        function sub(uint a, uint b) public
            returns (uint) {
            return a - b;
        }
    }

    /**
     * Contract which uses the calc library
     */
    contract Sample {

        /**
         * @dev Function to test addition
         * @return Boolean to denote success/failure
         */
        function testAdd() public returns (bool) {
            uint result = calc.add(5, 1);
            return (result == 5 + 1);
        }

        /**
         * @dev Function to test subtraction
         * @return Boolean to denote success/failure
         */
        function testSub() public returns (bool) {
            uint result = calc.sub(5, 1);
            return (result == 5 - 1);
        }
    }
```

6. Attach the `library` to a specific data type using the `using-for` directive:

```
library Lib {
    // ...
}

contract A {
    // Lib is the library and B is the type
    using Lib for B;
    // ...
}
```

7. The functions in the library will receive the object they are called on as the first parameter:

```
uint a = 10;
uint b = 5;
a.add(b); // equivalent to add(a,b);
```

8. To apply the library to all data types, assign it to *:

```
using Lib for *;
```

9. Modify the library used in step 5 to use `using-for`. A few extra lines are added to check integer over/underflow:

```
pragma solidity ^0.4.23;

/**
 * Calc library for addition and subtraction
 * This library is for illustration purpose only.
 * Do not use it in any contracts.
 */
library calc {

    /**
     * @dev Function to add two numbers
     * @param a first uint to add
     * @param b second uint to add
     */
    function add(uint a, uint b) public
        returns (uint c) {
        c = a + b;
        assert(c >= a);
        return c;
    }

    /**
     * @dev Function to find difference between two numbers
     * @param a uint value to subtract from
     * @param b uint value to subtract
     */
    function sub(uint a, uint b) public
        returns (uint) {
        assert(b <= a);
        return a - b;
    }
}

/**
 * Contract which uses the calc library
 */
contract Sample {
    using calc for uint;

    /**
     * @dev Function to test addition
```

```
        * @return Boolean to denote success/failure
        */
       function testAdd() public returns (bool) {
           return (uint(5).add(1) == 5 + 1);
       }

      /**
       * @dev Function to test subtraction
       * @return Boolean to denote success/failure
       */
       function testSub() public returns (bool) {
           return (uint(5).sub(1) == 5 - 1);
       }
   }
```

How it works...

Libraries are commonly used for code reusability. They are similar to contracts and the functions in a library are invoked using `delegatecall`. This allows the code to run from the caller's context and storage. Library functions can also be called directly if they do not modify the state.

Calls to library functions act like calls to an external contract (`delegatecall`). This is true for all cases except for library functions marked as internal. These functions are invoked with the internal calling convention (`JUMP`) in EVM.

There's more...

While compiling the contracts, the solidity compiler includes placeholders in the bytecode to add the location of libraries used. The placeholders are in the form of 40-byte substrings (`__LibraryName__`) including the name of the library. The address can be included by replacing those 40 symbols with the hex encoding of the address of the library contract.

The `solc` compiler provides an option to link the hex encoding during compile time. This can be done with the help of the `--libraries` attribute while compiling.

The input to the `--libraries` attribute can be a string:

```
--libraries "SafeMath:0x.. StringUtils:0x..."
```

Or it can be a file that includes each library and address as a separate line:

```
--libraries <filename>
```

Mathematical and cryptographic functions in solidity

Solidity provides a few inbuilt functions for performing mathematical and cryptographic operations. These functions can be used for a variety of tasks, including hash calculation and public key retrieval.

In this recipe, you will learn to use some of the common functions in solidity for performing mathematical and cryptographic tasks.

Getting ready

You need to have a working Ethereum installation for deploying and testing the smart contract. You can also use the Remix IDE to write and test solidity code.

It is required to have a basic knowledge of solidity to understand this recipe. Go through Chapter 2, *Smart Contract Development*, for more information.

How to do it...

1. To calculate the SHA-3 (keccak-256) hash of something, use the keccak256/sha3 function:

```
keccak256(...)
// OR
sha3(...) // alias to keccak256
```

2. The function returns the hash in bytes32 format:

```
keccak256(...) returns (bytes32);
```

3. Since the arguments to this functions are concatenated without padding, use any of the following input formats to yield the same value:

```
keccak256("hello", "world")
keccak256("helloworld")
keccak256(0x68656c6c6f776f726c64)
keccak256(68656c6c6f776f726c64)
```

4. Use solidity's `sha3` function to calculate the SHA-256 hash of the input. It works just like the `keccak256` function:

```
sha256(...) returns (bytes32);
```

5. Use the `ecrecover` function to verify the address associated with a public key. The function accepts a signed hash message along with v, r, and s values to calculate the address. For invalid inputs, it returns a *0*:

```
ecrecover(bytes32 hash, uint8 v, bytes32 r, bytes32 s) returns
(address);
```

6. Try running it in real time using a contract. Consider the following contract, which returns the address from the signed message:

```
pragma solidity ^0.4.23;

contract VerificationContract {
    function verifyAddress(
        bytes32 h,
        uint8 v,
        bytes32 r,
        bytes32 s) public pure returns (address) {
        return ecrecover(h, v, r, s);
    }
}
```

7. Let's test this function with an input message and address. First, create a hash from the input message using `web3JS`:

```
var message = "Hello World!";
var prefix = "\x19Ethereum Signed Message:\n";
var hash = web3.utils.sha3(prefix + message.length + message);
```

8. Sign the message using the address:

```
var address = "0x...";
var signature = await web3.eth.sign(message, address);
```

9. Calculate the v, r, and s values from the signed signature:

```
var r = signature.slice(0, 66);
var s = '0x' + signature.slice(66, 130);
var v = '0x' + web3.toDecimal(signature.slice(130, 132));
```

10. Pass the generated values to verify the address:

```
var result =
    await VerificationContract.verifyAddress
        .call(hash, v, r, s);
```

11. The returned result should be equal to the address used in step 8.
12. Apart from `keccak` and `SHA`, solidity can calculate ripemod-160 hashes as well:

```
ripemd160(...) returns (bytes20);
```

13. Solidity provides functions to calculate modulo operations on values that do not wrap around the `uint256` data type. This works for calculating modulus operations after addition or multiplication.

14. To compute *(a + b) % x; where x != 0*, use the solidity function called `addmod`:

```
addmod(uint x, uint y, uint k) returns (uint);
```

15. To compute *(a * b) % x; where x != 0*, use the solidity function called `mulmod`:

```
mulmod(uint x, uint y, uint k) returns (uint);
```

Cryptographic functions such as `sha256`, `ecrecover`, and `ripemd160` are a type of precompiled contract and they exist only after the first transaction to it. If you are using a private network, calling these nonexistent contracts can result in an out-of-gas error. Making some kind of transaction (such as sending some wei) can solve this issue in a private network. The main or test network already has these contracts in a working state and it doesn't require such a transaction.

There's more...

Apart from the inbuilt functions for cryptographic and mathematical operations, solidity provides ABI encoding functions as well. This helps in generating function signatures without actually calling these functions. The supported operations are given here:

- `abi.encode(...)`: To ABI-encode the given parameters

- `abi.encodePacked(...)`: For packed encoding of the given parameters

- `abi.encodeWithSelector(bytes4 selector, ...)`: To encode the given parameters, starting from the second, and prepend the given four-byte selector

- `abi.encodeWithSignature(string signature, ...)`: Similar to `encodeWithSelector`, but accepts the signature as first parameter

Creating upgradable smart contracts

Once a smart contract is deployed in the Ethereum network, its code cannot be changed at any point. State values can be modified if this was allowed in the original code. This brings the great advantage of immutability and trust, but with a cost. The addition of a new feature, or even a bug fix, cannot be performed due to the design of Ethereum.

In this recipe, we will focus on designing and creating upgradable smart contracts that can help maintain the application better.

Getting ready...

You need to have a working Ethereum installation for deploying and testing the smart contract. You can also use the Remix IDE to write and test the Solidity code.

It is required to have good knowledge of solidity before stepping through this recipe. Go through Chapter 2, *Smart Contract Development*, for more information.

How to do it...

1. Making a contract upgradable can be achieved through multiple methods. One of the popular implementations is to use a proxy contract that keeps track of the logic contract. The proxy will redirect calls to the latest contract that has the upgraded code.
2. To create a basic upgradable smart contract system, we will need three basic contracts. They are the following:

- Storage contract
- Proxy contract
- Logic contract

3. Use the logic contract to write the upgradable piece of code and the storage to keep track of all contract states. The proxy uses the latest code from the logic contract to update the state of the storage contract.

4. To keep things simple and easy to understand, consider a storage contract that has one state variable:

```
pragma solidity^0.4.24;

/**
 * Basic storage contract
 */
contract State {
    uint public result;
}
```

5. Create a simple logic contract that modifies the value of the state variable, for example, a contract that adds 1 to the current value of the state variable. Create the local variable in the logic contract with the same type and name:

```
pragma solidity^0.4.24;

/**
 * Basic logic contract
 * Increments the state variable value by 1
 */
contract AddOne {

    uint result;

    function increment() public {
        result = result + 1;
    }
}
```

6. Here comes the interesting part: the proxy contract. Create a simple contract that inherits the storage contract:

```
pragma solidity^0.4.24;

contract Proxy is State {
    ...
}
```

7. Add a state variable to store the address of the logic contract and a function to modify the value. This is the function that basically acts as the upgrade mechanism:

```
address logicContract;

function upgrade(address _newLogicContract) public {
    logicContract = _newLogicContract;
}
```

8. Handle the redirection using the `fallback` function inside the proxy contract. Use the low-level `delegatecall` method to invoke the logic.

9. The `delegatecall` method accepts a specific function signature and parameters to call the function. In the proxy contract, obtain these details from `calldata`.

10. Since the `delegatecall` method is used, the logic contract will run in the calling contract's context and storage. This helps in modifying the state of the calling contract with the logic written in the target contract.

11. The following contract shows the complete code of the proxy contract used in this example:

```
pragma solidity^0.4.24;

/**
 * Proxy contract which handles state and logic
 * Includes the ability to update the logic
 */
contract Proxy is State {
    address logicContract;

    /**
     * @dev Function to change the logic contract
     * @param _newLogicContract address of new logic contract
     */
    function changeLogic(address _newLogicContract) public {
        logicContract = _newLogicContract;
    }

    /**
     * @dev Fallback function to redirect calls
     */
    function fallback() public {
        require(logicContract.delegatecall(msg.data));
    }
}
```

12. To test this contract, deploy the proxy and logic contracts independently and use the `changeLogic` function in the proxy contract to update the `logicContract` address:

```
proxyContract.changeLogic(<logic_contract_address>);
```

13. Once the logic contract is updated, call the proxy contract with the function signature of the logic contract. In this case, that will be the first four bytes of the `keccak256` hash of the function name:

```
proxyContract.sendTransaction({
    input: <function_signature>
    ...
});
```

Function signatures are calculated from the first four bytes of the `keccak256` hash of a function. For example, to call the `increment` function, the signature can be calculated in solidity with `bytes4(keccak256("increment()"))`.

14. Since there is no function in the proxy contract that matches the `increment` function, the `fallback` function will be called. As per our `fallback` function logic, it will use the `msg.data` value to forward the call to the logic contract.

15. Assume that we need to modify the function to increment by 2 when called. To do this, deploy the same logic contract with modified logic:

```
/**
 * Logic contract
 * Increments the state variable value by 2
 */
contract AddTwo {

    uint result;

    /**
     * @dev
     */
    function increment() public {
        result = result + 2;
    }
}
```

16. Update the address of the logic in the proxy contract. This will start executing the new contract for subsequent calls.

17. This simple contract can be expanded to do more complex tasks. For example, we can create an interface for the logic contract to follow a certain standard, or add a versioning system on top of the proxy contract. This can vary based on the use case and requirements.

How it works...

The architecture of the upgradable contract discussed in this recipe can be explained as follows. A proxy contract keeps track of a logic contract that can be upgraded and requires states. When a transaction is submitted, the proxy uses the updated logic contract for any logic execution and stores the result in the state contract, as illustrated in the following diagram:

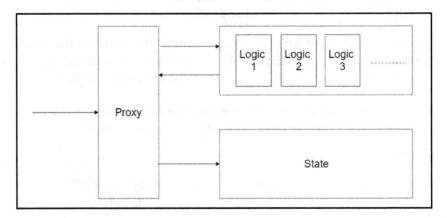

The design explained in this recipe can be considered as a basic example of how you can write upgradable smart contracts in Ethereum. The idea is to use proxy contracts to redirect transactions to the latest version of the code. You can modify the design based on your requirements.

The additional features explained in this recipe come with the cost of trust issues for users. Users can avoid such trust issues up to a certain point by verifying the contracts before actually using them. Using a more complex smart contract can also increase the overall gas cost involved for maintenance and usage. But, this can again be considered as a trade-off for upgradability.

Fetching data from APIs using solidity

Ethereum virtual machine (**EVM**), by design, cannot read data from the outside world. This restricts achieving certain functionalities in Ethereum blockchain. Since every node runs every calculation, it's not efficient to make arbitrary network requests from an Ethereum contract.

We can overcome this limitation with the help of oracles. These allow a smart contract to read data from an external source in an intelligent way. In this recipe, you will learn to create an Oracle service and read data from an external API.

Getting ready

You need to have a working Ethereum installation for deploying and testing the smart contract. You can also use the Remix IDE to write and test the solidity code.

It is required to have good knowledge of solidity before stepping through this recipe. Go through `Chapter 2`, *Smart Contract Development*, for more information.

How to do it...

1. Solidity does not allow you to pull data from an external API source. Use an Oracle service to achieve this functionality.
2. An oracle is an event listener that listens and responds to them by sending the results of a query back to the contract. In this way, contracts can interact with the external world.
3. As an example, assume that we have a smart contract that uses an external data service to select a random number. Let's see how we can implement it using a custom Oracle service.
4. Create a basic smart contract with a state variable to store the random number:

```
pragma solidity ^0.4.24;

contract OracleRng {
    uint public random;
    ...
}
```

5. The Oracle service listens to the event logged in the contract and then uses the log details to query data in blockchain. Create an event for the service to watch and another event to log the random number generated:

```
event LogOracle();
event LogNewRandom(uint random);
```

6. Create a function that acts as the Oracle calling method. This function will emit the Oracle triggering event:

```
function setRandom() public {
    emit LogOracle();
}
```

7. Finally, there should also be a `callback` function that will be called by the Oracle service to update the value:

```
function _callback(uint _random) public {
    random = _random;
    emit LogNewRandom(_random);
}
```

8. This is a very basic Oracle contract, which can read from external sources:

```
pragma solidity ^0.4.24;

/**
 * Random number generator contract
 * using oracles
 */
contract OracleRng {

    uint public random;

    event LogOracle();
    event LogNewRandom(uint random);

    /**
     * Function to emit the oracle event
     */
    function setRandom() public {
        emit LogOracle();
    }

    /**
     * Function called by the oracle service
     * @param _random Random value returned by the oracle
     */
```

```
function _callback(uint _random) public {
    random = _random;
    emit LogNewRandom(_random);
}
}
```

9. When the user calls the `setRandom` function, it initiates the whole Oracle service flow. There should be a service worker who listens and responds according to the events raised.

10. Create an event listener that listens to this event and queries the external world for data:

```
var oracle = oracleRng.setRandom();

// watch for logs
oracle.watch(function(error, result){
    ...
});
```

11. Once an event is fired, use some logic or an external API to create a random number:

```
// Use some logic or external API call to generate the number.
var random = 1232;
```

12. Call the source contract back to update the state with the generated random value:

```
oracleRng._callback(random, {
    from: "0x.."
});
```

13. This is how a basic Oracle service works. This service can be part of an existing application or can run as an external Oracle service to provide necessary data to the contract:

```
var oracle = oracleRng.setRandom();

// watch for logs
oracle.watch(function(error, result) {
    // Make API calls to generate random number
    var random = 1232;
    // Callback into source contract
    oracleRng._callback(random, {
        from: "0x.."
    });
});
```

How it works...

Since contracts don't have the ability to interact with the outside world directly, you can make use of the Oracle implementation to achieve this functionality. A simple Oracle server will listen to specific events occurring in the smart contract and will make API calls based on the parameters. The server will respond by making a callback transaction with the result of the API call.

The design can be illustrated as follows:

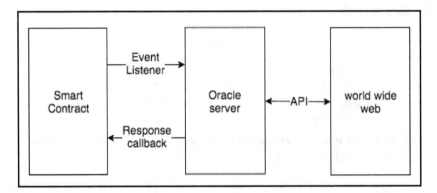

There's more...

The Oracle contract can be further modified to include more features. From a security perspective, we can use a modifier to accept callbacks only from trusted oracles:

```solidity
pragma solidity ^0.4.24;

contract OracleRng {

    // Address of trusted oracle
    address trustedOracle;

    // Modifier to restrict oracle calls
    modifier onlyTrustedOracle() {
        require(msg.sender == trustedOracle);
        _;
    }

    // Function to change trusted oracle
    function setTrustedOracle(address _oracle) {
        trustedOracle = _oracle;
```

```
    }

    function _callback(uint _random) public
        onlyTrustedOracle {
        //...
    }
}
```

Function as a type in solidity

In a statically typed language such as solidity, the type of each variable needs to be specified at compile time. To support this, solidity provides both inbuilt data types and user-defined data types. These elementary types include `integer`, `Boolean`, `mapping`, `struct`, and so on. Apart from these types, solidity allows defining functions a type. This helps to add several features such as invoking a dynamic `callback` function after a certain task.

In this recipe, you will learn to create and use functions as a type in solidity.

Getting ready

You need to have a working Ethereum installation for deploying and testing the smart contract. You can also use the Remix IDE to write and test the solidity code.

It is required to have good knowledge of solidity before stepping through this recipe. Go through `Chapter 2`, *Smart Contract Development*, for more information.

How to do it...

1. Define function types as either internal or external functions. These types can be used as a parameter while calling a function or while returning from a function:

```
function function_name(<function_type_parameters>)
    <internal | external>
    <pure | view | payable>
    returns (<function_return_types>) {
    // ...
}
```

Internal functions can only be called inside the current contract. External functions can be passed via, and returned from, external function calls. It consists of an address and a function signature.

2. Create a function that accepts a `uint` and a function type. Let's call the `uint` num and the function type `fun`. For this example, make the function type accept a `uint` and return a `uint`:

```
function calculate (
    uint num, // uint type
    function (uint) pure returns (uint) fun // function type
    ) { ... }
```

3. Use the received function type to calculate the result and return it:

```
function calculate (
    uint num,
    function (uint) pure returns (uint) fun
    ) internal pure returns (uint r) {
    r = fun(num);
}
```

4. Create another function that can be passed as a parameter. It should accept a parameter and return a value based on that:

```
function square(uint x)
    internal pure returns (uint) {
    return x * x;
}
```

5. This function can be used as a parameter to the `calculate` function. Let's write another function that invokes the operation:

```
pragma solidity ^0.4.16;

/**
 * Contract which uses function as a type
 */
contract Sample {
    function calc(uint num)
        public pure returns (uint) {
        return calculate(num, square);
    }

    function square(uint x)
        internal pure returns (uint) {
```

```
        return x * x;
    }

    function calculate(
        uint self,
        function (uint) pure returns (uint) f)
        internal pure returns (uint r) {
        r = f(self);
    }
}
```

Understanding solidity assembly

Ethereum supports an assembly language that can be used to gain fine-grained control over the EVM. This allows access to the EVM at a low level. This discards several important safety features of solidity. Assembly language can be either written inside solidity source code (inline assembly) or can also work as a standalone code (standalone assembly).

In this recipe, you will learn to write assembly-level code for accessing the EVM at a low level.

Getting ready

You need to have a working Ethereum installation for deploying and testing the smart contract. You can also use the Remix IDE to write and test the Solidity code.

It is required to have good knowledge of Solidity before stepping through this recipe. Go through Chapter 2, *Smart Contract Development*, for more information.

How to do it...

1. To write the assembly inline, use the assembly keyword:

```
assembly {
    // assembly code
}
```

2. Create local variables in the assembly by using the `let` keyword. For variables without any assignment, the default value will be assigned:

```
let x
let y := 2
```

3. Access the variables that are defined outside the assembly directly:

```
function f(uint x) public {
    assembly {
        x := sub(x, 1)
    }
}
```

 Assigning values to variables that point to memory or storage work differently inside solidity assembly. The assignment will only change the pointer and not the data.

4. Create a `for` loop in the assembly just like a regular loop:

```
assembly {
    for { let i := 0 } lt(i, 10) { i := add(i, 1) } {
        y := add(y, 1)
    }
}
```

5. Use the `if` statement to validate conditions inside the assembly. There is no `else` condition so use the `switch` statement for multiple conditions:

```
assembly {
    if lt(x, 0) {
        x := add(x, 1)
    }
}
```

6. Use the `switch` statement for executing statements based on conditions:

```
assembly {
    switch x
        case 0 {
            y := add(x, 1)
        }
        case 1 {
            y := add(x, 2)
        }
        default {
```

```
                    y := 0
            }
    }
```

7. Make function calls in the assembly just like you do with the normal function call:

```
assembly {
    function power(x, y) -> result {
        switch y
            case 0 {
                result := 1
            }
            case 1 {
                result := x
            }
            default {
                result := power(mul(x, x), div(y, 2))
                switch mod(y, 2)
                    case 1 {
                        result := mul(x, result)
                    }
            }
    }
}
```

8. Try using functional-style opcodes inside the assembly:

```
assembly {
    let x := add(1, 2)
    let y := mul(x, 3)
}
```

9. Some of the supported functional opcodes are listed here. The complete list is available in the Ethereum yellow paper:

- `stop`: stop execution
- `add(x,y)`, `sub(x,y)`, `mul(x,y)`, `div(x,y)`: Arithmetic operations
- `mod(x,y)`: x % y
- `exp(x,y)`: x to the power of y
- `not(x)`: Negation of x
- `lt(x,y)`, `gt(x,y)`: Less than or greater than; 1 for true and 0 for false
- `eq(x,y)`: 1 for true and 0 for false
- `and(x,y)`, `or(x,y)`, `xor(x,y)`: Bitwise AND, OR, XOR

- `shl(x,y)`, `shr(x,y)`: Logical shift left/right y by x bits
- `jump(label)`: Jump to label/code position
- `pc`: Current position in code
- `pop(x)`: Remove the element pushed by x
- `dup1...dup16`: Copy the ith stack slot to the top
- `swap1...swap16`: Swap the topmost and ith stack slot below it
- `mload(p)`: mem[p..(p+32)]
- `mstore(p,v)`: mem[p..(p+32)] := v
- `sload(p)`: storage[p]
- `sstore(p,v)`: storage[p] := v
- `msize`: Size of memory
- `gas`: Gas left for execution
- `address`: Address of the current contract
- `balance(a)`: Balance in wei at address a
- `caller`: Transaction/call sender
- `callvalue`: Value sent with the call
- `calldatasize`: Size of the calldata in bytes
- `call, callcode, delegatecall, staticall`: Call contract at given address
- `log0...log4`: Log with topics and data
- `timestamp`: Timestamp of the current block in seconds since the epoch

10. Try using the instruction style opcodes inside the assembly. The opcodes can be listed in the same way as they will end up in the bytecode. The following example adds *10* to the contents in memory at position *0x80*:

    ```
    10 0x80 mload add 0x80 mstore
    ```

11. Functional and instructional style expressions cannot be mixed together. They have to be written in either functional or instructional style:

    ```
    mstore(0x80, add(mload(0x80), 10))
    ```

    The order of arguments is in reverse order when comparing functional style and instruction style expressions. While using functional style expressions, the first argument will end up on the top of the stack.

12. The assembly language described so far in this recipe can also be used as standalone assembly code.

13. The assembly code can be used to achieve functionalities that are not possible with plain solidity. One good example is to check whether an address belongs to a contract or is owned externally:

```
pragma solidity ^0.4.24;

/**
 * Library contract with assembly code
 */
library AddressValidator {

    /**
     * Function to verify contract address
     * @param _address Address to verify
     * @returns isContract Returs verification result
     */
    function _isContract(address _address) public
        returns (bool isContract) {

        // Variable to store the code size
        uint codeSize;

        assembly {
            codeSize := extcodesize(_address)
        }

        isContract = codeSize > 0;
    }
}
```

There's more...

Yul (previously JULIA) is a new language that can be used for writing inline assembly code. This is an intermediate language that can compile to various backends, such as EVM and eWASM (upcoming). The components of Yul include functions, blocks, variables, literals, for loops, if and switch statements, and assignments.

Here's the power function explained in step 7, rewritten in the Yul language:

```
function power2(x:u256, y:u256) -> result:u256
{
    switch y
    case 0:u256 { result := 1:u256 }
    case 1:u256 { result := x }
    default:
    {
```

```
        result := power(mul(x, x), div(y, 2:u256))
        switch mod(y, 2:u256)
            case 1:u256 { result := mul(x, result) }
    }
}
```

The supported data types in Yul are `bool`, `u8`, `s8`, `u32`, `s32`, `u64`, `s64`, `u128`, `s128`, `u256`, and `s256`. Also, Yul does not provide any operators. It makes use of the opcodes as built-in functions to achieve the same result. Each of the backends can expose functions prefixed with the name of the backend. The prefixes `evm_` and `ewasm_` are reserved for the two proposed backends. These functionalities can be reimplemented if the backend changes under any circumstances.

Implementing multisig wallets in solidity

A multisig wallet is a smart contract that lives in the Ethereum blockchain. This wallet defines a set of rules to manage and transfer funds and requires approval from more than one participant before each action. This reduces risk if one person is incapacitated or loses their keys.

In this recipe, you will learn to create a basic multisig wallet and perform transactions using it.

Getting ready

The wallet is built on Ethereum and uses solidity as the language. You need to have a working installation of Ethereum for deploying and testing the code. You also need to have good knowledge of writing smart contracts to understand the solidity code explained in this recipe.

How to do it...

Every multisig wallet should have the following basic components:

- A list of addresses who have permission to do something
- A set of rules for approval
- An option to receive Ether
- Ways to submit/approve a request

1. Create a contract that can act as the `Multisig` wallet. Create a mapping to store the approver list:

```solidity
pragma solidity^0.4.24;

contract MultiSig {
    // Mapping to save the ownership status
    mapping (address => bool) public isOwner;
    // Owners array
    address[] public owners;

    // Returns list of owners.
    function getOwners() public view returns (address[]) {
        return owners;
    }

    // Modifier to restrict access
    modifier onlyOwner(address owner) {
        require(isOwner[owner]);
        _;
    }
}
```

2. Use a state variable to store the number of approvals needed before doing a transaction:

```solidity
uint public required;
```

3. Use the `constructor` to set the owner and approval details:

```solidity
constructor(address[] _owners, uint _required) public {
    for (uint i = 0; i < _owners.length; i++) {
        require(!(isOwner[_owners[i]] || _owners[i] == 0));
        isOwner[_owners[i]] = true;
    }
    owners = _owners;
    required = _required;
}
```

4. Create a transaction struct that will hold the submitted transactions:

```solidity
struct Transaction {
    address destination;
    uint value;
    bytes data;
    bool executed;
}
```

```
mapping (uint => Transaction) public transactions;
// Stores the confirmations from each address
mapping (uint => mapping (address => bool)) public confirmations;
// Total transaction count for calculating id
uint public transactionCount;
```

5. Create a function to add the transaction to the list:

```
function addTransaction(
    address destination,
    uint value,
    bytes data)
    internal returns (uint transactionId)
{
    transactionId = transactionCount;
    transactions[transactionId] = Transaction({
        destination: destination,
        value: value,
        data: data,
        executed: false
    });
    transactionCount += 1;
    emit Submission(transactionId);
}
```

6. Write a function to check whether the required number or confirmations is obtained:

```
function isConfirmed(uint transactionId)
    public constant returns (bool)
{
    uint count = 0;
    for (uint i=0; i<owners.length; i++) {
        if (confirmations[transactionId][owners[i]])
            count += 1;
        if (count == required)
            return true;
    }
}
```

7. Once enough confirmations are received, process the transaction using the executeTransaction function:

```
function executeTransaction(uint transactionId) public {
    if(isConfirmed(transactionId)) {
        Transaction storage trnx = transactions[transactionId];
        if (trnx.destination.call.value(trnx.value)(trnx.data)) {
            trnx.executed = true;
```

```
                    emit Execution(transactionId);
            }
        }
    }
```

8. To obtain confirmation from the owners, use the `confirmTransaction` function. This should call `executeTransaction` automatically based on the number of confirmations:

```
function confirmTransaction(uint transactionId)
    public onlyOwner(msg.sender)
{
    require(!confirmations[transactionId][msg.sender]);
    confirmations[transactionId][msg.sender] = true;
    emit Confirmation(msg.sender, transactionId);
    executeTransaction(transactionId);
}
```

9. After implementing these functions, a simple usable multisig wallet contract will look similar to the following contract. The contract is for demonstration purposes only. Do not use it in any production application:

```
pragma solidity ^0.4.24;

contract MultiSig {

    struct Transaction {
        address destination;
        uint value;
        bytes data;
        bool executed;
    }

    mapping (uint => Transaction) public transactions;
    mapping (uint => mapping (address => bool)) public
confirmations;
    uint public transactionCount;

    mapping (address => bool) public isOwner;
    address[] public owners;

    uint public required;

    event Confirmation(
        address indexed sender,
        uint indexed transactionId
    );
```

```
event Submission(uint indexed transactionId);
event Execution(uint indexed transactionId);

modifier onlyOwner(address owner) {
    require(isOwner[owner]);
    _;
}

// Fallback function to accept deposits
function() public payable { }

// Constructor sets owners and required confirmations.
constructor(address[] _owners, uint _required) public {
    for (uint i=0; i<_owners.length; i++) {
        require(!(isOwner[_owners[i]] || _owners[i] == 0));
        isOwner[_owners[i]] = true;
    }
    owners = _owners;
    required = _required;
}

// Allows an owner to submit and confirm a transaction.
function submitTransaction(
    address destination,
    uint value,
    bytes data)
    public returns (uint transactionId)
{
    transactionId = addTransaction(destination, value, data);
    confirmTransaction(transactionId);
}

// Allows an owner to confirm a transaction.
function confirmTransaction(uint transactionId)
    public onlyOwner(msg.sender)
{
    require(!confirmations[transactionId][msg.sender]);
    confirmations[transactionId][msg.sender] = true;
    emit Confirmation(msg.sender, transactionId);
    executeTransaction(transactionId);
}

// Allows anyone to execute a confirmed transaction.
function executeTransaction(uint transactionId) public {
    if(isConfirmed(transactionId)) {
        Transaction storage trnx = transactions[transactionId];
        if (trnx.destination.call.value(trnx.value)(trnx.data))
{
```

```
                trnx.executed = true;
                emit Execution(transactionId);
            }
        }
    }

    // Returns the confirmation status of a transaction.
    function isConfirmed(uint transactionId)
        public constant returns (bool)
    {
        uint count = 0;
        for (uint i=0; i<owners.length; i++) {
            if (confirmations[transactionId][owners[i]])
                count += 1;
            if (count == required)
                return true;
        }
    }

    // Adds a new transaction to the transaction mapping
    function addTransaction(
        address destination,
        uint value,
        bytes data)
        internal returns (uint transactionId)
    {
        transactionId = transactionCount;
        transactions[transactionId] = Transaction({
            destination: destination,
            value: value,
            data: data,
            executed: false
        });
        transactionCount += 1;
        emit Submission(transactionId);
    }

    // Returns list of owners.
    function getOwners() public view returns (address[]) {
        return owners;
    }
}
```

10. There are production-ready multiSig wallet implementations available for you to use. One good example is the ConsenSys multiSig Wallet. You can find it at https://github.com/ConsenSys/MultiSigWallet.

Smart Contract Security 8

In this chapter, we will cover the following recipes:

- Integer overflow and underflow
- Re-entrancy attack
- The parity hack
- Forcing Ether to a contract
- Using private variables
- Transaction Ordering Dependence
- Call to the unknown
- DoS using loops
- Security analysis tools for solidity
- Uninitialized storage pointer in solidity
- Best practices in solidity

Introduction

Ethereum and smart contracts are very new and highly experimental. Since smart contract engineering is different from traditional applications, it has to be done with care and precision. The cost of failure can be very high with smart contracts.

A deployed smart contract cannot be modified at a later stage. This brings increased trust and transparency, but the same applies to any bugs found after deployment. Before deploying the contract, it is important to ensure that no bugs are present in the contract and that a fail-safe mechanism to safeguard the funds is included.

This chapter covers known bugs that can occur while writing a smart contract and ways to avoid them.

Integer overflow and underflow

Overflow or underflow occurs when the value assigned to a variable exceeds the limit allowed for that data type. This is very common for the integer data type in solidity and has to be carefully verified during an assignment.

This recipe explains the situations in which integer overflow/underflow can occur and the ways to avoid them.

Getting ready

This recipe is all about solidity-based smart contracts. The Remix IDE (`https://remix.ethereum.org`) can help you quickly test and deploy a contract.

Also, you can use any Ethereum client (`geth`, `parity`, and so on) and the `solc` compiler to run this contract.

How to do it...

1. Consider the following basic token contract:

```
pragma solidity ^0.4.23;

contract TokenContract {
    mapping (address => uint) balances;

    event Transfer(
        address indexed _from,
        address indexed _to,
        uint256 _value
    );

    function sendToken(address receiver, uint amount)
        public returns(bool) {
        require(balances[msg.sender] < amount);

        balances[msg.sender] -= amount;
        balances[receiver] += amount;

        emit Transfer(msg.sender, receiver, amount);
        return true;
    }
```

```
function getBalance(address addr) public view returns(uint) {
    return balances[addr];
}
}
```

2. It is a very common and simple token contract, which has functions to transfer tokens and to check the balance of each account.

3. At first glance, there is nothing in this contract that can possibly go wrong. Incrementally add a quantity to the variable and, when it reaches the maximum value allocated to uint256 (2^256), it will circle back to zero. This is called integer overflow:

```
balances[receiver] += amount;
```

4. The same thing is applicable if the value is made to be less than zero. The value will circle back to the maximum value of uint256. This is called integer underflow:

```
balances[msg.sender] -= amount;
```

5. This may not occur in every condition and is completely dependent on the use case. Most of the time, the total supply will never reach the maximum value of uint256. But, it is always recommended to include enough validations to ensure that this cannot happen.

6. Try applying it for all integer types in solidity, including uint8, uint32, and uint64. These smaller values can easily hit the overflow value.

7. To avoid overflow or underflow situations, it is recommended to check whether the value after an arithmetic operation is the expected result:

```
balanceOf[_to] + _value >= balanceOf[_to]
```

8. Modify the transfer function in the following way to avoid any overflow during token transfer:

```
function sendToken(address receiver, uint amount)
    public returns(bool) {
    require(balances[msg.sender] < amount);
    require(balanceOf[_to] + _value >= balanceOf[_to]);

    balances[msg.sender] -= amount;
    balances[receiver] += amount;

    emit Transfer(msg.sender, receiver, amount);
    return true;
}
```

There's more...

There are best practices and reusable code that can be used to avoid such bugs in your smart contract. One perfect example is the `SafeMath` library of openzeppelin. This library introduces a few functions that can be used instead of the regular arithmetic operators. These functions include conditions to ensure that no overflow or underflow can happen:

```
pragma solidity ^0.4.24;

library SafeMath {
 /**
 * @dev Function to add two numbers
 */
 function add(uint256 a, uint256 b)
 internal pure returns (uint256 c) {
 c = a + b;
 assert(c >= a);
 return c;
 }

 function sub(...) { ... }
 function mul(...) { ... }
 function div(...) { ... }
}
```

To use this library, import `SafeMath` from the openzeppelin GitHub repository at `https://github.com/OpenZeppelin/openzeppelin-solidity`:

```
import "./contracts/math/SafeMath.sol";
```

Assign the library to the `integer` type you wish to use:

```
using SafeMath for uint256;
```

Now, all functions of the `SafeMath` library are part of the unsigned integer and are accessible directly. The `transfer` function can be modified as follows to use the `SafeMath` library:

```
function sendToken(address receiver, uint amount)
    public returns(bool) {
    require(balances[msg.sender] < amount);
    balances[msg.sender] = balances[msg.sender].sub(amount);
    balances[receiver] = balances[receiver].add(amount);
    emit Transfer(msg.sender, receiver, amount);
    return true;
}
```

Re-entrancy attack

One of the earliest bugs to be discovered in the Ethereum ecosystem is called the re-entrancy bug. This involves functions that can be called repeatedly before the first call to the function is finished. This allows the caller to withdraw all of the contract funds.

In this recipe, you will learn to avoid such issues in your smart contract.

Getting ready

It's expected that you have a basic understanding of the Ethereum blockchain and solidity before stepping through this recipe.

The Remix IDE (`https://remix.ethereum.org`) can help you quickly test and deploy the contract. Also, you can use any Ethereum client (`geth`, `parity`, and so on) and the `solc` compiler to run this contract.

How to do it...

1. Consider the following contract. This is a simple contract that allows the user to deposit and withdraw the amount:

```solidity
pragma solidity^0.4.24;

contract Victim {

    // Mapping to keep tract of user deposits
    mapping (address => uint) private balances;

    // Function to withdraw the contract balance
    function withdraw() public {
        uint amount = balances[msg.sender];
        msg.sender.call.value(amount)();
        balances[msg.sender] = 0;
    }

    // Function to deposit ether
    function deposit() public payable {
        balances[msg.sender] += msg.value;
    }
}
```

2. Here, the low-level `call` method is used to transfer funds to the caller address. If the target address is a contract, this method forwards all the gas remaining in the call to it. This executes any code present in the calling contract's `fallback` function.

3. To exploit this vulnerability, use the `fallback` function to call the `withdraw` function repeatedly until the contract becomes empty or runs out of gas.

4. Create a calling contract with the following functions:

```solidity
pragma solidity ^0.4.24;

contract Attacker {

    // Victim contract instance
    Victim victim;

    constructor(address _victim) public {
        victim = Victim(_victim);
    }

    // Deposit an amount and withdraw it immediately
    // Initiates the attack process
    function getJackpot() public payable {
        victim.deposit.value(msg.value)();
        victim.withdraw();
    }

    // Fallback function calls back into the contract again
    function () public payable {
        if (address(victim).balance >= msg.value) {
            victim.withdraw();
        }
    }

    // Function to withdraw the jackpot
    function withdrawJackpot() onlyOwner public {
        address(msg.sender).transfer(address(this).balance);
    }
}
```

5. Call the `getJackpot` function with a value to deposit the amount into the victim contract and make a withdraw request immediately. This invokes the `fallback` function of the attacker's contract, which calls the `withdraw` function again.

6. All these calls happen before changing the balance of the caller during the first call. This bypasses any balance check validation and allows the caller to withdraw the entire balance left in the contract.

7. There are several methods to avoid such issues. The first and foremost recommendation is not to use the low-level call function to transfer any amount. Use the `<address>.transfer` function to transfer funds to the account. This has a gas limit of 2,300, which is not enough for actual execution inside a contract:

```
// Function to withdraw the user balance
// Avoids using low-level call function
function withdraw() public {
    uint amount = balances[msg.sender];
    // Transfer function to transfer value
    // Gas limit of 2300
    msg.sender.transfer(amount);
    balances[msg.sender] = 0;
}
```

8. If you wish to keep the low-level call for some reason, then you could follow the checks-effects-interaction pattern to avoid this issue. This pattern asks you to make an external call only after all state modifications and conditions are completed. The victim contract can be modified as follows to avoid the issue:

```
pragma solidity^0.4.24;

contract NotVictim {

    // Mapping to keep tract of user deposits
    mapping (address => uint) private balances;

    // Function to withdraw the user balance
    // Follows checks-effection-interaction pattern
    function withdraw() public {
        // Checks-effects
        uint amount = balances[msg.sender];
        balances[msg.sender] = 0;
        // Interaction
        msg.sender.call.value(amount)();
    }

    // Function to deposit ether
    function deposit() public payable {
        balances[msg.sender] += msg.value;
    }
}
```

The parity hack

Parity provided a multisig wallet to manage your funds through an Ethereum-based contract. The contract had security flaws which were later exploited to steal the funds stored in it.

The parity wallet was attacked twice, and you will learn more about them and the methods to use to avoid similar attacks in this recipe.

Getting ready

It's expected that you have a basic understanding of the Ethereum blockchain and solidity before stepping through this recipe.

The Remix IDE (https://remix.ethereum.org) can help you quickly test and deploy the contract. Also, you can use any Ethereum client (geth, parity, and so on) and the solc compiler to run this contract.

How to do it...

1. A multisig wallet is a smart contract for transferring funds or interacting with other contracts. The transfers are done based on approval from multiple addresses.
2. You can use the smart contract and the associated library provided by parity as a multisig wallet for managing your funds.
3. The library contains an initWallet function. Use this to set the address of owners and other basic parameters:

```
function initWallet(
    address[] _owners,
    uint _required,
    uint _daylimit)
{
    initDaylimit(_daylimit);
    initMultiowned(_owners, _required);
}
```

4. While deploying a wallet contract, the `initWallet` function will be called from the `constructor` wallet contract. This is probably to bring some reusability to the `constructor` code.

5. You can use the wallet contract's `fallback` function to deposit Ether. The function also has a low-level `delegatecall` method, which forwards the calldata to the library contract:

```
function() payable {
    if (msg.value > 0)
        Deposit(msg.sender, msg.value);
    else if (msg.data.length > 0)
        _walletLibrary.delegatecall(msg.data);
}
```

6. You can also use the `delegatecall` method to call the `public` functions of the library through the wallet's `fallback` function.

7. To exploit this vulnerability, use the `delegatecall` method to call the `initWallet` function, which essentially changes the owner of the contract. The attacker simply makes a call with a new owner array containing only one address. This allows any transfer to take place with one approval.

8. Call the `kill` function present in the `wallet` library to destroy the contract and transfer all funds present in the contract:

```
function kill(address _to)
    onlymanyowners(sha3(msg.data))
    external {
    suicide(_to);
}
```

9. Also, use the `execute` function to transfer funds to a different address by providing approval from one account:

```
function execute(
    address _to,
    uint256 _value,
    bytes _data) {
    //...
}
```

10. The bug can be avoided in two ways: either by implementing the `constructor` function in the wallet contract itself, or by not using `delegatecall` to forward any incoming requests to the wallet contract.

11. To avoid an exploit like this, more care has to be taken while using low-level calls such as `delegatecall` in your smart contract.

Forcing Ether to a contract

A developer can choose to enable or disable the acceptance of value in a contract. This is done by flagging the named/unnamed functions as payable. But, there are ways one can send Ether to the contract by force.

This can affect some of the logic inside a contract, which was written based on the previous assumption. In this recipe, you will learn how to find and avoid such problems in your smart contract.

Getting ready

It's expected that you have a basic understanding of the Ethereum blockchain and solidity before stepping through this recipe.

The Remix IDE (`https://remix.ethereum.org`) can help you quickly test and deploy the contract. Also, you can use any Ethereum client (`geth`, `parity`, and so on) and the `solc` compiler to run this contract.

How to do it...

1. You can send Ether to a contract even if it does not implement a `payable` function. Generally, sending Ether to a non-payable function will result in a failed transaction.
2. A developer can easily overlook this and include some conditions in the contract that check for strict balance equality:

   ```
   require(this.balance == 1 ether);
   ```

3. Using such conditions can result in a permanent **Denial Of Service (DoS)** and can make the contract useless.
4. There are multiple methods to force Ether to a contract. It can either be sent through the self-destruct function or by guessing a contract address that might be created in the future.

5. The self-destruct function is generally used for removing the data of a contract from the blockchain. It also sends the Ether stored in the self-destructing contract to an address specified while calling the function:

```
contract SelfDestructable {

    function kill(address _target) public {
        selfdestrcut(_target);
    }

}
```

6. You can use the target as a contract address with the `fallback` function. But, sending Ether through self-destruct won't execute the `fallback` code.

7. This essentially allows anyone to send Ether to a contract that has no payable `fallback` function.

8. The second way of forcing Ether to a contract involves deterministically finding a contract address. You can guess a contract address from the RLP encoding of the sender's address.

9. To generate the contract address, take the rightmost 160 bits of the `keccak256` hash of an RLP encoding of the sender's address and its nonce:

```
// rightmost 160 bits of
sha3(rlp.encode([sender_address, nonce]))
```

10. Using this, a contract developer or someone who has access to this information can easily guess the address and send some Ether to it. This will make any logic that depends on the contract balance useless.

11. As a preventative measure, it is always recommended not to rely on a contract's balance for any logic. This is very uncertain and can be easily modified.

There's more...

Based on this property, a certain use case called the hidden Ether can be developed. This allows anyone to hide Ether that can be retrieved at a later stage.

Since a contract address can be easily guessed using the sender address and nonce, guess a future contract address that can be generated with the same address:

```
sha3(rlp.encode([0x1.., 10]))
```

Send some Ether to this address for safekeeping. To retrieve this Ether, deploy the following contract to this address:

```
pragma solidity^0.4.24;

/**
 * @dev Retrieve money stuck in the contract address
 **/
contract GetEtherBack {

    // Destroy the contract and send Ether to the creator
    constructor() public {
        selfdestruct(msg.sender);
    }
}
```

The contract will self-destruct while deploying and will return all the Ether stored there to the sender's address. This process has to be done with the same address and nonce value. If you fail to deploy it with the nonce, the Ether will be lost permanently and cannot be retrieved later.

Use of private variables

Solidity supports the `private` keyword for declaring private variables and functions. At first, this may look like a place where we can store values privately, but since all the data in Ethereum is public, values stored in these private variables can also be read.

In this recipe, you will learn to read the private values of a contract and ways to prevent such security vulnerabilities.

Getting ready

It's expected that you have a basic understanding of the Ethereum blockchain and solidity before stepping through this recipe.

The Remix IDE (`https://remix.ethereum.org`) can help you quickly test and deploy the contract. Also, you can use any Ethereum client (`geth`, `parity`, and so on) and the `solc` compiler to run this contract.

How to do it...

1. To learn more about reading private variables, consider the following odd-even contract. Each player chooses a number and, if the sum is even, then the first player wins; otherwise, the second player wins:

```
pragma solidity ^0.4.24;

contract OddEven {
    struct Player {
        address addr;
        uint number;
    }

    Player[2] private players;
    uint8 count = 0;

    function play(uint number) payable public {
        require(msg.value == 1 ether);
        players[count] = Player(msg.sender, number);
        count++;
        if (count == 2) selectWinner();
    }

    function selectWinner() private {
        uint n = players[0].number + players[1].number;
        players[n%2].addr.transfer(address(this).balance);
        delete players;
        count = 0;
    }
}
```

2. The contract uses the player's mapping to store previous bets. The contract assumes that using the private modifier makes the data stores actually "private" and not visible to anyone:

```
Player[2] private players;
```

3. Using the require condition prevents the player from placing a bet unless they transfer the specified bet amount:

```
require(msg.value == 1 ether);
```

4. Once the second player places their bet, the winner is selected based on the contract's logic. Finally, the winner receives the whole bet amount placed by both the first and second players.

5. You can easily win the game any number of times by exploiting a flaw. Wait for someone to make the first move, and play as the second player.

6. Now, although the variable is private, you can read the first player's bet by decoding the Ethereum transaction used. This allows you to choose a value that always makes you the winner.

 State changes in Ethereum are usually done through a transaction. If the receiving account is a contract in a transaction, the EVM runs the contract's code either to completion or until the execution runs out of gas.

7. The data field of a transaction is used to specify which method to call and the input parameters to the method. For example, to modify a private state variable in the contract, you need to pass the "private" value to the `setter` method through a transaction. Since the transaction data is visible to all the nodes, you can use this information to read the transaction data.

8. You can decode the transaction used to set the private variable and read the value stored in it. For example, consider the `play` function in the given game contract. Try calling this function with the following data:

```
0x6587f6ec00000000000000000000000000000000000000000000000000000000
0000064
```

9. The first 4 bytes of the transaction data point to the calling method's signature. You can calculate this by taking the first 4 bytes of the `keccak` hash of the method. In this contract, it is `bytes4(keccak256('play(uint)'))`, which is *0x6587f6ec*.

10. The remaining characters refer to the parameters of the calling method. Each parameter is represented by the `hex` value of the input padded to 32 bytes. For example, if 100 is the input parameter to the play method, then the transaction data for that parameter is as follows:

```
0x0000000000000000000000000000000000000000000000000000000000000064
```

11. If there are multiple parameters of both fixed and variable lengths, the transaction data can get more complex.

12. You may have the requirement to store private variables in your contract, but that's a rather complex problem. There have been a lot of attempts to simulate a private store of information, and one interesting approach is the use of a commit-reveal pattern.

13. In this method, you can ask users to first submit a hash of secret information. When everyone else has submitted theirs, each participant is asked to reveal their vote, which then can be verified.

Transaction-Ordering Dependence (TOD)

Given enough resources, someone can reorder the transactions in the mempool to arrive at the result they need. This is a big concern in a system with a high volume of public transactions. Protecting against this comes down to the specific contract, and there are multiple ways to do this.

In this recipe, you will learn more about TOD attacks and some common places where you can avoid them.

Getting ready

It's expected that you have a basic understanding of the Ethereum blockchain and solidity before stepping through this recipe.

The Remix IDE (`https://remix.ethereum.org`) can help you quickly test and deploy the contract. Also, you can use any Ethereum client (`geth`, `parity`, and so on) and the `solc` compiler to run this contract.

How to do it...

1. Transactions in the mempool are public and anyone can read the transaction data directly from it. This feature is there to help miners and bring transparency to the system.

2. This also allows the sender to replace a specific transaction with the same nonce and a higher gas price. This is only possible when the sender has permission and the transaction is not yet mined.

3. To demonstrate the effect of this issue, consider the example of an ERC20 contract. The contract has an approve function, which can be used to delegate an address to spend on your behalf:

```
pragma solidity^0.4.24;

contract ERC20 {

    // ...

    function approve(address _spender, uint256 _value)
        public returns (bool) {
        allowed[msg.sender][_spender] = _value;
        emit Approval(msg.sender, _spender, _value);
        return true;
    }

    //...

}
```

4. Changing a user's allowance using this method brings with it the risk of TOD. Someone can use both the old and the new allowance methods to transfer more tokens than the owner of the tokens ever wanted to allow the spender to transfer.

5. Try approving one address to transfer the tokens of some other address. For example, X allows Y to transfer A tokens. You can use the transfer function to perform the transfer operation:

```
ERC20.approve(address(Y), A); // from: X
```

6. After some time, x decides to reduce the allowance from A to B. This is again changed using the `approve` function by passing the new values:

```
ERC20.approve(address(Y), B); // from: X
```

7. Let's assume that Y notices this second approve transaction made by X and quickly does a transfer using the `transferFrom` function. This has to be done before the second approve transaction gets mined:

```
ERC20.transferFrom(address(Z), A); // from: Y
```

8. If Y's transaction gets executed before X's transaction, then *Y* transfers *A* tokens and gets permission to transfer another *B* tokens. Y can perform another transaction to transfer B tokens even before X notices it:

```
ERC20.transferFrom(address(Z), B); // from: Y
```

9. This attack is possible because of the logic implemented in the `approve` method. To avoid this issue, an easy way is to decrement the allowance value to zero and then set it to some other value:

```
ERC20.approve(address(Y), 0); // from: X
ERC20.approve(address(Y), B); // from: X
```

10. This solution requires more attention on the user's side. Another solution is to implement two functions, one to increment the allowance value and the other to decrement it:

```
pragma solidity ^0.4.24;

contract ERC20 {

    function approve(address _spender, uint256 _value) { }

    // Function to increase allowance
    function increaseApproval(
        address _spender,
        uint256 _addedValue)
        public returns (bool)
    {
        // Uses safeMath.sol
        allowed[msg.sender][_spender] =
            (allowed[msg.sender][_spender].add(_addedValue));
        emit Approval(
            msg.sender,
            _spender,
            allowed[msg.sender][_spender]
```

```
        );
        return true;
    }

    // Function to decrease allowance
    function decreaseApproval(
        address _spender,
        uint256 _subtractedValue)
        public returns (bool)
    {
        uint256 oldValue = allowed[msg.sender][_spender];
        if (_subtractedValue > oldValue) {
            allowed[msg.sender][_spender] = 0;
        } else {
            allowed[msg.sender][_spender] =
                oldValue.sub(_subtractedValue);
        }
        emit Approval(
            msg.sender,
            _spender,
            allowed[msg.sender][_spender]
        );
        return true;
    }

    // ...

}
```

Call to the unknown

DoS attacks are very common in Ethereum when a contract interacts with other addresses. These addresses can be either externally owned addresses or contracts. Performing validations based on these conditions can be very dangerous.

In this recipe, you will learn the pitfalls of interacting with other address and ways to avoid them. You will also learn about a design pattern that can help mitigate these issues, up to a certain point.

Getting ready

It's expected that you have a basic understanding of the Ethereum blockchain and solidity before stepping through this recipe.

The Remix IDE (`https://remix.ethereum.org`) can help you quickly test and deploy the contract. Also, you can use any Ethereum client (`geth`, `parity`, and so on) and the `solc` compiler to run this contract.

How to do it...

1. There are multiple ways a contract can interact with other contracts. Making validations around these interactions cannot be trusted, and the destination contract can manipulate them:

   ```
   require(<external_contract_call>);
   ```

2. It is recommended not to depend on untrusted third-party contracts for validations. The external call can make the contract useless.

3. A place where this can be easily overlooked is while transferring Ether. If the destination address is an externally owned account, then the transfer will be successful. If it is a contract address, then the transfer will call the `fallback` function of that contract and execute the code written inside it.

4. Write a `fallback` function that always cancels the transaction. This will make the calling contract's condition fail every time, making the contract useless.

5. Consider the following example contract, which allows anyone to become king by sending a higher value than the previous king. Once the new king is seated, the old king receives the invested value back:

   ```solidity
   pragma solidity ^0.4.24;

   contract BecomeTheKing {

       address currentKing;
       uint highestBid;

       function() payable {
           // Verify the value sent
           require(msg.value > highestBid);

           // Transfer the previous bid back
           require(currentKing.send(highestBid));

           // Update the king and value
           currentKing = msg.sender;
           highestBid = msg.value;
   ```

```
        }
    }
```

6. The contract looks very straightforward. For you to become king, place a bid that is greater than the previous bid. Once a new bid is validated, the old king gets his bid back.

7. The `send` function, which is used to send the previous bid, assumes that the destination is an externally owned account.

8. Create a contract to place a bid. Include a `fallback` function in the contract that always throws/reverts:

```
pragma solidity ^0.4.24;

// Attacker contract
contract AlwaysTheKing {

    // Call the function to become the king
    function becomeKing(address _address) payable {
        _address.call.value(msg.value);
    }

    // Always revert when some value is sent
    function() payable {
        revert();
    }
}
```

9. When a new player places a higher bid in the `BecomeTheKing` contract, it will try to transfer the older bid. Since the current king is your contract, which never accepts this transfer, the condition will fail every time. This allows you to stay as king forever.

10. To avoid such DoS attacks, it is recommended to use the `Withdraw` pattern. The pattern asks the recipient to withdraw the value rather than send it using the transfer function.

11. This avoids the possibility of DoS in the contract flow. Even if the recipient tries such an attack, it can only affect the specific transaction and it has nothing to do with other users.

12. Modify the `BecomeTheKing` contract as follows by using the `withdraw` pattern:

```solidity
pragma solidity ^0.4.24;

contract BecomeTheKing {

    address currentKing;
    uint highestBid;

    mapping(address => uint) balances;

    // Function to withdraw previous bids
    function withdraw() public {
        uint balance = balances[msg.sender];
        require(balance > 0);
        balances[msg.sender] = 0;
        msg.sender.transfer(balance);
    }

    function() public payable {
        require(msg.value > highestBid);

        // Save the previous bid for withdrawal
        balances[msg.sender] = highestBid;

        currentKing = msg.sender;
        highestBid = msg.value;
    }
}
```

DoS using loops

Like every Turing-complete programming language, solidity supports different types of loops to perform repeated tasks. Loops can be straightforward, but there are some situations where this can cause unexpected DoS.

In this recipe, you will learn to avoid a few accidental bugs that can occur even in the absence of an external attack.

Getting ready

It's expected that you have a basic understanding of the Ethereum blockchain and solidity before stepping through this recipe.

The Remix IDE (`https://remix.ethereum.org`) can help you quickly test and deploy the contract. Also, you can use any Ethereum client (`geth`, `parity`, and so on) and the `solc` compiler to run this contract.

How to do it...

1. Loops can be very tricky when it comes to solidty. There are two very common mistakes that anyone can easily overlook while writing smart contracts.

2. Create a function that uses a for loop to iterate through an array of addresses and transfer the payout:

```
pragma solidity ^0.4.24;

contract Payout {
    // Arbitrary length array to store addresses
    address[] private addresses;
    // Mapping to store payout value
    mapping (address => uint) public payouts;
    // Function to transfer payouts
    function payoutAll() public {
        for(uint8 i = 0; i < addresses.length; i++) {
            require(addresses[i].send(payouts[addresses[i]]));
        }
    }
}
```

3. The contract contains two potential bugs, which will arise when the length of the array exceeds a certain limit.

4. For example, the for loop uses a `uint` with size 8 to store the index. Since `uint8` can only store a very short range of integers, if the array length exceeds 255, an overflow can occur. This will result start transferring payout starting from index 0.

5. To avoid this, it is recommended to always use a data type that can accommodate the loop's needs. The function can be modified as follows to avoid this issue:

```
function payoutAll() public {
    for(uint256 i = 0; i < addresses.length; i++) {
        require(addresses[i].send(payouts[addresses[i]]));
    }
}
```

6. Using a different data type can solve the underflow issue, but it will still fail to satisfy the block's gas limit. It will take a lot of gas if there are more instructions to execute.

7. Since the array length is infinite, this issue can arise when the number of addresses in the array is more. This can also result in permanent DoS for the payout functionality.

8. It is recommended to perform a large set of instructions in batches to avoid such issues. The contract can be modified as follows:

```
pragma solidity^0.4.24;

contract Payout {

    // Using struct over mapping
    struct Recipient {
        address addr;
        uint256 value;
    }

    Recipient[] recipients;

    // State variable for batch operation
    uint256 nextIndex;

    // Function to transfer payout
    function payoutAll() public {
        uint256 i = nextIndex;

        while (i < recipients.length && gasleft() > 200000) {
            recipients[i].addr.send(recipients[i].value);
            i++;
        }

        nextIndex = i;
    }
}
```

9. It is recommended to verify all conditions before proceeding with this implementation. It depends on the use case you are planning to implement it with.

Security analysis tools for solidity

A few community-developed tools are available to find and solve security issues in smart contracts. Using these tools effectively can help identify known issues in solidity. In this recipe, you will learn about these popular tools and the ways to use them.

Getting ready

It's expected that you have a basic understanding of the Ethereum blockchain and solidity before stepping through this recipe.

This recipe might require the installation of various dependencies, based on the tools you choose to use. The requirements are given for each step.

How to do it...

1. One of the popular static analysis tools in the Ethereum ecosystem is `Mythril`. It is a security analysis tool that uses concolic analysis, taint analysis, and a control flow checking to detect a variety of security vulnerabilities.

2. Mythril is based on Python and you need a working installation of `Python v3` with `pip3` installed. Once you have those ready, run the following command to install Mythril:

    ```
    pip3 install mythril
    ```

    Concolic analysis is a hybrid code analysis technique that performs symbolic execution. It considers the program variables as symbolic variables along a concrete execution path. Symbolic execution is used in conjunction with new test cases to maximize code coverage. The main focus of this technique is to find bugs and vulnerabilities in a real-world scenario, rather than verifying code correctness.

    Taint analysis checks for variables that can be modified by an external user interaction. This helps in understanding the information flow characteristics of a contract.

3. You can also get it as a Docker image. Run the following command to pull it from `docker` Hub:

```
docker pull mythril/myth
```

4. Once you have installed `mythril`, perform analysis on a file to get a report:

```
myth -x erc20.sol
```

5. The Remix IDE (`https://remix.ethereum.org/`) also has inbuilt analysis capabilities to find common security flaws and best practices. To perform validation, go to the **analysis** tab and click **Run**. This will list all the issues in the given contract.

6. Oyente (`https://github.com/melonproject/oyente`) is a Remix-based IDE that focuses more on security. It provides both a UI and a command-line option to analyze smart contracts.

7. Generating a DOT graph can better help you visualize the contract. `Solgraph` is a tool that is built for this purpose. Install `solgraph` via `npm` using the following command. You need to have a working installation of `Node.js` for this:

```
npm install --save -g solgraph
```

8. After installing `solgraph`, use the smart contract file as an input to generate a DOT graph. It will generate a visualization explaining the control flow of the contract:

```
solgraph contract.sol > contract.dot
```

9. The community has also developed a lot of linting tools for solidity. Use any of the following tools to verify your code against best practices:

```
npm install -g solium
// OR
npm install -g solhint
```

Uninitialized storage pointer in solidity

Working with storage and memory variables can be a bit confusing in solidity. Using a storage variable inside a function can lead to unexpected behaviors.

In this recipe, you will learn to understand the importance of initializing a storage variable while declaring it.

Getting ready

It's expected that you have a basic understanding of the Ethereum blockchain and solidity before stepping through this recipe.

The Remix IDE (https://remix.ethereum.org) can help you quickly test and deploy the contract. Also, you can use any Ethereum client (geth, parity, and so on) and the solc compiler to run this contract.

How to do it...

1. Solidity allows you to choose the type of storage with the help of storage and memory keywords. A storage variable stores values permanently, whereas memory variables are persisted during the lifetime of a transaction.

2. Local variables of struct, array, or mapping type reference storage by default if no explicit specification is given inside a function. The function arguments are always in memory and the local variables, other than array, struct, or mapping, are stored in the stack.

3. Consider the following function. Here, the _a variable is of type memory and x is of type storage:

    ```
    function fun(uint _a) {
        uint[] x;
    }
    ```

4. The issue arises when these storage variables are uninitialized. An uninitialized storage variable can refer to the first memory location that will have some other data. This can lead to unexpected storage modifications.

5. Consider the following contract, which creates an uninitialized storage variable:

```
pragma solidity ^0.4.24;

// Contract to demonstrate uninitialized storage pointer bug
contract StorageContract {
    // Storage variable at location 0
    uint stateVaribale;

    // Storage variable at location 1
    uint[] arrayData;

    // Function which has an uninitialized storage variable
    function fun() public {
        // Storage variable which points to location 0
        uint[] x;
        // Modifies value at location 0
        x.push(0);
        // Modifies value at location 1
        arrayData = x;
    }
}
```

6. At first, this may look very straightforward. Since the function declares an uninitialized array, it will get created as a storage variable with the memory location pointing to location 0.

7. Storage variables are allocated memory in the order they are declared. In this contract, stateVariable is allocated to storage location 0 and arrayData is allocated to storage location 1.

8. When you define a new uninitialized storage variable, it points to the storage location of the first storage variable. This essentially allows two variables to share a single storage location.

9. This leads to unexpected storage modifications. This technique can be used by a developer to modify the value of a state variable without explicitly accessing it.

10. The Solidity compiler, by default, will show warnings for uninitialized storage variables. Make use of this to easily spot the bug.

11. To avoid any such storage modifications, fix the compiler warning by replacing it with an appropriate type based on the use case.

Best practices in solidity

Solidity is very new and undergoes rapid changes every day. You should expect new best practices and bugs to be suggested/discovered every day, which improves the platform as a whole. There are some best practices and software engineering techniques in solidity that you can follow to write bug-free and optimized smart contracts for Ethereum. This recipe focuses on this topic.

How to do it...

1. The first and most important technique is to keep the contract as simple as possible. Complex contracts increase the likelihood of bugs. The contract's logic should be simple and modularized.

2. Use already available, well-tested, and popular libraries to achieve common tasks. This can help you in writing bug-free and high-performing contracts.

3. Only use the blockchain where your application needs decentralization. It is okay to keep other things in a traditional centralized database. It is not advised to store everything in Blockchain.

4. Always keep your contract and the libraries up to date. This protects your contract from recently discovered bugs.

5. There are several Ethereum-specific properties that need to be considered while writing code for the Blockchain. This includes gas limitations, transparency, and trust.

6. Every instruction costs a value to run, and there is an upper limit enforced by each block. A transaction can use a maximum of the gas allowed for a block. The code has to be written in such a way that no transaction exceeds this limit in the future.

7. No value in Ethereum is private and anyone can read data from any contract. There are private access modifiers available for state variables, but they can still be read in other ways. Write your contracts considering this fact.

8. Relying on untrusted external contracts is very risky. It is always recommended not to do that for any task, since they can execute malicious code and do something bad.

Design Decisions

9

In this chapter, we will cover the following recipes:

- Serverless architecture for DApps
- Implementing your own wallet
- What if you find a bug after deployment?
- Generating random numbers in Solidity
- Keeping contracts simple, modular, and up to date
- Implementing user authentication in Ethereum

Introduction

So far in this book, we looked into various aspects of developing a secure distributed application, from setting up a network of your own and writing smart contracts, to securing the smart contracts from various bugs that might occur. You might need to take a wise decision between two different approaches in some scenarios while developing a blockchain application. For example, you may have to choose between implementing your own wallet or using an independent wallet such as MetaMask.

This chapter explores these design decisions further, and you will have a clear idea of what to choose by the end of each recipe. You will also learn to design better architecture for your decentralized applications based on these decisions. Having a basic idea about smart contracts and DApps will help you in getting the best out of this chapter.

Serverless architecture for DApps

Traditional client-server model applications are typically hosted in centralized servers and are managed in-house or by cloud service providers. The server component provides a service to one or more clients based on the requests received.

Blockchain can remove this centralized server and bring in more transparency to users. This can be achieved by interacting with the smart contracts directly through nodes or by using a third-party wallet such as MetaMask. In this recipe, you will learn how to choose between a client-server and serverless model for your Ethereum DApp.

Getting ready

It is required to have basic knowledge of writing smart contracts and building DApps using Web3JS. This recipe discusses the architecture of decentralized applications and is an advanced topic. Understanding the implementation of a basic DApp is essential to get more out of this recipe.

For those who are just getting started, it is recommended to read through the first three chapters of this book. It will help you understand the basics such as setting up an environment and building smart contract and DApps.

How to do it...

1. The entire business flow of a typical serverless Ethereum DApp happens between the **Client** and the **Blockchain**. Based on the business requirements, you can create a more complex DApp with multiple layers involving both centralized and decentralized components.

2. You can create a client as simple as a static HTML file that interacts directly with the **Blockchain** using HTTP calls, or a rich application with complex architecture. You can distribute them as a standalone application or through protocols such as swarm or the **InterPlanetary File System (IPFS)**.

 IPFS and SWARM are different decentralized file distribution protocols. They allow the storing of any static files including images, HTML/CSS, and JS, and can be shared with the larger community.

3. In simple terms, the architecture can be visualized as follows. The **Blockchain** module represents one or more nodes in an Ethereum network the client can connect and interact with. The **Transaction** updates the blockchain state and *query* returns the current state:

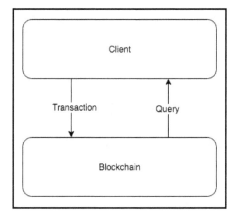

4. Use the **Client** to send transactions directly and query details from the **Blockchain** without having to rely on any intermediaries.

5. Since there is no restriction on reading the data stored in Ethereum, you can directly **Query** the data using Web3JS or other RPC methods:

```
// Solidity contract
contract Test {
    function getData() returns(string data) {
        return "Hello world!";
    }
}

// Web3JS
var TestContract = new web3.eth.contract(<abi>, <address>);
TestContract.methods
    .getData()
    .call()
    .then(console.log);
```

6. Sending transactions can be a little tricky since the private keys of user accounts have to be managed independently. The quick and popular way is to depend on a wallet such as MetaMask. It can help the user to manage their private keys locally without having to trust a third-party service.

7. Use MetaMask to sign the transaction using the user's private key and broadcast it to the blockchain network. Use the injectable web3 instance provided by MetaMash from the DApp:

```
if (typeof web3 !== 'undefined') {
    // Use Mist/MetaMask's provider
    web3 = new Web3(web3.currentProvider);
```

```
    } else {
        // if no provider is available
        web3 = new Web3(new
                Web3.providers.HttpProvider("http://localhost:8545"));
    }
```

8. Listen to the events logged from the client for real-time updates. This can help to inform the user of any state changes happening in the Ethereum blockchain:

```
TestContract.events.TestEvent({
    filter: { ... },
    fromBlock: 0
}, function(error, event){
    console.log(event);
})
```

9. If the application does not require a wallet or provider such as Mist/MetaMask, you can connect to any known Ethereum node or use a service such as INFURA. For more information regarding the node connection, refer to the `Chapter` `1`, *Getting Started*, of this book.

10. For more complex applications, you need to rely on servers for performing some tasks. For example, interacting with other services can be a little cumbersome with a serverless approach.

11. Introducing a server can be very useful in terms of features, but can bring some sort of centralization to the whole model. Take the decision based on the requirements of the application being built.

12. For applications such as games and social networks that require a huge volume of transactions, the throughput of Ethereum can act as a bottleneck. This has to be considered while designing such an application. One recommendation is to move transactions away from the blockchain to a different service. Since this processing and storage is happening outside the blockchain, they can be referred to as off-chain transactions and storage.

13. Everything boils down to the requirements and the balance between decentralization and application features.

Implementing an application-specific wallet

For every transaction signing, a DApp can make use of wallets such as MetaMask, or can handle the private keys itself. Handling the private keys can be a more user-friendly and optimal solution at first, but the user won't always trust the DApp when it comes to handling private keys.

In this recipe, you will understand the key points of implementing application-specific wallets and using third-party solutions.

Getting ready

This recipe helps you decide on a design decision that can arise during the development of a fully functional DApp. It is an advanced topic, and knowledge of Ethereum and DApps in general are required to get the most out of this recipe.

Stepping through the first three chapters of this book is recommended if you are just getting started on this topic.

How to do it...

1. Designing and implementing an application-specific wallet can help the user in many ways. Use this approach to avoid the need for the user to install additional wallet software for managing private keys and signing transactions.
2. Use an application-specific wallet to do tasks such as creating/managing the user's private keys and signing/broadcasting the transaction to the network. Doing these tasks from the application avoids the need for a third-party wallet such as MetaMask.
3. Build the wallet from scratch by implementing Ethereum wallet functionalities or use a library such as `ethereumjs-wallet` (`https://github.com/ethereumjs/ethereumjs-wallet`) for implementations of these tasks.
4. Use the `ethereumjs` library for functionalities such as creating a new private key, importing an existing private key, creating an HD wallet, and so on. For signing transactions, `ethereumjs-tx` can be used along with the wallet.

> The user can send some Ether from other wallets or exchanges to seed the newly generated accounts. As an additional feature, Shapeshift (`https://shapeshift.io/`) APIs can be integrated into your application to converting other cryptos to Ether.

5. Handle the signing of each transaction in the background using private keys. The authentication can be done either for individual transactions or through the DApp master login.

6. Implementing a dedicated wallet can involve a lot of development effort when compared with third-party wallet implementations such as MetaMask. Store the private keys and other account credentials very securely since a security breach can cost a lot.

7. As a result of the wallet implementation, the interaction from the user side will be greatly simplified and they can easily interact with the application without having to install any third-party software.

8. Implementing a wallet can also bring trust issues. You have to ask users to trust your DApp to handle accounts and their private keys, which is not recommended for all scenarios.

9. The decision on which approach to use will depend completely on the kinds of users using the application and the use case for building the application. The frequency of transactions can also matter while implementing the wallet.

What if you find a bug after deployment?

As discussed in Chapter 8, *Smart Contract Security*, the immutability of smart contracts can bring some disadvantages, such as when fixing a bug that is found after deployment. The contracts can be designed in a way that the effect of a bug can be reduced to a minimum, which can help in overcoming such limitations.

In this chapter, you will learn about various design techniques to minimize the effect of a bug found after a deployment process.

Getting ready

It is required to have at least a basic knowledge of writing smart contracts and building DApps using Web3JS. Understanding the implementation of a basic DApp is essential for getting the most out of this recipe.

For those who are new to this, it is recommended to read through the first three chapters of this book. It is also recommended to refer to Chapter 8, *Smart Contract Security*, for more information on common bugs that can occur while writing smart contracts.

How to do it...

1. It is not possible to fix the bug by updating the code in the smart contract due to the immutable nature of Ethereum smart contracts. Upgradable smart contracts are a way to overcome this issue for a certain limit. But, it reduces the user's trust in the smart contracts.

2. There are several design techniques that can be considered while writing smart contracts to minimize the effect of a potential bug.

3. Let's consider a simple contract that allows the deposit and withdrawal of Ether from a contract. We can try implementing various design techniques to avoid the loss of funds up to a certain limit:

```solidity
pragma solidity ^0.4.24;

contract VulnerableContract {

    function deposit() public {
        // Code to accept Ether
    }

    function withdraw() public {
        // Code to transfer Ether
    }

}
```

4. Include the rate limiting functionality in your contract, which will limit the task performed to a certain time period. For example, the contract will allow a user to withdraw only a certain amount of Ether/tokens per day. Additional withdrawals can be prevented completely or allowed only through elevated or multi-signature approval. This will greatly reduce the loss and give enough time for the user or owner to find a resolution.

5. Model this contract in the following way to implement the functionality. The modifier verifies the time between the current and last withdrawal:

```solidity
pragma solidity ^0.4.24;

contract ControlledContract {

    // Simplified withdraw tracker
    // Can include amount for more precise tracking
    mapping(address => uint) lastWithdraw;

    // Modifier to limit the rate of withdraw
```

```
modifier verifyWithdraw() {
    require(lastWithdraw[msg.sender] + 1 days > now);
    _;
}

function deposit() public {
    // Code to accept Ether
}

function withdraw(uint _value) verifyWithdraw public {
    // Code to transfer Ether
    require(_value < 1 ether);
    lastWithdraw[msg.sender] = now;
}

}
```

6. Another approach is to pause or stop contract functionality as soon as a bug is discovered. This prevents the attacker from performing malicious actions on the contract. The example contract can be modified as follows to include the pause functionality:

```
pragma solidity ^0.4.24;

contract ControlledContract {
    bool pause;
    address owner;

    modifier onlyOwner() {
        require(msg.sender == owner);
        _;
    }

    modifier whenNotPaused {
        require(!pause);
        _;
    }

    function pauseContract() onlyOwner public {
        pause = true;
    }

    function unPauseContract() onlyOwner public {
        pause = true;
    }

    function deposit() whenNotPaused public {
        // some code
```

```
        }

        function withdraw() whenNotPaused public {
            // some code
        }
    }
```

7. Consider delaying contract actions as an approach in order to minimize the effect
   of an attack. Each contract action can either be performed after a certain time
   period or through an approval. The withdrawal contract can be further modified
   to include the mentioned method:

```
pragma solidity ^0.4.24;

contract ControlledContract {

    struct WithdrawalReq {
        uint value;
        uint time;
    }

    mapping (address => uint) balances;

    mapping (address => WithdrawalReq) requests;

    uint constant delay = 7 days;

    function requestWithdrawal() public {
        require(balances[msg.sender] > 0);
        uint amountToWithdraw = balances[msg.sender];
        balances[msg.sender] = 0;
        requests[msg.sender] = WithdrawalReq(
            amountToWithdraw,
            now
        );
    }

    function withdraw() public {
        require(now > requests[msg.sender].time + delay);
        uint amountToWithdraw = requests[msg.sender].value;
        requests[msg.sender].value = 0;
        msg.sender.transfer(amountToWithdraw);
    }
}
```

8. The decision on which design to choose depends heavily on the targeted user base and the requirements. You can either implement a fail-safe method or all of them. You can also come up with a fail-safe method based on your requirements, but make sure that the code is well-audited and error-free before deploying it to production.

Generating random numbers in Solidity

Some applications might need a **random number generator** (RNG) to perform specific tasks. There are many use cases where randomness is an essential part. For example, a decentralized lottery requires a random number to select the winner. Randomness can also be used to provide suggestions to the users of the application.

Generating a random number can be tricky in a decentralized system such as Ethereum for various reasons. Such functionality has to be achieved through design workarounds. In this chapter, you will learn how to build an RNG that can be used in your DApp.

Getting ready

It is required to have at least a basic knowledge of writing smart contracts and building DApps using Web3JS. Understanding the implementation of a basic DApp is essential to get more out of this recipe.

For those who are new to this, it is recommended to read through the first three chapters of this book.

How to do it...

1. Programs in Ethereum have to be deterministic since they run on multiple nodes, and everyone running the EVM has to get the same result. This prevents the implementation of a true random number generator for Ethereum-based DApps.
2. A common method of implementation for the random number generator is by using deterministic, miner-defined parameters such as difficulty or timestamp:

```
pragma solidity^0.4.24;

// Contract to generate random number
// Uses timestamp and difficulty
// Not recommended
```

```
contract RNG {
    function generateRandom() view returns (uint) {
        return uint256(keccak256(
            abi.encodePacked(block.timestamp, block.difficulty)
        ));
    }
}
```

3. Modify this further to generate a random number from the block hash of a future block, which is harder to predict. This is commonly used across various Ethereum DApps.

4. Consider the example of a decentralized lottery that selects the winner based on a future block. The winning lottery number can be determined in such a way:

```
pragma solidity^0.4.24;

contract Lottery {

    // Structure of a bid
    struct Bid {
        uint num;
        uint blockNum;
    }

    // Mapping to store bods
    mapping(address => Bid) bids;

    // Function to select the winner based on future block hash
    function isWon() public view returns (bool) {
        uint bid = bids[msg.sender].num;
        uint blockNum = bids[msg.sender].blockNum;

        require(blockNum >= block.number);

        uint winner = uint(keccak256(
            abi.encodePacked(blockhash(blockNum + 3))
        ));

        return (bid == winner);
    }
}
```

5. To bring in more randomness, implement and use an external service for generating a random number. A contract can read this data with the help of Oracle services.

Oracle services help Ethereum smart contracts to read data from the World Wide Web. For example, it can query an API and return the result. It is different from the Oracle database. For more information, refer to the *Fetching data from APIs using solidity* recipe from `Chapter 7`, *Advanced Solidity*.

6. It is also required to trust the third-party service to provide valid results every time. If the service is compromised, it is more harmful to use the service than build one in the contract itself.

7. There are a lot of proposals, and research is happening in this field, and one of the recent proposals from the Ethereum community is *RANDAO: A DAO working as the RNG of Ethereum*.

8. RANDAO is a DAO that allows anyone to participate, and the random number is generated by all participants together. It includes three phases.

9. In the first phase, ask the participant to send a transaction to the contract with a certain amount of Ether as a pledge in a specified time period (for instance, a six-block period, approximately 72 seconds) and the result of *sha3(s)*, where the value of *s* is not revealed by the participant.

10. In the second phase, ask anyone who submitted the result of *sha3(s)* to send a transaction with the number *s* to contract *C* within a specified time period. Use the contract to check whether *s* is a valid number by comparing the result of *sha3(s)* with the previously committed data. Save valid s values to the collection of *s* to generate a random number.

11. Use the contract to generate the random number from collected seed *s* values and write it to storage. The result will be sent to all contracts that requested the random number.

12. Finally, send back the pledge and the profit to the participants from the contract. Calculate the profit from the fees that are paid by other contracts for consuming the random number and divide it into equal parts.

13. The choice depends completely on the targeted users and the use case. The trade-off has to be considered while choosing one option over the other.

Keeping contracts simple, modular, and up to date

Smart contracts and solidity are relatively new, and the best practices and tools are still under proposal or at an early stage of implementation. A lot of bugs and security vulnerabilities are still being discovered and the platform needs to evolve. To prevent any potential bugs from surfacing, it is always recommended to follow existing guidelines and general software design principles.

In this recipe, you will learn the importance of keeping the contract simple, modular, and updated.

Getting ready

It is recommended to have a basic understanding of writing smart contracts before going through this recipe. It covers various guidelines that you have to consider which will make your smart contracts better. For a better development environment, use the tools and libraries recommended in the first chapter of this book.

How to do it...

1. Likelihood of an error increases when the complexity of the code increases. To reduce this, it is always recommended to keep the contract code to a minimum and stick to the core functionality.
2. Ensure that the contract's logic is simple and easy to understand. It is important to keep the contract very readable.
3. While comparing with traditional software engineering practices, the code has to be reusable, modular, and upgradable. This may not always be the case when it comes to smart contracts in a blockchain system. Write the contracts in a balanced manner to follow best practices and yet consider trust and immutability factors.
4. An upgradable contract can look very usable and ideal when considering general software engineering principles. But, this increases the complexity of the contract and makes it more prone to bugs. Make a proper trade-off between a more complex, error-prone, upgradable contract and a simple bug-free contract.

5. Contracts can be written in various modules or by keeping all contract code in a single place and minimizing the control flow between multiple functions. It is recommended to choose an approach that is more readable and easy to review, based on the requirements.

6. A modular contract helps a lot in code reusability and avoids duplication on the network. Multiple contracts can refer to a single library deployed on the network to achieve a common task. It is always recommended to verify the previously deployed contract code for safety before using it across many contracts.

7. There are a lot of well-tested and audited smart contract libraries to provide common functionalities. A perfect example is OpenZeppelin contracts. Use them to reduce the risk of potential bugs in the contract.

8. OpenZeppelin provides contracts for common tasks such as ERC20/ERC721 token standards, initial coin offerings, performing arithmetic operations, and so on. You can find more information about the library here: `https://github.com/OpenZeppelin/openzeppelin-solidity/`.

9. Solidity and its best practices undergo rapid changes daily, and it is recommended to adopt them as soon as possible. Update the libraries used frequently to avoid any newly discovered bugs.

Implementing user authentication in Ethereum

Every application requires some sort of authentication and authorization to restrict unauthorized usage. In Ethereum, most of this happens through the **externally owned account** (**EOA**) from which the transactions originate. EOAs are generated through strong cryptographic algorithms that are hard to hack unless the hacker has access to the private keys.

In this recipe, you will learn various authentication and authorization methods that can be implemented in your Ethereum DApp.

Getting ready

It is required to have at least a basic knowledge of writing smart contracts and building DApps using Web3JS. Understanding the implementation of a basic DApp is essential to get more out of this recipe.

For those who are new to this, it is recommended to read through the first three chapters of this book.

How to do it...

1. Every DApp is authenticated and authorized by the user's address. The address is the key to accessing a decentralized application built on Ethereum.

2. Consider the example of CryptoKitties, a popular crypto collectable game built on Ethereum. The application identifies the user using their Ethereum address. A user can purchase kitties using their address and the ownership of the asset will be transferred to them.

3. The application lists all the kitties owned by the currently logged in address on a different page. You can easily track the assets using the address:

```
mapping(address => uint[]) kitties;

function getKitties(address _owner) returns(uint[]) {
    return kitties[_owner];
}
```

4. Any tasks involving the kitties can only be performed by their respective owners. This ensures proper authentication:

```
mapping(uint => address) kittyToOwner;

modifier onlyOwner(uint _id) {
    require(kittyToOwner[_id] == msg.sender);
    _;
}

function transfer(uint _id, address _to) onlyOwner(_id) {
    // Code to transfer the kitty
}
```

5. Similar procedures are followed throughout smart contracts to achieve authentication and authorization in the Ethereum DApp.

6. Since the addresses can be used to sign transactions externally without the need for a transaction, you can use this for other methods of authentication.

7. For example, use the `ecrecover` function to extract the address from a signed transaction. This allows anyone to verify the transaction origin and thereby authenticate the address:

```
ecrecover(hash, v, r, s);
```

8. You can use key files generated for each account as a method of authentication. Successful unlocks can be considered as a proper authentication and the address used can be assigned to the logged in user.

9. In an Ethereum DApp, authorization for actions performed happens mostly in the smart contract, and the private key acts as the authenticator. Some additional layer of security can be implemented as per the application's requirements. It finally boils down to the targeted users and the type of interactions they have with the application.

10
Other Protocols and Applications

In this chapter, you will learn the following topics:

- Registering on Ethereum Name Service
- Whisper–communication protocol for DApps
- Swarm–distributed storage platform
- Watching Bitcoin transactions using BTCRelay
- Scheduling Ethereum transactions using an alarm clock
- Using the openzeppelin library

Introduction

The Ethereum ecosystem is relatively new and is constantly evolving at a very high rate. New services and platforms are being added to it every day. The system has its own limitations, which can be either due to the lack of platform maturity or some design choices that have to be made for a distributed system. There are workarounds for some of the limitations, for example, by using Oracle services to interact with an external data source.

The community is building new applications and protocols to help users and developers to get more out of Ethereum. In this chapter, you will learn about other Ethereum protocols that can be used in multiple scenarios, and various reusable applications available in the Ethereum ecosystem. This will help you in building feature-rich distributed applications based on Ethereum.

Registering on Ethereum Name Service

Ethereum Name Service (ENS) is a decentralized naming system that is built on top of Ethereum blockchain. The service allows anyone to create human-readable names for machine-readable Ethereum addresses and makes them easily identifiable.

In this recipe, you will learn to register your own ENS domain and learn more about how it works. You will also learn to integrate the ENS service into your wallet application.

Getting ready

It is required to have basic knowledge of setting up an Ethereum node and working with the `web3` JavaScript console before stepping through this recipe. For more information on node setup and interaction, refer to the first chapter of this book.

How to do it...

1. Let's try registering a name in the ENS for learning purposes. First, download the test helper file (`https://github.com/ensdomains/ens/blob/master/ensutils-testnet.js`) for the initial bootstrapping process. The file contains contract definitions and Ropsten testnet addresses for easy interaction. Use this file only for testing purposes.

    ENS is already deployed in the Ethereum main and test networks. You can find them at the following addresses:

   Mainnet: `0x314159265dd8dbb310642f98f50c066173c1259b`
   Ropsten: `0x112234455c3a32fd11230c42e7bccd4a84e02010`
   Rinkeby: `0xe7410170f87102df0055eb195163a03b7f2bff4a`

2. Once the download has completed, open the `geth` console, which is connected to the Ropsten test network and load the downloaded JavaScript file. It will create ENS contract instances that you can interact with:

   ```
   > loadScript('../ensutils-testnet.js');
   ```

3. Now, before registering a name in the ENS, ensure that it is not already owned by some other address. This can be verified by checking the expiry date of the name. If the returned date is earlier than the current date, the name is available and you can claim it:

```
> var time = testRegistrar.expiryTimes(web3.sha3('packt'));
> new Date(time.toNumber() * 1000);
```

 If the expiry time is earlier than the current date, it can mean one of two things: either the name is not yet claimed by anyone or the previous claim has crossed the expiry date.

4. Next, set the public resolver to resolve your name. Ensure you unlock your account before performing any state changing functions:

```
> ens.setResolver(
    namehash('packt.test'),
    publicResolver.address,
    { from: eth.accounts[0] }
  );
```

5. Once the resolver is assigned successfully, update the mapping with the address of your choice:

```
> publicResolver.setAddr(
    namehash('packt.test'),
    '0x111...', // Or any other address
    { from: eth.accounts[0] }
  );
```

6. You can also create a subdomain and map an address by following similar steps.
7. Finally, verify that your ENS name resolves to the address you have selected.

```
> var address = ens.resolver(namehash('packt.test'));
> resolverContract.at(address).addr(namehash('packt.test'));
```

8. The `.test` **Top-Level Domains** (**TLDs**) in a test network use **First In First Server** (**FIFS**) registrars. They are also configured to expire 28 days after the claim date. The main network follows an auction-based registry, which asks the users to place bids for each name.

9. The auction usually runs for 5 days. It includes 3 days of bidding and 2 days of revealing the bids. The status of the name and the bid can be checked using the following command:

```
> ethRegistrar.entries(web3.sha3('packt'))[0]
```

10. It will return a status ID ranging from 0 to 5. The meaning of each ID is as follows:

- 0: Name is available and the auction hasn't started
- 1: Name is available and the auction has started
- 2: Name is taken and currently owned by someone
- 3: Name is forbidden
- 4: Name is currently in the *reveal* stage of the auction
- 5: Name is not yet available due to the *soft launch* of names

11. Based on the status, you can start the auction, place a bid, reveal your bid, or finalize the auction. For more information regarding placing a bid and auctions in general, refer to the official ENS documentation here: `http://docs.ens.domains/`.

How it works...

ENS is used to map a human-readable name, such as `packt.eth`, to more complex identifiers such as an Ethereum address. ENS shares its goal with the **Domain Name Service** (**DNS**) of the internet, which maps IP addresses to easily recognizable strings of characters. ENS contains two important components: the registry and the resolver. A registry is a smart contract that owns a domain and issues subdomains of that domain to users. The user has to follow the set of rules defined in the contract for registering a domain.

The registry maintains a list of all domains/subdomains and the following information about each of them:

- The owner, which can be an externally owned account or contract address
- The resolver
- The lifetime for all records saved under that domain

The owner of each domain will have access to set the resolver and **time-to-live** (TTL) for that domain. They can transfer the ownership of each domain or subdomain to another address. The resolver handles the process of translating names into addresses. Any contract that implements the relevant standards can act as a resolver contract in ENS.

On the Ethereum main network, you can register your names under the `.ens` TLD. It uses an auction-based registrar for allocating names to owners. The Ropsten test network allows both `.eth` and `.test` TLDs. The `.test` domain allows anyone to claim an unused name for testing purposes. The names claimed, expire after 28 days. The Rinkeby network also supports ENS but only for the `.test` TLD.

Whisper–communication protocol for DApps

Whisper is a communication protocol for DApps, which they use to communicate with each other. There are various use cases in which a communication protocol like Whisper is essential. With the help of this protocol, applications like chat rooms can be built on Ethereum.

In this recipe, you will learn more about the Whisper protocol.

Getting ready

You need to have knowledge of Ethereum network setup and usage to get the best out of this recipe. You can learn more about these initial configurations in Chapter 1, *Getting Started*.

Whisper is still in the development stage and is not yet recommended for production applications.

How to do it...

1. Whisper uses the `shh` protocol to send messages between DApps. In `Web3JS`, you can directly access the object from the root:

   ```
   web3.shh
   ```

2. Create a new identity using the `shh` object. Call the `newIdentity` function to do this:

```
var identity = web3.shh.newIdentity();
```

3. Use the `post` method to broadcast the messages:

```
web3.shh.post({
    // ...
});
```

4. Every `post` method accepts a `JSON` object with the following parameters:

   - **topic**: One or multiple arbitrary data items that are used to encode the abstract topic of this message. It can be used to filter messages based on requirements.
   - **payload**: Unformatted byte array that provides the data to be sent. Similar to topic.
   - **TTL**: Time for the message to live on the network in seconds. This defaults to 50.
   - **priority**: Priority you want the packet to have on the network. It is specified in milliseconds of processing time on your machine. This defaults to 50.
   - **from**: Message sender; optional.
   - **to**: Message receiver; optional.

5. With these parameters, the `ssh` post method can be described as follows:

```
shh.post({
    "from": identity,
    "topics": [ web3.fromAscii("whisper app") ],
    "payload": [
        web3.fromAscii("Ethereum"),
        web3.fromAscii("Whisper")
    ],
    "ttl": 100,
    "priority": 1000
});
```

6. Listen to messages by using the `watch` method:

```
var listner = shh.watch({
    "topics": [
        web3.fromAscii("whisper app"),
        identity
    ],
```

```
        "to": identity
   });
```

7. Use a `callback` function to execute some logic when a new message is received:

```
listner.arrived(function(message) {
    // Executed when a new message received
    console.log(web3.toAscii(message.payload))
    console.log(message.from);
});
```

8. This can be further customized to perform *1 - 1* or *1 - N* communications based on the application requirements and use case.

Swarm–distributed storage platform

Swarm is a native base layer service for Ethereum, which provides a distributed storage platform and content distribution service. The goal of Swarm is to provide a decentralized store of Ethereum's public records. It can store DApp code and data, or even blockchain data.

To a user, Swarm may look very similar to the internet but files are not uploaded to a specific server. The objective is to have a peer-to-peer storage and serving solution that is DDOS resistant, has zero downtime, is fault tolerant, and is censorship resistant. The system can self-sustain due to a built-in incentive system that uses peer-to-peer accounting and allows trading resources for payment.

In this recipe, you will learn to use Swarm for storing and retrieving data.

Getting ready

You need to have a working installation of Ethereum on your system before stepping through this recipe. It is also required to have `git` and `golang` installed as prerequisites. You can learn more about the initial configurations in `Chapter 1`, *Getting Started*.

Swarm is still under constant development and is not yet recommended for use in production applications.

How to do it...

1. Download and install Ethereum by running the following command if you do not have it configured:

```
$ sudo add-apt-repository -y ppa:ethereum/ethereum
```

2. Once Ethereum is installed, download and install the stable version of Swarm:

```
$ sudo apt-get update
$ sudo apt-get install ethereum-swarm
```

3. Verify the installation of Ethereum using the `version` command. It should return the currently installed version of Swarm:

```
$ swarm version
```

4. Now, to connect and start using Swarm, you need to have an Ethereum address. Follow the commands given here to create an account and use it with Swarm:

```
// Password will be asked and returns the address
$ geth account new

$ swarm --bzzaccount <account_address>
```

5. Once the node is started, verify it by navigating to `http://localhost:8500` in your browser.

6. Now, to start a `swarm` cluster with a single node, use the `maxpeers` flag with a 0 value:

```
$ swarm --bzzaccount <account_address> --maxpeers 0
```

7. In a multi-node cluster, you can add peers by specifying their `enode` address. To get the enode address of a node, use the `admin.nodeInfo.enode` command:

```
$ geth --exec "admin.nodeInfo.enode" attach ipc:/path/to/bzzd.ipc
```

8. We can add a peer just like in Ethereum. Use the `admin.addPeer` command with `enode_address` as the parameter:

```
$ geth --exec='admin.addPeer(<enode_address>)' attach
ipc:/path/to/bzzd.ipc
```

9. To upload a file, use the `swarm up` command:

```
$ swarm up ../filename.txt
// will return a hash value
```

10. The hash value returned is the hash of a JSON file that contains the example file as its only entry, and is called as the manifest. Both the file contents and the manifest are uploaded by default.

 You can avoid the creation of the manifest file by specifying it explicitly. It uploads the content as is. However, if you wish to retrieve this file, the `bzz:/` scheme will result in a `404 Not Found error`. In order to access this file, you would have to use the `bzz-raw:/` scheme.

11. To access the uploaded file, use the `hash` along with the Swarm endpoint:

```
http://localhost:8500/bzz:/<hash_value>/
```

12. To upload a directory, you can use the `--recursive` command:

```
$ swarm --recursive up ./path/to/directory
```

13. To download any uploaded file, use the `swarm down` command:

```
$ swarm down bzz:/<hash_value>
```

14. A directory can also be downloaded with the same command and the `--recursive` flag:

```
$ swarm down --recursive bzz:/<hash>
```

15. Apart from uploading and downloading files through the **Command Line Interface (CLI)**, Swarm supports file uploads through HTTP as well. Use the HTTP endpoint provided by Swarm to do this:

```
$ curl -H "Content-Type: text/plain"
       --data "data_for_uploading"
       http://localhost:8500/bzz:/
```

16. It will return the hash value, which can be used to read the file through HTTP, as described in step 11.

17. Apart from `bzz` and `bzz-raw`, Swarm supports four more URL schemes:

    - `bzz-list`: It returns the list of files contained in manifest under `<path>`, grouped into common prefixes by using / as a delimiter.
    - `bzz-hash`: It responds with the hash value of the raw content, which is the same content returned by requests with the `bzz-raw` scheme.
    - `bzz-immutable`: A particular `bzz-immutable` URL will always address the exact same fixed immutable content.
    - `bzz-resource`: It allows you to receive hash pointers to content that the ENS entry resolved at different versions.

18. Apart from the CLI and HTTP methods, Swarm also supports interaction directly from the filesystem. This is achieved through **FUSE (Filesystem in Userspace)**.

19. Windows is not supported by FUSE. So, the method will work only with Linux, macOS, and FreeBSD. To install FUSE, run the following commands:

    ```
    // Linux
    $ sudo apt-get install fuse
    $ sudo modprobe fuse
    $ sudo chown <username>:<groupname> /etc/fuse.conf
    $ sudo chown <username>:<groupname> /dev/fuse

    // MacOS
    $ brew update
    $ brew install caskroom/cask/brew-cask
    $ brew cask install osxfuse
    ```

20. To upload files through FUSE, upload some content to Swarm using the `swarm up` command. Once you get the returned manifest hash, use it to mount the manifest on a mount point:

    ```
    $ swarm fs mount --ipcpath <path-to-bzzd.ipc> <manifest-hash> <mount-point>
    ```

21. For more information about using Swarm, refer to the official documentation at https://swarm-guide.readthedocs.io/.

Watching Bitcoin transactions using BTCRelay

Ethereum supports the transfer and verification of Ether by default. If the target users use Bitcoin more than Ethereum, then interoperability between Bitcoin and Ethereum becomes a problem. To solve this issue, Ethereum has a smart contract that stores and relays Bitcoin transactions so that Ethereum DApps can verify Bitcoin transactions.

In this recipe, you will learn to use BTCRelay, which acts as a bridge between the Bitcoin blockchain and Ethereum smart contracts.

 To discover new and popular DApps in the Ethereum network, you can use *State of the DApps* (https://www.stateofthedapps.com/), which is a DApp registry. You can also submit your own DApp to the registry.

Getting ready

You need to have an understanding of Ethereum and smart contracts to get more out of this recipe. Refer to the first three chapters of this book to get a basic understanding of Ethereum and building DApps.

How to do it...

1. The service provides several APIs through its contract, which we can use to verify or relay Bitcoin transactions. These APIs can be used in your DApp to achieve Bitcoin-related verification. Let's understand the important functions exposed by the BTCRelay contract through an example that uses them.

2. Use the `verifyTx` function to verify a Bitcoin transaction. A transaction is considered as verified only if it has at least six confirmations. The function returns the hash of the verified bitcoin transaction. It returns 0 if the verification fails:

```
verifyTx(
    rawTransaction, // Raw transaction bytes - bytes
    transactionIndex, // Index of the transaction in Block - int256
    merkleSibling, // Merkle proof sibling hashes - int256[]
    blockHash // hash of the transaction block - int256
) returns (uint256)
```

3. To verify and relay the transaction to a specific contract, use the `relayTx` function provided by BTCRelay. The function is very similar to `verifyTx` but accepts one more parameter as `contractAddress`. The target address should have a function called `processTransaction`. The `relayTx` function returns either the result of `processTransaction` or an error code:

```
relayTx(
 rawTransaction, // Raw transaction bytes - bytes
 transactionIndex, // Index of the transaction in Block - int256
 merkleSibling, // Merkle proof sibiling hashes - int256[]
 blockHash, // hash of the transaction block - int256
 contractAddress // Address of the target contract
) returns (int256)

// Target contract function
// Will be invoked by relayTx
processTransaction(
 bytes rawTransaction,
 uint256 transactionHash
) returns (int256)
```

4. Use the following functions provided by the service to set and get the block header of a block hash:

```
// Get header
getBlockHeader(
    blockHash // Hash of the block
) returns (bytes)

// Set header
storeBlockHeader(
    blockHeader // raw block header - bytes
) returns (int256)

// Set multiple headers at once
bulkStoreHeader(
    bytesOfHeaders, // raw block headers one after another - bytes
    numberOfHeaders // number of headers
) returns (int256)
```

5. `getBlockHeader` returns the header as bytes if it is found. It returns a 0 result with a length of 80 bytes if the header does not exist. The result is 0 if the payment is insufficient. The payment can be calculated by calling the `getFeeAmount` function:

```
getFeeAmount(blockHash) returns (int256)
```

6. There are other functions that are used to read and write more data about bitcoin transactions:

```
// Returns the hash of given block height
getBlockHash(blockHeight) returns (int256)

// Returns the difference between the chainwork
// of latest and 10th prior block
getAverageChainWork()

// Returns the hash of latest block
getBlockchainHead() returns (int256)

// Returns the block height of latest block
getLastBlockHeight() returns (int256)
```

7. BTCRelay also includes functions to help relayers with incentives. Relayers are those who update the contract with recent blockchain transactions:

```
// Store single block header and store its fee
storeBlockWithFee(blockHeader, fee) returns (int256)

// Sets fee and the recipient for the given block hash
changeFeeRecipient(blockHash, fee, recipient) returns (int256)

// Get the fee recipient for the given block hash
getFeeRecipient(blockHash) returns (int256)

// Get the amount of fee for changeFeeRecipient
getChangeRecipientFee() returns (int256)
```

8. The service can be used in your application by specifying its deployed address and ABI. Consider the following example as a template for calling the functions:

```
var btcRelayAddr = "0x...";
var btcRelayAbi = [...<BTCRelay_ABI>...];

var btcRelay = web3.eth.contract(btcRelayAbi).at(btcRelayAddr);

btcRelay.verifyTx.call(
    transactionBytes,
    transactionIndex,
    merkleSibling,
    transactionBlockHash,
    { from: '0x..', ...}
);
```

9. Refer to the official GitHub repo (`https://github.com/ethereum/btcrelay`) for more information related to Ethereum contract and internals.

Scheduling Ethereum transactions using an alarm clock

Ethereum needs an external actor to perform transactions. This restricts anyone to schedule a transaction which will get executed in the future. Ethereum has a scheduling smart contract, which helps in solving such problems. This contract helps to design and implement more complex DApps that depend on future transactions.

In this recipe, you will learn to schedule transactions that will be executed in the future and develop DApps around those future transactions.

Getting ready

You need to have an understanding of Ethereum and smart contracts to get more out of this recipe. Refer to the first three chapters of this book to get a basic understanding of Ethereum and building DApps.

How to do it...

1. **Ethereum Alarm Clock (EAC)** is a smart contract that lives in the Ethereum blockchain. This makes the service trusted and accessible from other smart contracts.

2. To interact with the EAC service, you need to use the `scheduler` interface. The interface provides some function signatures that can identify the required functions from the EAC contract:

```solidity
pragma solidity ^0.4.21;

/**
 * @title SchedulerInterface
 * @dev The base contract that the higher contracts:
 * BaseScheduler, BlockScheduler and TimestampScheduler
 * all inherit from.
 */
contract SchedulerInterface {
```

```
function schedule(
    address _toAddress,
    bytes _callData,
    uint[8] _uintArgs
) public payable returns (address);

function computeEndowment(
    uint _bounty,
    uint _fee,
    uint _callGas,
    uint _callValue,
    uint _gasPrice
) public view returns (uint);
}
```

3. Use the `scheduler` function with the required parameters to schedule a transaction. Create a new contract that will make use of the scheduling service:

```solidity
pragma solidity ^0.4.24;

import "./SchedulerInterface.sol";

contract DelayedPayment {
    SchedulerInterface public scheduler;
}
```

4. Use any function, or the constructor, to set the address of the EAC contract:

```solidity
constructor(address _scheduler) public payable {
    scheduler = SchedulerInterface(_scheduler);
}
```

5. The `scheduler` function accepts three parameters. The first parameter is the target address. Let's consider it as the scheduling contract's address:

```solidity
_toAddress = address(this); // address of scheduling contract
```

6. The second parameter accepts `calldata` to send along with the transaction. This depends on the type of transaction being sent. Leaving it blank will call the `fallback` function of the target address:

```solidity
_callData = ""; // or specify any function signature
```

7. The third parameter is a `uint` array, which accepts a series of other parameters. They are specified as follows:

   - `callGas`: The amount of gas that will be sent with the transaction
   - `callValue`: The amount of Ether (in wei) that will be sent with the transaction
   - `windowSize`: The number of blocks after windowSize during which the transaction will still be executable
   - `windowStart`: The first block number that the transaction will be executable
   - `gasPrice`: The gas price (in wei) that must be sent by the executing party to execute the transaction
   - `fee`: The fee amount (in wei) included in the transaction for protocol maintainers
   - `bounty`: The payment (in wei) included in the transaction to incentivize the executing arguments
   - `deposit` (optional): Required amount of Ether (in wei) to be staked by executing agents

8. After applying these parameters, a basic scheduler contract will look like this:

```
contract ScheduledPayment {

    SchedulerInterface public scheduler;

    address public scheduledTransaction;

    constructor(address _scheduler) public payable {
        scheduler = SchedulerInterface(_scheduler);
    }

    function scheduleTransaction(uint _numBlocks) public {
        uint lockedUntil = block.number + _numBlocks;

        scheduledTransaction = scheduler.schedule.value(0.1 ether)
        (
            address(this),
            "",
            [
                200000,
                0,
                255,
                lockedUntil,
                20000000000 wei,
                20000000000 wei,
```

```
                    20000000000 wei,
                    30000000000 wei
            ]
        );
    }

    function () public payable {
        // ...
    }
}
```

Using the openzeppelin library

There are many open source libraries available for Ethereum smart contracts re-usability. One of the most commonly used libraries is openzeppelin. It provides well audited and modularized smart contracts that achieve common tasks in the Ethereum blockchain. Using this can improve your overall DApp standards and security.

In this recipe, you will learn more about the smart contracts provided by the openzeppelin library. You will also learn to install and use this library in your DApp.

Getting ready

You need to have an understanding of Ethereum and smart contracts to get more out of this recipe. Refer to the first three chapters of this book to get a basic understanding of Ethereum and building DApps.

How to do it...

1. Openzeppelin is distributed through npm. Install it using the npm install command:

   ```
   npm install -E openzeppelin-solidity
   ```

    npm does an automatic semantic version update for improved security and bug fixes while installing. This is not suggested for openzeppelin, since minor changes in a contract can make it work differently. To avoid semantic version updates, use --save-exact or the -E attribute while installing.

2. The files will be downloaded to the `node_modules` folder. Reference them directly by specifying the contract's file path:

```
import 'openzeppelin-solidity/contracts/ownership/Ownable.sol';

contract NewContract is Ownable {
  // ...
}
```

3. Since solidity allows references from GitHub, you can also import the library directly from its repository:

```
import "github.com/OpenZeppelin/openzeppelin-
solidity/contracts/ownership/Ownable.sol";

contract NewContract is Ownable {
  // ...
}
```

4. Let's look into each of the contract categories in detail. The access contracts allow selective restrictions and basic authorization control functions for a solidity contract. Use this to gain access to common functionalities such as address whitelisting, signature-based permission management, and RBAC (Role-Based Access Control):

```
import "openzeppelin-
solidity/contracts/access/SignatureBouncer.sol";
import "openzeppelin-solidity/contracts/access/Whitelist.sol";
import "openzeppelin-solidity/contracts/access/RBAC/..";
```

5. The ICO set provides most of the contracts to run an ICO. Either use the basic crowdsale contract or modify it further by using the other modules provided with it. There are modules to control distribution, emission, price, and validation:

```
import "openzeppelin-solidity/contracts/crowdsale/...";
```

6. The introspection provides an interface that can be used to make an ERC-165 standard contract:

```
import "openzeppelin-solidity/contracts/introspection/...";
```

 ERC-165 creates a standard method to publish and detect what interfaces a smart contract implements. It is sometimes useful to query whether a contract supports the interface and which version of the interface, in order to adapt the way in which the contract is to be interacted with.

7. The life cycle set provides a collection of base contracts that you can use to manage the existence and behavior of a contract and its funds:

   ```
   import "openzeppelin-solidity/contracts/lifecycle/...";
   ```

8. The math section contains the most used and most popular libraries. Use these contracts to help perform safe arithmetic operations that protect against integer overflow and underflow:

   ```
   import "openzeppelin-solidity/contracts/math/...";
   ```

9. Use the ownership smart contracts to manage contract and token ownership:

   ```
   import "openzeppelin-solidity/contracts/ownership/...";
   ```

10. Use the collection of smart contracts in the payments section to manage payments through escrow arrangements, withdrawals, and claims:

    ```
    import "openzeppelin-solidity/contracts/payment/...";
    ```

11. To build the commonly used standard token implementations, use the tokens collection. It includes both ERC-20 and ERC-721 token implementations:

    ```
    import "openzeppelin-solidity/contracts/token/ERC20/...";
    import "openzeppelin-solidity/contracts/token/ERC721/...";
    ```

12. There are a few more utility contracts present in the library that can be used to achieve smaller tasks, such as address validation and guarding against reentrancy.

13. For more information on the library, refer to the official GitHub repository at https://github.com/OpenZeppelin/openzeppelin-solidity. Because of the constantly changing nature of Ethereum and its ecosystem, it's always a good idea to use the latest version of the library to avoid any security issues.

11
Miscellaneous

In this chapter, we will cover the following recipes:

- Using Vyper to write smart contracts
- Debugging smart contracts with Remix
- Deploying contracts using Remix
- Generating documentation for solidity code
- Writing better code with the help of a linter
- Sharing solidity code with others

Introduction

So far in this book, you have learned to set up an Ethereum network, write highly scalable smart contracts, build decentralized applications, secure smart contracts from bugs, and much more. The ecosystem is evolving very rapidly and new features and modules might be added at any time. It is strongly recommended to keep an eye on the latest releases and their change logs to build better applications with more security and features.

A decentralized ecosystem will also force you to think a bit differently while building applications, due to its core design. Not all traditional client-server concepts will work in this scenario. It is highly recommended to do a bit of research before finalizing the architecture for your application.

This chapter includes a few additional recipes that will come in handy during your development process. It includes an introduction to a new programming language for writing smart contracts and other generic tools to support the development process.

Using Vyper to write smart contracts

Vyper is a new programming language that compiles to EVM bytecode. It is an experimental language developed with the goal of increasing simplicity, security, and auditability. Vyper also includes additional features such as overflow checking, decimal fixed-point numbers, support for more data types, and much more.

In this recipe, you will learn to write better smart contracts using Vyper and its new features.

Getting ready

Vyper can only be built if you have Python 3.6 or higher installed in your system. It is also recommended to set up a virtual Python environment so that package installments are isolated. Run the following commands to create a Python environment:

```
virtualenv -p python3.6 --no-site-packages ~/vyper-venv
source ~/vyper-venv/bin/activate
```

How to do it...

1. Run the following command to download and install vyper from its GitHub repository:

   ```
   git clone https://github.com/ethereum/vyper.git
   cd vyper
   make
   make test
   ```

2. After installation, verify it by compiling an example contract. To compile the contract, run the following command from the console:

   ```
   vyper examples/name_registry.vy
   ```

3. To modify the required compiler output, use the -f flag with an array of output parameters:

   ```
   vyper -f ['abi', 'json', 'bytecode'] fileName.vy
   ```

4. In Vyper, each contract is stored in a distinct file. Files in Vyper are similar to classes in object-oriented programming languages.

5. To create a state variable in the Vyper contract, use the following syntax. The name and the data type have to be specified for each declaration:

```
beneficiary: address
index: int128
```

6. The basic data types supported by Vyper are as follows:

- **Unsigned**: `uint256`
- **Signed**: `int128`
- **decimal**: Holds a decimal fixed point value
- **address**: Holds an Ethereum address (20-byte value)
  - **balance**: Gets the balance of the address in `wei_value`
  - **codesize**: Gets code stored at this address and returns `int128`
- **timestamp**: Holds the time
- **timedelta**: Time difference
- **wei_value**: Holds amount of Ether in its smallest denomination
- **bool**: `true` or `false`

7. Vyper supports the creation of custom data types using a `struct`. A `struct` can be created by specifying its name, followed by the list of members and its types:

```
// syntax
<struct_name>: {
    <value>: <data_type>,
    <value>: <data_type>,
    ...
}

// example
voters: {
    isVoted: bool,
    delegate: address
}
```

8. The language also supports the creation of a mapping to store key-value pairs. To create a mapping, use the syntax given here:

```
// syntax
<mapping_name>: <value_type>[<key_type>]

// example
isAllowed: address[bool]
```

9. A more complex mapping can be created by specifying a `struct` type as the value. The `struct` type can be implemented separately, or along with the mapping:

```
userDetails: {
    name: bytes32,
    age: int128
}[address]
```

10. Vyper supports the creation of functions and each function should start with the `def` keyword:

```
@public
@payable
def function_name():
    // ...
```

 Functions can be called either internally or externally and have different levels of visibility. Each function in a Vyper contract must be decorated with either `@public` or `@private`. A contract can also have `@payable` to accept the value transferred.

11. Functions can accept parameters and return values after processing. The types of input and output parameters have to be specified. The state variables can be accessed by prefixing them with the `self` keyword:

```
@public
@payable
def buy():
    self.buyer = msg.sender
```

12. To create a constructor in Vyper, use the __init__ function. The constructor function gets executed whenever the contract is created:

```
@public
@payable
def __init__():
    self.value = msg.value
    self.owner = msg.sender
```

13. A contract can also have a default function, which is executed on a call to the contract if no other functions match the given function signature. It is similar to the `fallback` function in solidity. Use this syntax to create a default function:

```
@public
@payable
def __default__():
    ...
```

14. To create an event in Vyper, use the `event` keyword. The event parameters can also be indexed. While logging, events created can be called by prefixing them with the `log` keyword:

```
Deposit: event({value: int128, from: indexed(address)})

@public
@payable
def invest():
    log.Deposit(msg.value, msg.sender)
```

15. Validations can be done using the `assert` keyword. To validate a variable, use the following `assert` keyword along with the condition:

```
@public
def doSomething():
    assert not self.isAllowed
    assert msg.sender == self.isOwner
    ...
```

There's more...

Vyper's goal is to increase security and simplicity while writing smart contracts. To achieve this, the language brings some restrictions when compared with Solidity. These are listed here:

- **Modifiers**: Vyper does not support modifiers, because it makes it too easy to write misleading code. Modifiers encourage people to write code where the execution jumps around the file and increases complexity. The recommendation is to write these checks as asserts in functions where they are required.
- **Inheritance**: Contract inheritance makes code too complicated to understand, which negatively impacts auditability.

- **Inline assembly**: Inline assembly restricts the reader or developer to search for a variable name in order to find all instances where that variable is read or modified.
- **Function overloading**: The problem with function overloading is that it increases complexity and makes the code much harder to search through, as you have to keep track of which call refers to which function.
- **Operator overloading**: Operator overloading allows "+" to be overloaded so that it executes commands that are not visible at first glance, such as sending funds the user did not want to send.
- **Recursive calling and infinite length loops**: This makes it impossible to set an upper bound on gas limits, which allows gas limit attacks.
- **Binary fixed point**: Binary fixed point approximations are often required and they do not have an exact representation.

Debugging smart contracts with Remix

As discussed in earlier chapters, Remix is a rich IDE for writing, testing, and deploying smart contracts. It provides all the essential features required for an effective development environment. In addition to these features, Remix also includes a useful debugger built right into it.

Debugging a contract using sent transactions can be a bit tricky. By using the Remix IDE, one can easily debug a specific transaction. In this recipe, you will learn to debug an Ethereum smart contract step by step. It will help you to identify and fix bugs easily.

Getting ready

Remix is a browser-based IDE. You need to have an up-to-date web browser, such as Chrome, Firefox, or Edge, to access the online IDE. Remix comes with a test Ethereum network where you can deploy and test your contracts. It also allows you to connect to an existing network.

How to do it...

1. Access Remix by navigating to `https://remix.ethereum.org/`.

2. Let's use the following smart contract to test the debugging functionality. The contract uses a function to set the value of state variables and doesn't do anything complex:

```
pragma solidity^0.4.24;

contract Sample {
    uint value;
    address sender;
    function setValue(uint _value) public {
        value = _value;
        sender = msg.sender;
    }
}
```

3. Navigate to the **Run** tab in the right panel and click **Deploy** to deploy the contract. Be sure to set the **Environment** as JavaScript VM. It will deploy the contract to a built-in Ethereum instance and will generate an interface to interact with the contract in the right panel, as shown in the following screenshot:

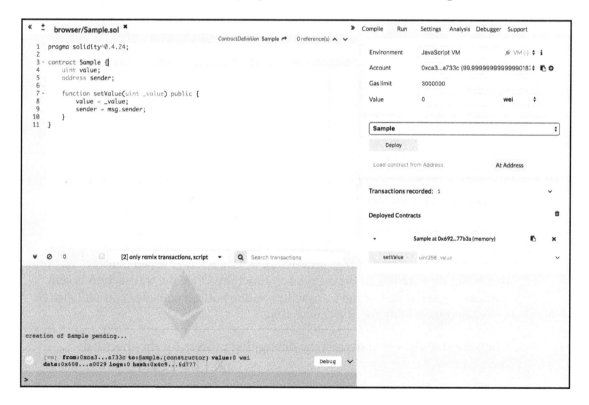

4. You can access the debugger by navigating to the **Debugger** tab in the right panel. It allows you to specify a transaction hash or a block with a transaction index to start the debugging process, as shown in the following screenshot:

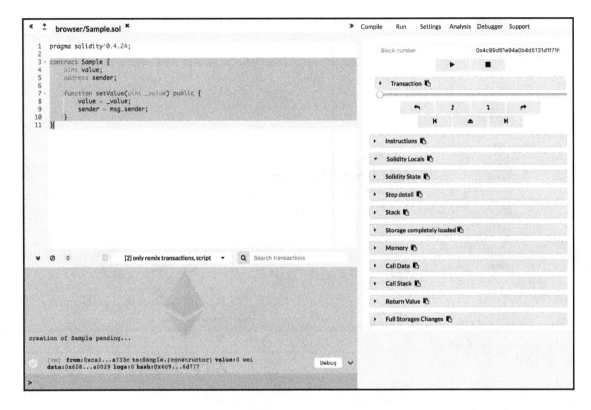

5. The debugger gives you the option to navigate the code by each instruction. You can also read the current state of the machine from the debug window. This window provides options to read the instructions, local states, step details, values in the stack, values in memory, call data, call stack, and more.

6. Let's try to make a transaction and debug it. Use the **Deployed contract** section under the **Run** tab to call the `setValue` function. Once the transaction is sent, you can see the status of the transaction on the bottom console. You will also be given an option to debug the transaction.

7. Click the **Debug** button to start the debugging process for the specified transaction.

8. Navigate through the instructions by moving the slider or by clicking the buttons right below it. The debugger will highlight the code that represents the current instructions in the editor window. You can also see the values of states being changed for each instruction, as shown in the following screenshot:

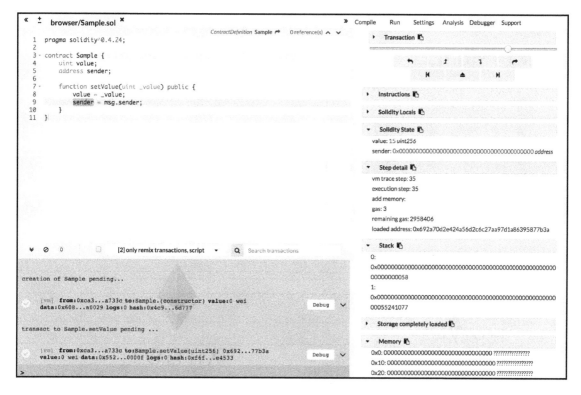

9. You can stop the debugger at any point by clicking the stop icon in the debugger window.

Deploying contracts using Remix

Remix supports connecting and interacting with multiple Ethereum networks. You can connect to these networks either directly or through providers. Remix also provides options to do transactions such as contract deployment and state changes.

In this recipe, you will learn to connect and deploy contracts to multiple Ethereum networks. This allows the developer to quickly test the contracts without the hassle of writing code or interacting with command-line tools.

Getting ready

Remix is a browser-based IDE. You need to have a modern web browser such as Chrome, Firefox, or Edge to access the online IDE. Remix comes with a test Ethereum network where you can deploy and test your contracts. It also allows you to connect to an existing network.

How to do it...

1. Access the Remix IDE by opening the link (`https://remix.ethereum.org/`) in your browser.
2. To connect to an existing Ethereum network, navigate to the **Run** tab and select **Environment**.
3. Environment provides the following options as shown in the following screenshot:

   - JavaScript VM
   - Injected Web3
   - Web3 provider

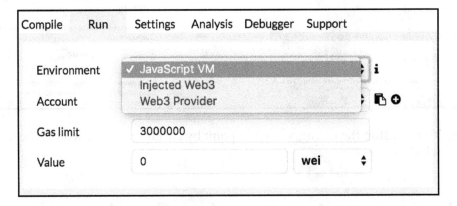

4. Selecting the JavaScript VM option will connect the node to a built-in mock Ethereum network. It is the best suitable network for quick testing.

5. The injected `Web3` option connects to a provider supplied by MetaMask or other wallets. The `Web3` provider option connects to a node directly using its RPC URL.

If you are using Remix through an HTTPS URL, then the RPC should also be an HTTPS service. If you don't have access to an HTTPS RPC, then navigate to `http://remix.ethereum.org/` for the connection.

6. Once you have connected a network successfully, you can see the list of accounts and their respective balances in the **Account** dropdown shown as follows:

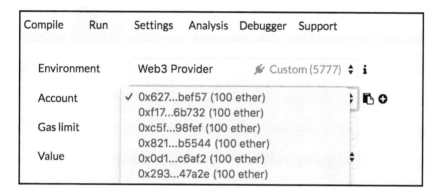

7. Select the account from which you have to perform the transaction and click **Deploy**. If you have multiple contracts written in a single file, then select the contract to deploy from the list of contracts near the **Deploy** button.

8. If the contract has a constructor that accepts parameters, then you will be asked to specify the values while deploying, as shown in the following screenshot:

9. If you already have a deployed contract, then you can interact with it by specifying the contract address in **Load contract from Address**.

Generating documentation for solidity code

Proper source code documentation is essential for every well-maintained project. It helps the reader to understand the code better. A developer who is trying to improve the code with new features will find this very useful. The solidity community has come up with a document generator that helps developers to build intuitive documentation for the smart contract. This recipe will help you create such documentation for your contract using Doxity.

Getting ready

Doxity is a documentation generator that is built using JavaScript and is distributed through npm. You need to have NodeJS (any recent version) installed on your machine to use this.

How to do it...

1. First, install doxity in your system using npm. You can either do it globally or locally, based on your requirements:

```
// Global installation
npm install -g @digix/doxity
// Local installation for a project
npm install @digix/doxity
```

2. Once you have installed doxity, you can use it to generate documentation based on the comments provided for each function.

3. It is recommended to follow the general comment pattern (natspec) for all functions, which explains each function's definition.

4. Consider the following function as an example of proper commenting:

```
/**
 * @dev Technical explanation
 * @param <param1_name> Description of param1
 * @param <param2_name> Description of param2
```

```
    */
    function functionName(...params...) {
        ...
    }
```

5. Since support for multiple return types has to be implemented, use JSON to specify it for documentation:

```
    /**
     * @dev Function to calculate the sum & difference of two numbers
     * @param _a First number
     * @param _b Second number
     * @return {
     *      "_sum": "Sum of first and second number",
     *      "_difference": "Difference between first and second number",
     * }
     */
    function calc(uint _a, uint _b) { ... }
```

6. To set up a doxity project, use the init command. It will clone and initialize a boilerplate for your project:

    doxity init

7. To generate the documentation for your contract, use the build command. It will generate static HTML files and will save them to the docs folder in your project:

    doxity build

8. If you had to change the code after generating the documentation, use the compile command to update it:

    doxity compile

9. Doxity also provides a development server for editing the project. Run the following command to start it:

    doxity develop

10. Finally, once you have finished your project, run the publish command to generate deployable documentation. You can use the files in the docs folder of your project:

    doxity publish

11. The final documentation will look something like this. It will have different tabs for each contract, and each tab will have all the details of that specific contract:

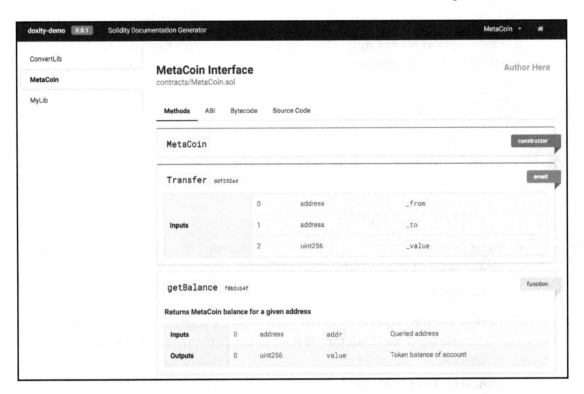

Writing better code with the help of a linter

It is very important to follow best practices while writing code. This is more important when it comes to smart contracts, specifically solidity, because of the security issues that can arise. It is easy for a new smart contract developer to miss minor details. To avoid this, it is recommended to use a linter, which verifies your code against best practices.

This recipe will introduce you to the popular linters used in solidity to help you write better code. This can improve the overall readability and security of your smart contracts.

Getting ready

These linters are built using JavaScript and are distributed through `npm`. You need to have `NodeJS` (any recent version) installed on your machine to step through this recipe.

How to do it...

1. Solium is a popular linter used by many to validate their code against best practices. Solium is distributed through `npm` and you can install it using the following command:

   ```
   npm install -g solium
   ```

2. Run the following command to verify the installation. It will return the details of the currently installed version:

   ```
   solium -V
   ```

3. Use the `init` command to set up your project to support Solium linting:

   ```
   solium --init
   ```

4. This command will create two files (`.soliumignore` and `.soliumrc.json`) in the project directory. The `soliumignore` file contains the names of files and directories to ignore while linting and the `soliumrc` file contains configuration that includes rules, plugins, and shareable configs.

5. Once `solium` is set up, you can start linting your project by specifying a single file or a directory that contains multiple solidity contract files:

   ```
   // Lint a specific file
   solium -f fileName.sol

   // Lint files present in the folder
   solium -d contracts/
   ```

6. Solium also fixes recommendations automatically. To do this, add a `--fix` flag while linting:

   ```
   solium -d contracts/ --fix
   ```

7. You can also run Solium in the background in watch mode. It will watch the directory for any changes and will print the results immediately:

```
solium --watch --dir contracts/
```

8. While linting, you can specify rules for each line through comments. For example, you can instruct Solium to ignore a line/file or to ignore a specific recommendation:

```
// Avoid linting for the next line
/* solium-disable-next-line */

// Avoid the whole file
/* solium-disable */
```

9. For more information about Solium, refer to its official documentation at `http://solium.readthedocs.io/`.

Sharing solidity code with others

You might be required to share your contract files with someone at some point during development, or during any later phase. A well-maintained project will have its own source control repository that can be shared with people. There are some tools and services that you can use to quickly share small contract snippets with others quickly. In this recipe, you will learn about those services, which will make your life easier while sharing code.

Getting ready

This recipe introduces you to some browser-based tools. It is required to have a recent browser (Chrome, Firefox, Edge, and so on) installed in your system to step through this recipe.

How to do it...

1. To share/store small snippets of code, you can use `gist`. The process is mostly manual and requires you to copy and paste the code and then share it with someone. You can access `gist` from `https://gist.github.com/`.

2. The Remix IDE ships with an option to publish your contract files directly to an anonymous public `gist`. Click the **publish to Gist** option in the top-left panel of the Remix IDE. Clicking it will publish all your contract code to a public `gist`. Take extra care while doing this for your confidential files, as it will make everything public.

3. You can also use `EthFiddle`, which is a minimalistic IDE with code sharing features. It is targeted at solidity smart contracts and you can access it from `https://ethfiddle.com/`, as shown in the following screenshot:

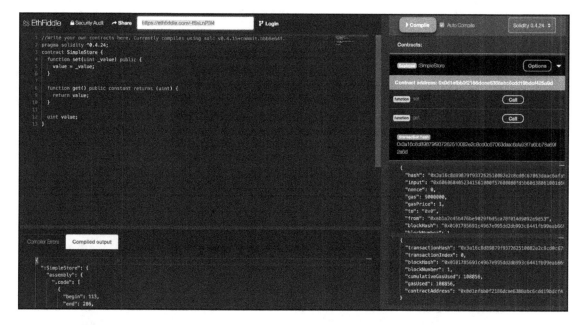

4. Once you have the source code in place, you can share the code by clicking the **share** button on the top panel. It will display a link that can be shared with others.

5. The tool also comes with a built-in solidity compiler, which can be used to compile your contract. Click the **Compile** button in the top-right panel to do so. You can enable the auto-compile checkbox to compile the contract in real time.

6. To change the compiler version, click on the dropdown next to the **Compile** button.

7. Click on the **Compiler Errors** tab in the bottom panel to check whether your code has any syntax errors.

8. Click on the **Compiler Output** tab to see the output of the successfully compiled code.

9. Once the contract compiles successfully, you can deploy the contract by clicking the **Deploy** button.

10. You can change the from address, value, and gas, or proceed with the default values. It will deploy the contract to the tool's built-in Ethereum network, as shown in the following screenshot:

11. To interact with the deployed contracts, use the contract panel on the right-hand side of the tool. You can use it to read/write from the contract. Click the **Call** button to perform transactions, and you can see the relevant details right below the button, shown as follows:

12. Apart from these features, EthFiddle also stores code shared recently. You can access it by clicking the **Recent Fiddles** button in the bottom panel.

Other Books You May Enjoy

If you enjoyed this book, you may be interested in these other books by Packt:

Ethereum Projects for Beginners
Kenny Vaneetvelde

ISBN: 978-1-78953-740-6

- Develop your ideas fast and efficiently using the Ethereum blockchain
- Make writing and deploying smart contracts easy and manageable
- Work with private data in blockchain applications
- Handle large files in blockchain applications
- Ensure your decentralized applications are safe
- Explore how Ethereum development frameworks work
- Create your own cryptocurrency or token on the Ethereum blockchain
- Make sure your cryptocurrency is ERC20-compliant to launch an ICO

Ethereum Smart Contract Development
Mayukh Mukhopadhyay

ISBN: 978-1-78847-304-0

- Know how to build your own smart contracts and cryptocurrencies
- Understand the Solidity language
- Find out about data types, control structure, functions, inheritance, mathematical operations, and much more
- See the various types of forks and discover how they are related to Ethereum
- Get to know the various concepts of web3.js and its APIs so you can build client-side apps
- Build a DAO from scratch and acquire basic knowledge of DApps on Ethercast
- Be guided through the project so you can optimize EVM for smart contracts
- Build your own decentralized applications (DApps) by taking a practical approach

Leave a review - let other readers know what you think

Please share your thoughts on this book with others by leaving a review on the site that you bought it from. If you purchased the book from Amazon, please leave us an honest review on this book's Amazon page. This is vital so that other potential readers can see and use your unbiased opinion to make purchasing decisions, we can understand what our customers think about our products, and our authors can see your feedback on the title that they have worked with Packt to create. It will only take a few minutes of your time, but is valuable to other potential customers, our authors, and Packt. Thank you!

Index

Drizzle 160, 162, 164

E

enums
  working with 57, 60
ERC20 token
  creating 168, 169, 172
  URL 175
ERC223 token
  creating 186
error handling
  assert() 252
  in solidity 250
  require() 250
  revert() 251
Eth-netstats
  URL 34
Ether
  sending, to contract by force 304, 305
Ethereum Alarm Clock (EAC) 352
Ethereum Improvement Proposal (EIP) 172, 251
Ethereum Name Service (ENS)
  registering 340, 342
Ethereum Request for Comment (ERC) 172
Ethereum transactions
  scheduling, with alarm clock 352
Ethereum Virtual Machine (EVM) 100, 277
Ethereum wallet
  URL 31
  using 31
Ethereum
  client, selecting 8, 9
  URL 9
EVM logger 75, 78
Externally Owned Addresses (EOA) 33, 336

F

fallback function 54, 56
First In First Server (FIFS) 341
function modifiers
  using 70, 71, 72
FUSE (Filesystem in Userspace) 348

G

game
  creating 230, 231, 232, 233
ganache GUI
  URL 24
Geth
  about 9
  used, for deploying contracts 83, 85

H

HD wallet
  using, in Truffle 164

I

IBFT (Istanbul Byzantine Fault Tolerance) 8
INFURA
  URL 17
  using 17, 18
Initial Coin / Initial Token Offering (ICO/ITO) 168
Initial Coin Offering (ICO)
  building 188, 189, 190, 191
  features, adding 193, 196
integer overflow
  avoiding 296, 298
integer underflow
  avoiding 296, 298
Integrated Development Environments (IDE)
  selecting 40, 41, 42
interaction ways, contract
  Nethereum 119
  Web3J 119
interface contracts 253
  about 254
InterPlanetary File System (IPFS) 324
investors
  bonus tokens, providing 197, 198, 199

J

JavaScript Runtime Environment (JSRE)
  working with 13, 16
JSON-RPC
  used, for interacting with Ethereum 113, 115, 118